OBJECTIVES & STRATEGY

OBJECTIVES & STRATEGY

An analytical and evaluative approach to business studies

Andrew Gillespie & Simon Harrison

Hodder & Stoughton

A MEMBER OF THE HODDER HEADLINE GROUP

Orders: please contact Bookpoint Ltd, 78 Milton Park, Abingdon, Oxon OX14 4TD. Telephone: (44) 01235 827720, Fax: (44) 01235 400454. Lines are open from 9.00 – 6.00, Monday to Saturday, with a 24 hour message answering service. Email address: orders@bookpoint.co.uk

A catalogue record for this title is available from The British Library

ISBN 0 340 758 368

First published 2000
Impression number 10 9 8 7 6 5 4 3 2 1
Year 2005 2004 2003 2002 2001 2000

Cover illustration by Jon H. Hamilton
Typeset by Fakenham Photosetting Ltd, Fakenham, Norfolk
Printed in Great Britain for Hodder & Stoughton Educational, a division of Hodder Headline Plc, 338 Euston Road, London NW1 3BH by J. W. Arrowsmith Ltd, Bristol.

Contents

Acknowledgements

Thanks once more to Ali, from Andrew Gillespie, for her ongoing understanding and constant smiles.

Simon Harrison would like to thank his wife Liz for her support, good humour and clever ideas.

The authors and publisher would like to thank the following for permission to reproduce copyright material:

Financial Times, pp. 16, 95, 104, 127, 129, 160, 166.
Key Note Ltd./Trade Sources, p. 90.
The Economist, pp. 126, 160, 162.

Every effort has been made to trace copyright holders but this has not always been possible in all cases; any omissions brought to our attention will be corrected in future printings.

If you have any comments on this book or suggestions for future editions, the Series Editor would be pleased to hear from you on: **gillsp@hotmail.com**

General introduction

Using this series

This series of six books is designed specifically to develop the higher levels of skill needed for exam success and, at the same time, to provide you with a critical and detailed insight into the subject as a whole. The books are written by a team of highly experienced examiners and authors to provide you with the information and approach to achieve the best results. Whereas a traditional textbook tends to provide an explanation of topics, this series concentrates on developing ideas in a more analytical manner. When considering a topic such as business strategy, for example, the book will focus on issues such as:

- Why is business strategy significant for firms?
- What determines a firm's strategy?
- To what extent is strategic planning useful and desirable?
- Can a firm succeed without a strategy?

The whole approach of the series is intended to develop a questioning and evaluative understanding of business issues. The emphasis is on why certain factors are important, rather than merely describing what they are. Reading these books will provide you with new insights into topics and help you to develop a critical view of the issues involved in the different areas of the subject.

Using this book

This particular book critically examines issues involved in business objectives and business strategy. It covers the following areas:

- decision-making
- starting up and business format
- business mission, objectives and culture
- business strategy
- managing growth
- change in ownership
- contingency planning and crisis management.

Throughout the text we provide up-to-date examples of business behaviour in the form of **fact files** and **numerical investigations**. There are also numerous **progress checks** in each chapter to help you to review your understanding of the topics you have covered so far. Each chapter includes sample exam questions, students' answers (including marks awarded and marker's comments) and advice on how to answer specific types of question in the exam. The answers to the sample questions can be found in the *Teacher's Handbook* which accompanies this series. Chapter 10 is designed to help you interpret and analyse numerical data from this syllabus area. Chapter 11 provides information on how the business concepts covered in the book are usually assessed in examinations and focuses on the key underlying issues in each topic; this will be invaluable when it comes to preparing for your exams.

Chapter 9 focuses on the most recent issues in this area of the syllabus to make sure you are completely up-to-date in your understanding and to provide you with the latest ideas to include in your answers.

Not only will this book provide you with a thorough understanding of the significance of topics involved in business objectives and strategy, it will also help you develop the approach you need to achieve top grades. It is an invaluable resource for students who want to achieve exam success.

The 'levels of response' approach to marking

In AS and A Level Business Studies candidates are assessed by their ability to demonstrate certain key skills. A student's final grade will depend on the extent to which he or she has shown the ability to analyse points, structure ideas and come to a reasoned conclusion. An A grade candidate is someone who demonstrates these skills consistently, whereas a C grade candidate shows them intermittently. To do well at AS and A Level, students not only have to know the issues involved in each topic area, they also have to be able to develop their ideas. It is very important, therefore, that candidates provide some depth to their answers, rather than leaving many ideas undeveloped. In most cases students do better by analysing a few key points in their answers, rather than by listing many different ideas. Unfortunately, many students find it difficult to expand on their initial points; although they often demonstrate a good knowledge of the issues involved, they do not necessarily find it easy to explore these ideas further. The aim of this series of books is specifically to help you develop your ideas in more depth, which will enable you to do better in the exam.

The basic approach to assessment at A Level is the same for all the examination boards and is known as 'levels of response' marking. In its simplest form this means that the mark you get depends on the skill you have demonstrated. The higher the skill shown in your answer the higher your final mark.

There are four main levels of skill assessed at A Level. These are:

- synthesis and evaluation (the highest level skill)
- analysis

- explanation and application
- identification (the lowest level).

As you can see the 'identification' of relevant factors is the lowest level skill. This means that listing ideas will not in itself achieve a high grade. What is important is that you explain these points (i.e. show what they mean) or apply them to the context of the question, analyse them (i.e. show why they are significant) and evaluate them (i.e. weigh up their relative importance).

In a typical question worth 9 marks, the mark scheme may look something like this:

- candidate *evaluates* relevant factors 9–7 marks
- candidate *analyses* relevant factors 6–5 marks
- candidate *explains* relevant factors 4–3 marks
- candidate *identifies* relevant factors 2–1 marks.

As you can see, a candidate who simply identifies factors can only achieve a maximum score of 2 out of 9. Regardless of how many different points he or she makes, if all the student has done is to list ideas they cannot get more than 2 marks in total. To move up the levels and gain more marks candidates need to demonstrate the higher level skills. Unfortunately, most textbooks spend so much time explaining ideas that they cannot do much to help develop the ability to analyse and evaluate. This series focuses throughout on these higher level skills to help you move up the levels of response in the exam and maximise your grade.

Imagine you were faced with a question which asked you to 'Discuss the factors which might influence a firm's strategy'. A good answer would identify a few relevant factors, explain what is meant by them, analyse their relevance and then discuss their importance. For example:

'A firm's strategy may be influenced by its resources. If a firm has low unit costs (perhaps because of economies of scale or technological advances) it may decide to compete by setting low prices in relation to the benefits offered. Its ability to do this will depend on the extent to which its unit costs are lower than its competitors and their likely reaction. It will also depend on the extent to which customers are sensitive to price (e.g. price elasticity of demand) and value lower prices. Strategy must be linked to market opportunities – there is no point offering a low price if customers actually want better quality products and are willing to pay for them.'

This is a strong answer which takes a couple points and develops them in some depth. For comparison, consider this answer:

'Strategy depends on resources, competitors, market opportunities, a firm's strengths and the match between what a firm can do and what is needed by customers.' This answer has many ideas but all of them are left undeveloped and so it is a much weaker answer.

More recent mark schemes adopt a slightly different approach in which content, analysis and evaluation are each given a mark, as in the example below. As you can see in this case (which is the mark scheme for an essay) you can gain up to 8 marks for content, 8 for application, 8 for analysis and 16 for evaluation. Within each category the levels approach is used so that strong evaluation can be awarded up to

SKILL	CONTENT	APPLICATION	ANALYSIS	EVALUATION
MAXIMUM NUMBER OF MARKS	8	8	8	16
Level of response	8–5 marks Three or more relevant factors identified	8–6 marks Full explanation of factors	8–6 marks Full analysis using theory appropriately and accurately	16–11 marks Mature judgement shown in arguments and conclusions
	4–3 marks Two relevant factors identified	5–3 marks Some explanation of two or more factors	5–3 marks Analysis with some use of relevant theory	10–5 marks Judgement shown in arguments and/or conclusions
	2–1 marks One relevant factor identified	2–1 marks Some explanation of one factor	2–1 marks Limited analysis of question	4–1 marks Some judgement shown in text or conclusions
	0 marks No knowledge shown	0 marks No application or explanation	0 marks No analysis present	0 marks No judgement shown

Table 1.1 Example mark scheme

16 marks, whereas more limited evaluation may only get 1 or 2 marks. The basic principles of this scheme are similar to the original levels of response model; certainly the message to candidates is clear: the higher marks require analysis and evaluation; the best marks require good analysis and evaluation! A content laden answer would only get a maximum of 7 marks.

The key to success in examinations is to consistently demonstrate the ability to analyse and evaluate – this involves exploring a few of the points you have made. All of the books in this series take an approach which should develop your critical ability and make it easier for you to discuss your ideas in more depth.

The higher level skills

What is analysis?

To analyse a point you need to show why it *matters.* Why is it relevant to the question? Why is it important? Having made a point and explained what it actually means, you need to discuss its significance either by examining what caused it or by exploring its effect on the business. This is illustrated below.

Question: *Analyse the possible benefits of having a management by objectives system.*

Answer: A management by objectives system can be motivating (*point made*) because it provides a target for people. Therefore, both subordinates and managers can measure performance relative to the target. Without this type of guideline, it is difficult to know whether employees have done well or not because there is nothing to judge it against. So objectives provide something to aim for (*explanation*). However, if the targets are too high and unobtainable the objective may be demotivating because people will not see any point in trying (*analysis*).

To develop the analysis further you could go on to discuss other possible issues, such as how the objectives are determined and whether rewards are linked to achieving the targets.

The answer above provides a logical chain of thought: management by objectives provides a clear target which can be motivating provided the targets can be achieved.

What is synthesis?

Synthesis occurs when an answer is *structured effectively*. Essentially, it involves writing well organised answers rather than leaving it up to the reader to make sense of the argument. In a 'discussion' question this means putting an argument for a case, an argument against and then a conclusion.

Synthesis tends to come from planning your answer, rather than starting writing immediately. Whenever you face a question, try to sort out what you want each paragraph to say before you begin to write the answer out in full. This should lead to a better organised response. A final paragraph to bring together the arguments is also recommended.

What is evaluation?

Evaluation is the highest skill and involves demonstrating some form of *judgement.* Once you have developed various points you have to show which one or ones are most important or under what circumstances these issues are most likely to be significant. Evaluation involves some reflection on the arguments for and against and some thought about which aspects are most important.

This often involves standing back from your argument to decide what would make your ideas more or less relevant. Ask yourself under what circumstances would one course of action be chosen rather than another? This process is illustrated below.

Question: *Discuss the possible benefits to a firm of having a business plan.*

Answer: A business plan sets out what the firm wants to achieve and how it wants to achieve its targets (*point made*). This is useful because it involves an analysis of the present and future situation which may mean that decision-making is improved and risk is reduced (*explanation*).

The actual process of producing the plan should force managers to think about the future and to research all the possibilities. This is extremely valuable because it should avoid decisions made purely on the basis of gut feeling (*analysis*).

However, this depends on whether managers do undertake research – they may simply make up the numbers based on experience and intuition. Also, the plan does not guarantee success because the environment can change so rapidly. What looks like a good business idea one minute may prove to be a failure if market conditions change due to technology or new competition for example. The value of a plan depends on the quality of the information and the extent to which managers have foreseen change (*evaluation of points*).

To evaluate your arguments you need to think carefully about whether the points you have made earlier in your answer are *always* true. What makes them more or less true? What makes the impact more or less severe? To what extent can the firm avoid or exploit the situation you have described? To evaluate effectively you have to imagine different organisations and think about what factors would influence them to act in one way or another. What would make the impact of change greater or smaller? Evaluation, therefore, requires a broad appreciation of the factors which influence a firm's decisions and an awareness of the variety of organisations present in the business world.

We hope you find these books useful. They are designed to be very different from typical textbooks in that they will help you to use ideas and think about their importance. At the same time, these books will provide you with new insights into topics and, we hope, will convey some of the passion and enthusiasm we have for such a fascinating subject.

CHAPTER 1

Overview

It is very easy to get caught up in the detail of business and lose sight of the bigger picture. Whenever we pick up the newspapers there are stories of price cuts, advertising campaigns, new products and special offers. Whilst these are undoubtedly important, what really matters is the *decisions* which lie behind them:

- What made a firm decide to compete in one market as opposed to another?
- Why has the firm decided to compete by offering additional services rather than trying to cut price?
- Why does it provide some products but not others?

Vision and leadership

These are the kinds of strategic decisions which ultimately determine a firm's success. They rely on the vision of the management team to match the firm's strengths with the opportunities in the market. It was vision and leadership which enabled Lou Gerstner to take IBM from an ailing manufacturer of computer equipment to a successful provider of 'business solutions', which helped Richard Branson to extend the Virgin brand and which allowed Rupert Murdoch to identify the potential for satellite TV. It was Bill Gates' technical skill and his awareness of the potential of personal computers and the Internet which drove Microsoft forward to become the biggest company in the world. It is the skilful but possibly less well-known managers at Coca Cola, Unilever, 3M, General Electric and Sony which have kept these businesses on top for many years.

The secret of success

Of course the detail matters, but the first thing is to make sure the firm is in the *right markets* at the *right time.* Successful organisations are the ones which have clear objectives and a strategy which matches their skills and resources to market opportunities. Unsuccessful firms get stuck fighting in declining markets or competing in ways which lack any competitive advantage.

Objectives and strategy, decision-making and planning

This book considers the importance of issues such as objectives, strategy, decision-making and planning. These broad themes underly every business – in some cases they involve formal processes (e.g. devising a strategic plan or producing a five year business plan); in other cases the ideas may simply exist in the head of an entrepreneur. What really matters is not whether the plans are written down, but whether managers have a clear idea of what they want the firm to do and how they intend to achieve their objectives. They also need a good understanding of their markets and strengths. As the internal and external environments of firms change so must the strategy: just think how Sainsbury's has changed from being a food retailer to a provider of DIY goods, banking and insurance; look at the way banks are moving off the high street and onto the internet; consider the way the Virgin brand has been extended into all kinds of business areas. These examples demonstrate how businesses are continually reshaping and developing.

Opportunities are always opening up, sometimes slowly, sometimes with incredible speed, as with the internet. Managers have to be ready to exploit these opportunities. The UK today is radically different from even 10 years ago – think of the use of faxes, email, mobile phones, computer games, the increase in eating out, the rise of coffee shops, the growth of overseas foods, the introduction of cable and digital TV and you will appreciate that business opportunities appear all the time.

The packaging of a particular brand, the price of a particular item and the advertising of a new product all matter, but they are the consequence of more significant strategic decisions which determine whether the firm is operating in the right area to begin with. It is the ability to see the 'big picture', to stand back and decide what really matters in the market and which markets are going to count that is really important. People like Peter Wood, who saw the potential for direct insurance, Jeff Bezos, famous for setting up the Internet bookseller Amazon.com, Charles Dunstone, who saw the possibilities in being an independent seller of mobile and car telephones are truly great business leaders. This book focuses on some of the issues the great business minds consider when leading their firms forward:

- What business are we in?
- What are our strengths and weaknesses?
- What should we do next?
- How can we create a culture of success which encourages employees to take the initiative, to exceed customer expectations and to learn from each other and the external environment?

It is these decisions which separate out the winners and the losers. In particular, the book covers the following areas:

- *Decision-making* – in Chapter 2 we consider the nature of decision-making and compare the value of different approaches to making a decision. Some decision-makers rely mainly on data; others trust their own intuition more. We examine the process of decision-making and consider how the process might depend on the manager, the situation and the nature of the decision itself. Was the decision to produce or launch the Sony Playstation likely to have been based on information or intuition, for example? What about the decision by Ford to buy Kwik-Fit? To what extent should you trust data if your heart tells you something different?
- *Starting up* – in Chapter 3 we consider some of the main issues involved in starting up in business, such as developing a successful idea and choosing an appropriate format, company or sole trader for example. An enormous number of businesses fail in their first few years and so we consider what firms can do to help ensure that they survive.

- *Business mission and objectives* – successful business has a clear sense of direction. In Chapter 4 we consider the typical objectives set by managers and discuss the importance of objectives in determining business success. If firms do not have a clear idea where they are going, it will not be surprising if they never get there!
- *Business strategy* – once managers have determined the firm's objectives they must consider the way in which these targets are achieved, the strategy. In Chapter 5 we consider the factors which influence a firm's strategy and the contribution of the strategy to business performance. We also examine the nature of strategic planning, including the problems it can cause for firms.
- *Managing growth* – business growth brings many opportunities, including cost advantages and the chance to promote staff. It also brings with it many challenges, such as the difficulties of controlling larger numbers of employees. In Chapter 6 we examine the opportunities and threats which growth can provide.
- *Change in ownership* – organisations are continually reshaping, increasing or decreasing the size of their operations, entering new markets, leaving other ones. In Chapter 7 we examine some of the ways in which firms change their shape – such as through take-overs and mergers – and we examine the various issues involved in such change.
- *Contingency planning* – firms need to plan for events in the future. A particular type of planning is contingency planning in which firms prepare themselves for disaster scenarios which may never happen, such as a fire at their suppliers or a major computer crash. In Chapter 8 we consider how firms might plan for such contingencies and whether such investment is actually worth it.

This book covers some very important integrating themes which lie at the very heart of business success. Setting objectives, planning, reshaping and preparing for unexpected events are all crucial issues to be addressed for a firm's future development and success. An understanding of these topics and their significance is vital to anyone who wants to develop a critical appreciation of business performance.

Figure 1.1

Decision-making

Introduction

Decision-making lies at the very heart of management. Managers must decide what the firm does, how it should be done and who needs to do what. They must decide on the firm's strategy, what resources the firm needs and how these should be allocated. Good decision-making is absolutely crucial to a firm's success. Make the wrong decision about which market to be in and, no matter how hard you try, you will struggle to do well. Identify the right market and the right time to enter, and life will be that much easier.

Good decision-making lies at the heart of business success.

The management process

The management process involves:

- Planning: deciding what the firm should be doing and how it should try to achieve its objectives.
- Organising: deciding what resources are needed and when they are required.
- Co-ordinating: ensuring the various resources are ready at the right time and that they work together properly.
- Controlling: making sure that all is going according to plan.

The cycle

Management is a dynamic process. Managers must continually review the firm's progress relative to the targets which have been set and take action if there is any deviation from the plan. At the very heart of this process is good decision-making: managers have the responsibility for deciding what to do and for getting it done. This involves a whole host of decisions; some long term, some short term; some complex, some relatively simple. Managers must decide which decisions really matter and do everything possible to make the right decision every time. In reality, they are bound to make mistakes sometimes, but the good managers are the ones who get it right more often than they get it wrong and who make sure they get it right when it really matters. Bad managers are bad decision-takers; good managers get the key decisions right.

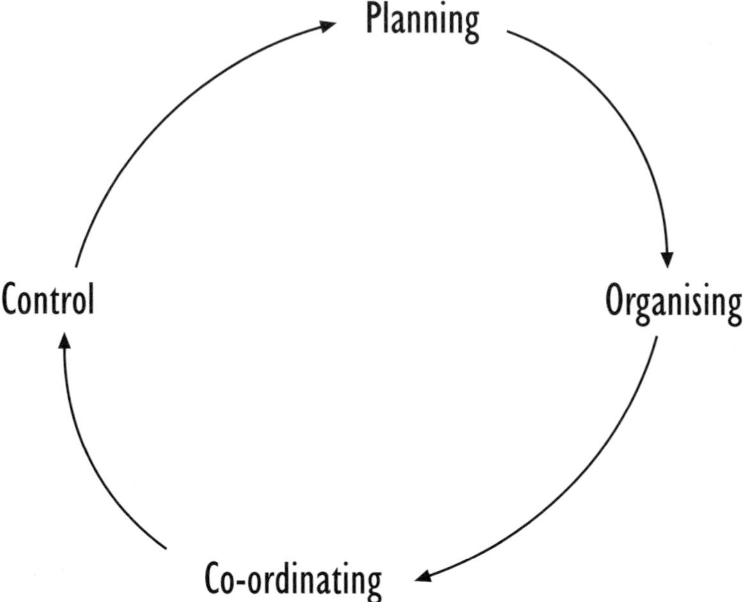

Figure 2.1 The management process

Informing decisions

When it comes to choosing a particular course of action, there are three ways in which a decision can be made. It can be based on:

- the manager's own experience
- his or her intuition (or gut feeling)
- data (the 'hard' facts).

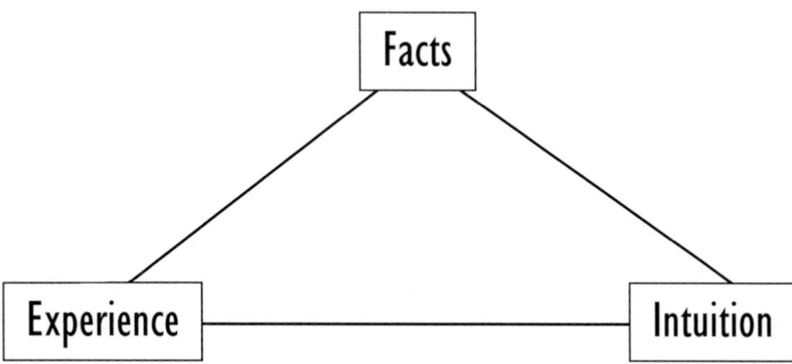

Figure 2.2 Elements of decision-making

FACT FILE

According to management writer Roger Dawson, great decision-makers: have a high tolerance for ambiguity; have a well ordered sense of priorities; are good listeners; always build consensus around a decision; avoid stereotypes; remain resilient; are comfortable with soft and hard input (*intuition and fact*) and are realistic about costs and the difficulty of a decision.

A good decision is likely to involve a combination of all three factors, although the relative importance of these will change according to the manager's personality, the nature of the decision and the extent to which data is available. Risk-takers who doubt the validity of the evidence before them are more likely to use their intuition. A more cautious person may look harder at the data.

KEY POINTS

Managers are more likely to base a decision on research if:

- the decision involves a high risk
- a large number of resources are involved
- data is readily available
- they do not have confidence in their gut feelings
- they lack experience
- the decision may be difficult to reverse.

Given the importance of decision-making, it is not surprising that managers are interested in knowing whether there is a right or wrong way of doing it. Should they stick with their gut feeling? Or is it always better to refer to the data? In practice, there are no simple answers to these questions; a 'good' decision may be reached in many different ways depending on the people and issues involved. In the end, only time will tell whether the decision was right or wrong (even then, different people may hold conflicting views about whether or not the course of action worked).

Scientific decision-making

A scientific approach to decision-making is one which bases a decision purely on data. Data is gathered and analysed to ensure that the final decision is rational and is based on facts. By comparison, an intuitive decision is based on gut feeling; this means the decision-taker feels instinctively that the decision is right, whether or not this is supported by the data.

A scientific model

A scientific approach to decision-making is based on the model below:

- *Set objectives* – what is it we are trying to achieve?
- *Gather data* – what data is there which can help us make the decision?
- *Analyse data* – what does the data mean?
- *Select a strategy* – what should we do?
- *Develop a plan* – how should we implement the strategy?
- *Implement the plan* – how should we put the plan into action?
- *Review* – can we check the progress of the plan relative to the objectives?

Setting objectives

The first step in this process is to clearly identify the objective; before taking any decision it is vital to know what it is you are trying to achieve. The success of the decision will depend ultimately on the extent to which it helps the firm to fulfil its objectives. If the targets themselves are not clear effective decision-making is impossible. There is no point cutting prices to boost sales if the firm's objectives are to promote an exclusive image, for example. Similarly, there is little point investing heavily in a promotional campaign to revive sales, if senior managers want to move out of this market and into another one. The success of any decision must, therefore, be placed in the context of the original objectives. Is a 10% increase in profits successful? Only if the firm wanted to increase profits by 10%. If it had aimed to increase profits by 40% it has underachieved. Typical business objectives might be to increase sales, to gain market share or to increase profitability.

Gathering data

The second stage of the decision-making process is to gather data – by researching the problem the manager should get a better overview and gain greater insight into the issues involved. The data may be gathered externally (for example, using market research agencies) or internally (using past company records). The decision about how and where to gather data will depend on how much time and money the firm has and how important it thinks the decision is. A manager is unlikely to spend much time on reordering light bulbs but will probably research the purchase of new premises very carefully. Primary research generally requires more time and money than secondary but is more likely to relate specifically to the firm's informational needs.

KEY TERMS

Primary research
involves gathering new data. It involves field research.

Secondary research
involves the use of data which has already been gathered. It involves desk research.

Decision-making is dynamic – managers must continually review their decisions and make new ones.

One of the dangers of gathering data is that managers may end up having too much of it! In an attempt to make the right decision, they sometimes gather as much data as they can and end up being swamped by it. This is why it is important for managers to define their objectives as clearly as possible. If they have defined very precisely what the target is, they will know what information is needed. Good decision-makers usually spend time thinking about the information required and how it can best be gathered. Poor decision-makers tend to pick up what data they can and then try and decide which parts are useful.

FACT FILE

Harold Geneen built up ITT into a major US conglomerate. He is said to have made his decisions based only on 'unshakeable facts'. He did not want opinions; he wanted facts and only facts. He insisted his employees had a firm grasp of the facts and figures involved in the areas for which they were responsible.

Analysing data

The next stage in decision-making is one of analysis. This is important in order to turn the raw data into something useful. Managers look for trends, causes and effects within the data to try and understand its significance. Techniques such as investment appraisal and ratio and break-even analysis are analytical tools which managers use to make sense of numerical data. The purpose of such techniques is to help turn the data into information, to help interpret the numbers so that their significance becomes clearer.

KEY POINTS

Primary research is more likely to be used in making a decision when:

- the firm has the necessary funds
- the decision does not have to be made immediately
- the impact of making a wrong decision would be serious
- the manager believes in gathering data before deciding.

Selecting a strategy and developing a plan

The final decision, and therefore strategy and plan, will depend on the options available, the firm's own strengths and resources and the overall objective.

Implementing a plan

Once a strategy and plan have been chosen, managers have to implement them. This can prove to be the most difficult stage in the process. Many managers would argue that the problem is not knowing what to do but actually getting it done. If the firm is limited by its resources it may end up choosing a second best plan. Alternatively, there may be resistance to the plan from within the firm. Change can be difficult to implement internally and the firm's own employees can often present a barrier to change. This is because the plan may involve a loss of status for some employees, require extra work or new skills.

FACT FILE

Shakespeare in Love was a major film hit in 1999 but the concluding scenes were not the ending which was filmed originally. Having trialled the film with a test audience, the film makers altered the ending. This is fairly common practice in the film industry, where film companies make sure they research the market reactions thoroughly before releasing a film. Even so, some films become hits even though this would not have been predicted from test results.

Reviewing progress

Once a plan has been implemented, the manager needs to keep a check on progress. It is not enough to put a plan into action; it is also the manager's responsibility to make sure the plan is carried out in the correct manner and that the desired results are achieved. Decision-making must be seen as an ongoing process in which results, objectives and strategies are constantly reviewed.

Summary

Good decision-making, therefore, involves a clear definition of the objectives, effective gathering of relevant data and a good analysis of the situation. The decision then has to be successfully implemented and reviewed.

PROGRESS CHECK

Consider the possible problems a firm might have in implementing a decision to expand rapidly.

KP

KEY POINTS

A decision is more likely to be successful if:

- the objectives are clear
- relevant data is gathered
- the analysis of the data is effective
- the decision can be easily implemented.

Bill Gates advocates scientific decision-making

The importance of examining quantifiable data and taking a scientific approach to decision-making is emphasised in Bill Gates' book *Business At the Speed of Thought*:

> 'The business side of any company starts and ends with hard-core analysis of its numbers. If you don't understand what's happening in your business factually and you're making business decisions based on anecdotal data or gut instinct alone, you'll pay a big price … Numbers give you the factual basis for the directions in which you take your products. Numbers tell you in objective terms what customers like and don't like. Numbers help you to identify your highest priorities so that you can take fast tactical or strategic action … The analysis should always support action not just more action. Analysis should lead you step-by-step to a decision and to action. You have to think, act, evaluate, adapt.'

PROGRESS CHECK

1 **Outline the stages of the decision-making process.**
2 **Examine the potential benefits of adopting a scientific approach to decision-making.**

By following the various stages of the decision-making model managers hope to reduce the risk of making a mistake. However, this process does not guarantee success. After all, the manager could have chosen the wrong objective to begin with, in which case the decision itself is bound to be flawed. Imagine a manager had decided to expand into a market which then went into a major decline; it does not matter how effectively the decision to expand was taken, it may still be extremely difficult to make a profit.

The quality of the data is also a major influence on the effectiveness of the decision. If the data is out of date, inaccurate or irrelevant, the final decision is likely to be incorrect.

'Paralysis by analysis'

Managers must also avoid 'paralysis by analysis'. This can occur when managers focus for too long on the data, gathering more and more, to try and improve the quality of their decision. The result is that they are actually unable to reach a conclusion because they are overwhelmed by the amount of information available to them. Even if they do finally make a decision, they may have spent so much time gathering and analysing the data that conditions have changed and the chosen course of action no longer appropriate.

'Programmed' decisions

Although the scientific decision-making process seems entirely logical, this does not mean that it is always used by decision-takers. In some situations, managers may not see the need for a detailed analysis of the issues and may prefer to rely more on their own experience. This is particularly likely to be the case with what are called **'programmed' decisions**; these are routine decisions which have been made many times before, such as re-ordering stock. A manager may automatically use the same supplier and order the same quantity each time without looking at all the alternatives. The manager may argue that the decision was achieved scientifically the first time and so there is no need to change it. This could be a valid view (assuming the decision was actually reached scientifically the first time!) but also depends on whether conditions have changed since the decision was first taken; over a number of years (if not months) new suppliers may have entered the market, the terms and conditions of their contracts may have changed and the precise requirements of the firm may have altered. If there have been a number of new developments, it may not be appropriate to rely on experience. Managers would make better decisions if they took a fresh look at the data. Even routine decisions are worth examining scientifically once in a while. Whether managers do this depends on how important they think the issue is and how busy they are.

Using intuition

Despite the logical appeal of the scientific approach, many successful business people refer to the importance of their gut feeling in making the right decision. What matters is not what the data appears to say but what you feel is right, they would argue. Although relying on intuition is highly risky, because it has no basis in actual data, it may be an attractive way of making a decision if time is limited and something has to be done quickly. It may also be appropriate if the relevant data does not exist or is too expensive (relevant to the expected gains) to gather.

Intuition may be more appropriate than a scientific approach if a high degree of creativity or originality is needed – when a fashion designer comes up with a new trend-setting design, for example, it is more likely to be based on gut feeling than a rigorous analysis of the market. When there is a major breakthrough in the world of music or art this is often because someone has done something which no-one has thought of before or done something in a way which others would have thought did not make sense. In situations where a new approach is required, intuition may be the key rather than an obsessively logical approach.

KEY POINTS

A manager is more likely to use intuition if:

- time is limited
- the decision does not carry a high degree of risk
- the necessary data is not available or too expensive
- the decision needs to be highly creative.

In reality, effective decisions are likely to be made with a combination of hard facts, experience and gut feeling. By gathering data the risk of error is reduced, but there is still an element of doubt – you do not really know your expected sales or costs, for example, you can only estimate them. Good managers will use the data available and combine this with their own experience and intuition to select the right course of action. To take a decision without thinking about the data or blatantly ignoring it is foolhardy; however the data which does exist should always be placed in context. If the data suggests the project will be profitable but is based on assumptions which you believe are false, then you would be wrong to go ahead with it.

FACT FILE

When John Conlan, Chief Executive of First Leisure (which owns a range of clubs, bingo halls, gymnasiums and bowling alleys), was asked how he tested new ideas he said, 'You can't, frankly. You do the homework, the market research, the focus groups. But at the end of the day, the customer doesn't know what he wants until he sees it. If you went by customer feedback, you'd end up with a very strange leisure camel that nobody wanted.' One way of reducing risk he thinks is to copy rivals. 'I take the view that the man who invented the wheel was a bit of an idiot. The genius was the guy who came up with the other three.'
Financial Times 23 January 1997

Imagine you were going to place a bet on a horse. A logical approach would be to study the form in detail – you would look at how the horses have run in the past and how they performed under similar conditions in similar races. An approach based on experience might be to look at the horses just before the race begins. Then to decide which one to pick based on how other winning horses have looked before the race. An intuitive approach might be to look at their names or colours and pick on the basis of which one 'sounds or looks right'. In reality you may use a combination of all three methods – you may look at the form, see the horses on the day and also be influenced by the name (how many of us would bet on a horse called 'Sad Loser'?). Even then, success cannot be guaranteed (ask the betting shops!) a fact which highlights the difficulties facing all decision-makers.

PROGRESS CHECK

Questions

1 **To what extent do you think investors buy shares on the basis of hard facts?**
2 **Examine the potential problems of 'scientific' decision-making as opposed to hunch.**

Decision trees

Probability

A technique which is used to help managers make decisions is known as a **decision tree**. A decision tree is based on probability theory and sets out diagrammatically the likelihood of different outcomes occurring together with the associated financial consequences. By considering the probability of different outcomes and possible financial results, a manager can calculate the expected value of a particular course of action. He or she can then compare these expected values to decide which action to take.

KEY TERM

The **probability** of an event is how likely it is to occur. The probability can range between 0 (definitely will not happen) and 1 (definitely will happen).

The advantages of decision trees

The value of drawing a decision tree is that it highlights all the possible outcomes of an action, together with the likelihoods and possible gains or losses of each one. This makes it easy for managers to see the different options open to them. The actual *process* of drawing up the tree is as important as the chart itself. This is because the process forces managers to think about the various options and the consequences of each one. There may be disagreements about the various values allocated to the probabilities and financial outcomes, but the important thing is that it makes people *think* about what happens when they make a decision.

KEY TERM

The **expected value** of an event is the weighted average of the possible outcomes and the likelihood of each of them occurring. If there is a 0.7 chance of winning £100 and a 0.3 chance of winning £50 the expected value is: (0.7 × £100) + (0.3 × £50) = £85

The health warning

When it comes to using decision trees, the mathematics involved is not particularly complex and it is possible to identify the course of action with the highest potential value. However, managers must be aware that these numbers are only *estimates.* Like any decision involving the future, the data is a forecast and, therefore, the validity of the decision will depend on the reliability of the estimates. If the manager has incorrectly estimated the likelihood of different outcomes and incorrectly estimated the consequences of each, it is not surprising if the final decision is wrong. Decision trees should, therefore, be treated with some caution.

The reliability of the estimates will depend on how they were derived – were they based on past data, a test market, or just intuition? Reliability will also depend on the type of outcome under review – if a firm is launching a new product in a rapidly changing and unfamiliar market, any estimate of the probability of success is likely to very tentative. However, if it is undertaking a mailshot which is similar to ones which have been undertaken before, the estimated response rate is likely to be quite accurate.

FACT FILE

In March 1999 the Office for National Statistics (ONS) admitted there were errors in the official pay statistics it had produced. Publication of the average earnings index (one of the most sensitive economic indicators used by the Bank of England to set interest rates) was suspended in November 1998 after different figures gave conflicting views. The ONS admitted it had got it wrong.

Although decision trees do have a logical appeal they rely on *quantifiable* data. When making a decision there may be many *qualitative* factors to consider as well:

- How does a particular project fit with the image of the company?
- What will the reaction of employees be?
- What will be the impact on employees' morale?
- Is it ethical?

The results of any decision-tree analysis have to be taken in context; it may be that managers finally decide to make the decision based on qualitative rather than quantitative factors. Investment in a new sports complex may not appear to be as profitable as a re-launch of an existing product, but the impact on employer–employee relations may be more desirable, for example.

KEY:
□ = a decision has to be made
○ = the outcomes of a decision
p = probability of a particular outcome
EV = expected value if that option is chosen. This is a weighted average of the possible outcomes (e.g. for option A EV = (0.5 × £30,000) + (0.5 × £20,000) = £25,0000

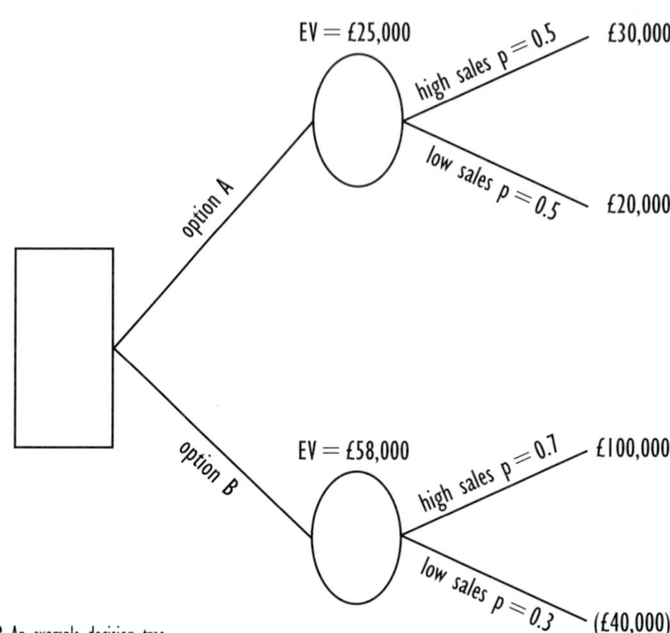

Figure 2.3 An example decision tree

KEY POINTS

Decision trees are more likely to be useful when:

- the estimates of the probabilities of the outcomes are accurate
- all relevant courses of action are considered
- the manager can actually implement the decision
- qualitative factors are not significant.

Risk

It is important to consider the risks involved in a particular decision. In the example above the expected value of choosing B is higher than A; this is because there is a good chance of gaining £100,000. However, there is a danger of losing £40,000. A risk-averse organisation (i.e. one which does not like risk) may choose A. Although this has a lower expected value, there is no possibility of losing money according to the firm's estimates.

Decision trees are a tool which can help to formalise the decision-making process and so make managers quantify the consequences of any particular course of action. Instead of just talking generally and without focus, they are forced to address each option in turn and in detail. As we have mentioned, the use of decision trees does not guarantee that the final decision is right. If, for example, the manager fails to include all the relevant courses of action, the wrong decision may be taken. You may be choosing between advertising more or lowering the price when you should be considering a change of packaging. Similarly, if the manager's estimates of the probabilities and financial outcomes are incorrect the decision may be wrong. Lastly, as with any decision-making technique, making the decision is only part of the process – it then has to be implemented. Deciding to launch a new product may be the easy bit – actually launching it to the right specifications, within budget and on time may be the real challenge.

How do firms estimate probabilities?

To calculate the expected value of a particular decision managers must estimate the probability of a given outcome. These estimates may be based on **backdata.** If, in the past, only one in four products launched has succeeded, then the firm may use a probability of 0.25 for success and 0.75 for failure.

Alternatively, the firm may try a product in a test market and use the results from this area as an estimate for the market as a whole. These figures will only be reliable if the test market is representative; if the test market is known to have a particular bias the results will have to be adjusted.

If backdata is not available and it is not possible to test out the decision, the firm will have to rely on its managers' own judgement and intuition. The more routine the decision, the more likely it is to be right; the more unfamiliar the decisions, the greater the chance of error.

KEY TERM

Backdata
consists of past research findings which can be used to predict future outcomes.

FACT FILE

Experience is more likely to lead to the right decision if:

- the manager has got it right many times before
- the decision is similar to decisions made in the past
- the conditions have not changed much since the last time.

PROGRESS CHECK

Questions

1 **Analyse how firms might estimate the likelihood of a new product surviving in the marketplace.**
2 **Discuss the possible benefits of using decision trees in decision-making.**

Fishbone diagrams (the Ishikawa method)

A fishbone diagram is another technique which can be used to help solve problems and make better decisions. These diagrams were originally developed by Professor Ishikawa at Tokyo University. They are intended to highlight the cause of a particular problem. Refer to the diagram below. The box at the end on the right shows the issue under investigation. Each of the ribs is a potential cause of the problem and then the rays feeding into each of these are possible contributory factors. By drawing a diagram such as this a decision-maker can get an overview of an issue. It is a useful exercise to do in a group with all those involved, since it forces a discussion of the factors causing the problem and helps to identify what lies behind the difficulty.

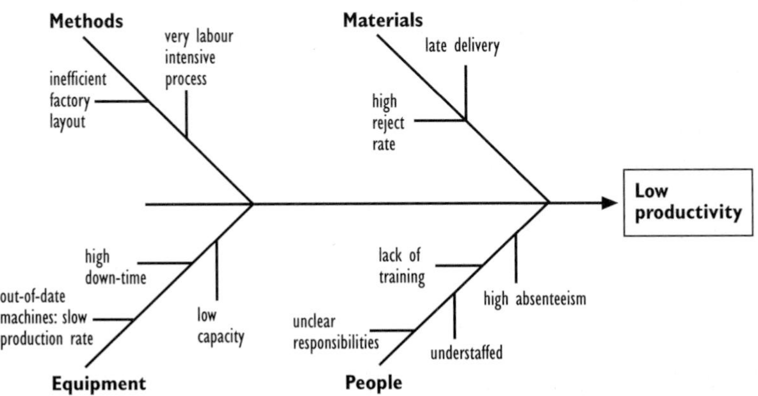

Figure 2.4 A fishbone diagram

Scenario planning

Scenario planning is an attempt to identify two or three possible situations in the future and to plan accordingly. Firms such as Shell attempt to build a limited number of views of the future, based on different assumptions. Scenario planning forces managers to think about the future and to consider possible future occurrences. This is a useful exercise as it raises managers' awareness of likely events and helps them to prepare. It is particularly useful in times of rapid change, when extrapolation from past data would be meaningless and even misleading. Scenario planning aims to create the 'big picture' of how the industry may develop – it does not rely on detailed data. Managers attempt to identify the fundamental driving forces in their industry which will determine the future business environment and imagine what could happen.

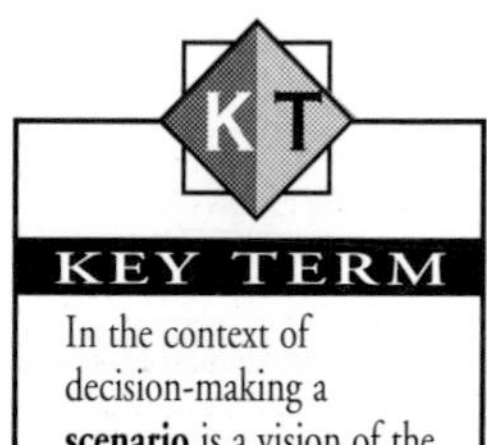

KEY TERM

In the context of decision-making a **scenario** is a vision of the future.

The origins of scenario planning lie in the work of Herman Kahn who worked for the Rand Corporation and the Hudson Institute. His famous phrase was 'thinking the unthinkable'.

PROGRESS CHECK

Questions

1 **Examine the differences between decision trees and scenario planning.**
2 **How useful are decision-making aids such as decision trees, fishbone diagrams and scenario planning in helping managers to make better decisions?**

Other factors in decision-making

Qualitative factors

When making a decision managers will usually take into account qualitative factors as well as quantitative ones. Whether the manager is using decision trees, investment appraisal, ratio analysis or any of the mathematical techniques to help analyse the data, there will also be a range of other less well defined factors to take into account. For example, the manager may be concerned about:

- *Reputation:* the impact of the decision on the firm's corporate image. Basing production operations in an emerging economy and paying low wages may make economic sense, but may also make the firm vulnerable to negative publicity. Sponsoring a sports event may not be a commercial proposition but may be popular with the public or internally.
- *The reaction of employees:* if a particular, potentially profitable, proposal is likely to prove very unpopular and cause friction in the workplace, managers may decide not to go ahead. Long-term success requires the support of employees; it may not be worth upsetting them for a minor one-off gain. Imagine a manager faced two options, one involving redundancies and the other involving the recruitment of more staff. He or she would probably prefer to be recruiting.

Making people redundant, freezing their wages, moving them to a new job that they do not want, increasing their workload when they are clearly stressed – these are all things managers would want to avoid if they could. They will do it if they have to, but if they can find an alternative solution they probably will.

- *Ethical issues:* the ethical stance of the managers or the firm's owners may mean that investment is made in some projects which are not particularly profitable (such as investment in the community) or that the firm does not invest in other schemes which could be very profitable (e.g. arms trading).

The final decision is likely to be a combination of both quantifiable and qualitative data. The numerical analysis is bound to count, but the less quantifiable factors can also play a major role.

KEY TERMS

Quantitative factors are measurable, such as the number of sales, costs and profits.

Qualitative factors are not easily measurable (but nevertheless very important). These include peoples' attitudes, the culture of the organisation and the ethics of the managers.

PROGRESS CHECK

Analyse the qualitative factors a firm might take into account when considering a major capital investment project.

Opportunity cost

KEY TERM

The **opportunity cost** of any decision is the benefit foregone, i.e. what else has been sacrificed as a result. The decision to enter one particular market may mean funds are not available for more product development.

Opportunity cost is a crucial concept in business in general and in decision-making in particular. When making a decision, a manager should not only consider what is involved in the particular course of action but also what other decisions are prevented as a result. If, for example, you decide to invest £100 m setting up a new production line, the money is no longer available to invest in a new marketing campaign. When making a decision, it is easy to focus on the two or three options in front of you and ignore the many other things you could be doing instead.

Managers need to take a broad view of any decision and consider the sacrifices involved. This is very important when deciding whether a project is actually worthwhile – a 10% return may seem desirable, but what if you could be earning 14% elsewhere? The concept of opportunity cost is also important in the context of **time management**. When managers get involved in a particular problem which eats into their time, they need to consider what else they could be doing; spending two weeks sorting out a relatively minor problem may involve a huge opportunity cost in terms of the strategic decisions which could have been made during this period.

What you are doing is not all that counts – what else you could be doing also matters.

Risk

All decisions involve risk. The outcomes cannot be guaranteed and so there is inevitably an element of uncertainty. However, the degree of risk will vary from project to project. If you put money into a bank at a fixed rate of interest you will almost certainly be paid the interest you expect; if, however, you bet on a horse, the

FACT FILE

Each day billions of pounds of currency is bought and sold by speculators. In 1995, for example, $1.2 trillion dollars of foreign exchange swapped hands per day; this is around 50 times the value of world trade in goods and services. Speculators are making decisions on possible future currency movements using a combination of mathematical analysis, experience and intuition. One of the most famous speculators is George Soros who made millions of pounds on one day in September 1992 when he sold pounds; later that day the pound left the exchange rate mechanism and fell in value. Soros was able to buy them back and make a profit immediately. On a good day he is said to make $1 billion by speculating.

chances of getting a return are much lower. When making a decision a manager must, therefore, consider the risk involved – how likely is it to succeed and what if it goes wrong? Some managers will be more risk-averse than others; they will not like risk and tend to choose safer projects. Other managers will be more willing to 'gamble' and go for the higher prizes, even if the likelihood of winning is less certain. Faced with the same data, two managers may choose different projects purely because of their view of the risk involved and their attitude to risk.

A manager's attitude to risk will be influenced by:

- the *culture* of the organisation – are managers encouraged to try things out and see what happens?
- the manager's own *personality* and *experiences*
- the *money* involved – we are likely to be more carefree when only a small amount of money is at stake
- the personal impact if it goes wrong – will the manager be held responsible?

Business success almost inevitably involves taking risks. If you wait until you are sure, you may miss the opportunity.

PROGRESS CHECK

Analyse the factors which might make one firm more willing to take risks than another.

FACT FILE

In the 1980s Danone wanted to launch a range of yoghurts in Japan. Extensive research by their own research company showed very favourable results, yet when the products were launched they were unsuccessful. An investigation showed that Japanese consumers had been reluctant to upset the researchers and so had told them the yoghurts tasted nice even when they hated them!

Why do people make wrong decisions?

Whenever you have to make a major decision you are unlikely to feel 100% sure about what you do. You may not have enough information; you may have too much. You may have too little time or you may not be entirely sure what are the key factors to focus on. Even the best managers make mistakes; the difference is that they make less mistakes and less costly mistakes than bad managers. Ultimately, whatever data you gather, however many people you ask for advice, making a decision involves professional judgement. A manager must gather together all the different elements of the puzzle and put them together to reach a conclusion. The way that different managers analyse the data will depend on their experiences, their creativity, their vision and their ability to distinguish the factors which really matter from those that are less significant. Whatever happens managers must avoid being bombarded by too much data and letting this prevent action being taken.

The pace of change

Even if a decision is properly researched and thought through, the external environment can soon make it inappropriate. A good decision can soon become a bad one. Even a good decision to target a particular market segment can quickly become inappropriate if a competitor manages to beat you to it. Tax changes can make a decision unprofitable; technology can overtake a firm and make a product obsolete. Decision-making must, therefore, be seen as an dynamic process. Decisions must be reviewed, adjusted and developed. What was right in the past may not be right now and decision-makers must react as their objectives, resources and environment changes.

FACT FILE

In 1999 NATO attacked Yugoslavia. Despite using the most modern military hardware available, several mistakes were made when the wrong targets were hit. When the Chinese embassy was bombed in error, NATO admitted that this had happened because the maps it had used were out of date.

Drift

Management writer Roger Dawson identifies several problems which typically cause problems in decision-making and cause the decision-maker to drift off course. For example:

- *Availability drift* – this occurs when the decision-maker gives too much importance to information which is readily available.
- *Experience drift* – this occurs when people see things in their own terms. If their background is in marketing, managers may overemphasise its importance, for example.
- *Conflict drift* – this occurs because people tend to reject information which conflicts with their own views.
- *Anchoring drift* – this occurs when people are dealing in an unfamiliar area. They may latch on to the first data they get and always use this as a reference point.

Effective decision-makers must be aware of these problems of drift which prevent them identifying and analysing the relevant information effectively.

KEY POINTS

Bad decisions are more likely to occur when:

- managers fail to identify the key issues
- there is too much or too little information
- the information is inaccurate
- the manager lacks experience and good judgement
- circumstances change rapidly.

PROGRESS CHECK

Examine the possible barriers to making the 'right' decision.

Groupthink

One particular problem which occurs when several people come together to make a decision is known as **groupthink**. This occurs when a group of people get together and talk themselves into making a decision which they would not normally have made as individuals. This phenomenon can be seen with juries, for example. Often individual members end up voting in a way which they would not have done if asked to make a decision alone. By working in a group, they end up convincing each other of a particular way of thinking.

KEY TERM

The **culture** of an organisation refers to the values, attitudes and beliefs of the people who work within it.

Many managers leave a meeting and wonder how they all ended up reaching a particular decision. Groupthink is something which firms have to watch out for because it can lead to the wrong decisions being made. To avoid groupthink occurring, organisations have to create a climate in which people do not feel afraid of criticising the established view.

PROGRESS CHECK

Explain the possible implications of 'groupthink' for decision-making.

FACT FILE

The **ringi process** is typical of the way decisions are made in Japan. Proposals are circulated within the firm so that decisions are made with a consensus. This approach means that employees 'buy in' to the decision as it is being made, rather than having to be convinced of its worth later on.

Culture and decision-making

Managers who have worked in different countries have often commented on the different ways in which decisions are made around the world. Typically American and British managers want a relatively quick decision. In these countries people tend to respect the leader or manager, who knows his or her own mind and who listens, but is able to take a decision for themselves. A good meeting in these countries involves some discussion but leads to a definite decision. Although there has been a noticeable move in many companies towards a more democratic process, the general approach still involves a dominant character who takes on board different views but reaches his or her own conclusion.

Decision-making is different in other countries such as Japan where there is a much more consensual approach. Meetings in Japan often go on for much longer than in the West and Western managers sometimes get frustrated that nothing seems to be being decided. Ideas go round and round so that everybody has an input. This obviously takes more time. By the end everyone has had the opportunity to comment on the decision and so, in theory, should be more committed to it. In the Western model there is a danger that individuals do not feel properly consulted and feel that a decision has been imposed on them. This may lead to resentment and frustration. On the other hand the Japanese approach may be too slow and result in market opportunities being missed.

FACT FILE

Harold Leavitt divides decision-makers into three types:

- **Type 1:** *Visionaries* – bold, charismatic, original and often eccentric, e.g. Winston Churchill.
- **Type 2:** *Logical and analytical* – they deal with facts not opinions, e.g. Harold Geneen of ITT.
- **Type 3:** *Doers* – these people are concerned with fixing things and implementing plans.

Imagine that a new production line is being set up, for example. In the West, the aim would be to get it up and running as quickly as possible. Once it was working, faults would be found and these would then have to be fixed. By comparison, a Japanese approach to this project would tend to get everyone who was likely to be affected involved in the planning stage. This means the planning would take longer, but once the line is established there is less chance of anything having been overlooked. These cultural differences to decision-making can be a major issue when firms merge or are involved in a take-over – a failure to understand how others make decisions can result in frustrations, anger and a poor working relationship.

The culture within a particular firm will also have a big impact on decision-making. Faced with a range of options a manager will consider the firm's objectives and also decision values. What does the company believe is important? How much risk are employees expected to take? Is the firm looking for short-term or long-term rewards? Two managers in two different companies with the same data in front of them may make completely different decisions because of the culture of their organisations – one may choose a safer option, another may be willing to spend more and risk more in the pursuit of profits.

PROGRESS CHECK

Examine the ways in which culture might influence a firm's decision-making.

FACT FILE

Des Dearlove in his book *Key Management Decisions* identifies five types of decision-maker:

1 *flamboyant* – pride themselves on making bold, snap decisions
2 *practical* – pride themselves on making sensible, workable decisions
3 *analytical* – pride themselves on making logical decisions
4 *defensive* – prefer not to make decisions
5 *creative* – enjoy making decisions but only if they utilise new ideas and break new ground.

How is decision-making changing?

Information technology

In some ways decision-making should be becoming easier as information technology develops. Improvements in information gathering, analysing and distribution systems should mean that better information is available more readily and at a cheaper cost. Many organisations have developed Management Information Systems which aim to give managers the information they need, when they want it, and in a form they can use. With more good quality information one might hope for better decision-making. Unfortunately this is not necessarily the case. As ever, there is the danger of collecting the wrong information. Information technology may encourage the gathering of data, but does not guarantee that the right information is collected or that it is interpreted or used in an effective manner.

FACT FILE

You can find out almost anything you want to on the internet. In 1999 a list of 100 alleged British MI6 spies was made available on the internet. No-one was sure who had put the list there but some blamed a disaffected employee.

The speed of change

The speed of change in the external environment is undoubtedly making decision-making more complicated. The rapid arrival of new products, the increasing fragmentation of markets and the never ending changes in the business environment mean that managers face an increasingly difficult task, with or without developments in information technology.

The role of the manager

Whether or not decision-making is getting easier there has been a general change in the role of a manager in the decision-making process. Managers are expected increasingly to involve employees in the decision-making process rather than deciding what to do and then telling the workforce that they have to do it. This move towards more democratic management reflects the increasing emphasis being placed on the knowledge, skills and insight of employees and a realisation that their contribution can enhance decision-making. Increasingly, managers are being asked to act as facilitators rather than active decision-makers.

KEY POINTS

Decision-making is likely to be more effective if:

- the manager is experienced
- good quality information is available
- employees are involved and agree with the decision.

PROGRESS CHECK

Analyse the ways in which information technology might help decision-making.

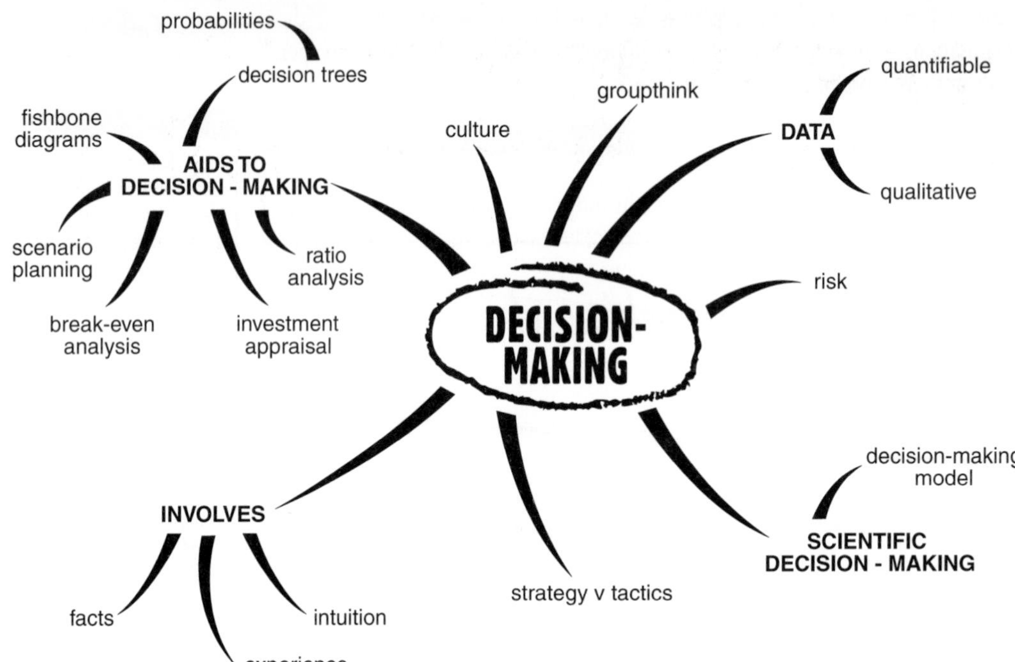
probabilities
decision trees
fishbone diagrams
AIDS TO DECISION - MAKING
scenario planning
break-even analysis
investment appraisal
ratio analysis
culture
groupthink
DATA
quantifiable
qualitative
risk
DECISION-MAKING
decision-making model
SCIENTIFIC DECISION - MAKING
strategy v tactics
INVOLVES
facts
experience
intuition

Figure 2.5

Approaching exam questions: Decision-making

Consider the value of intuition to a decision-maker.

(11 marks)

This is a fairly straightforward question in which you need to discuss how intuition could be beneficial. You also need to be aware of its limitations. A good answer will explain what intuition is, highlight the contribution it can make to good decision-making and also discuss the problems with this approach. The question asks you to *consider*, so to achieve full marks you must show *judgement* – what makes intuition more or less likely to be useful? What type of decision is more likely to need intuition? What sort of decision is most likely to benefit from a more scientific approach?

Answers may include the following ideas:

- Intuition may enable a manager to make 'leaps of imagination' and come to radical solutions to problems which might not otherwise have been found.
- Intuition might enable a firm to stay ahead of its competitors.
- Decisions made by intuition may be hard to second guess.
- Intuition is most likely to be used if:
  - it has worked in the past
  - there is limited data available
  - the market conditions are changing extremely rapidly.
- However, intuition also brings with it risk because it is only 'gut feeling'. A more scientific approach would be based on data which could reduce the chances of mistakes. However, even this approach does not guarantee success.
- The value of intuition will depend on the decision being made, the risks involved and the attitude of the decision-maker.

'Decisions should be based on hard data. Nothing else matters.' Discuss.

(40 marks)

This question is essentially about the relative importance of data in decision-making. It is deliberately provocative ('Nothing else matters') and is inviting candidates to argue against the case. A good answer will highlight the importance of 'hard' data (in that it provides a factual basis for decision-making) but will also consider situations where other factors, such as intuition and qualitative aspects may have a role; for example:

- if data is not available or is too expensive to obtain
- if the manager does not trust the data or trusts his or her own intuition more
- if the manager is deliberately trying to break with a trend and be unpredictable
- if factors such as employee morale or ethics are important.

A good answer would weigh up the value of 'hard' data and highlight that it can be more or less useful depending on the decision-maker and the situation.

'With increasing amounts of data available thanks to information technology, there is no reason why decisions should ever be wrong.' Critically assess this view.

(40 marks)

This question makes a fairly extreme statement suggesting that decisions should never be wrong because of the developments in information technology. A good answer would analyse the statement. Why should information technology help? In what ways can it improve decision-making? How can developments improve decision-making? The answer would then go on to discuss whether the statement is actually valid. To what extent can information technology help? Is good information technology enough? If not, why not?

Areas which could be covered include the fact that developments in information technology have made more information available, more quickly and at a much lower cost in the past. In many ways this should make decision-making easier. However, various other points need to be considered:

- Just because more information is generally available, it does not mean that the information you want exists.
- More data does not help in itself – it still has to be analysed and interpreted correctly.
- It is possible to have too much data, leading to 'paralysis by analysis'.

It is important to remember that, no matter how much information is available, unexpected changes in the environment can turn a 'good' decision into a 'bad' one. It is not always possible to predict changes in interest rates, competitors' actions or social attitudes and so decisions do go wrong. A good answer could also discuss some of the problems of implementing a decision: a decision can be right at the decision-making stage but fail to be successful because of problems putting it into practice.

Also, the quantity of information is just one part of the equation – you also need to consider the quality of it, the process of implementation and possible changes in the environment.

'The good decision-maker is the one who listens.' Discuss this view.

(11 marks)

This is a question which requires *discussion*, so you need to outline two sides of the argument and show *judgement*:

'listening is valuable because . . .

On the other hand too much listening may mean . . .

It depends on . . .'

Areas which could be usefully discussed include the importance of consultation and being prepared to learn from others when making a decision. However good the decision-maker, it is unlikely that he or she knows everything they need to about the particular issue. They can improve their understanding of an issue by listening to others. By involving others in the process, managers can gain new insights into a problem and gain a different perspective on how it could be solved.

However, too much listening can bring problems – it may slow up the decision-making process and lose a valuable time advantage. Consultation can cause conflict – people whose ideas are rejected may feel disappointed or frustrated. Consultation may be unnecessary. If the decision is relatively minor, the decision-maker may feel confident that sufficient data is available and that they have the experience to make the decision themselves. A 'listening' approach may simply delay the obvious decision.

A good answer will highlight the value of listening but also the potential problems. The extent to which listening is necessary or even desirable will depend on the circumstances – with a highly risky, unfamiliar decision in which success relies on peoples' co-operation listening may be crucial.

Student answers

Consider the advantages of adopting a scientific approach to decision-making.

(11 marks)

Student answer

Scientific decision-making is logical and rational. Decisions are based on data rather than intuition. It is systematic and follows the process of deciding what you want to achieve, gathering data, analysing it, implementing it and reviewing it. By making sure you have the facts and by studying them carefully this should mean that less mistakes are made. It should reduce the risk.

If a manager does not do this and just decides things because he or she feels like it, this is much more dangerous. Scientific decision-making prevents mistakes occurring because it makes sure it is logical and right. Scientific decision-making involves many different techniques such as investment appraisal, ratio analysis, break-even analysis, elasticity of demand and many other topics which analyse data to make a decision. By using these things we can make sure we have looked at a problem from many different angles and so choose the right decision. If we do not do this, we will probably get it wrong because we are not using data.

Marker's comments

This answer starts off well. It correctly describes the decision-making process and highlights some of the advantages of the scientific approach. However, it fails to fulfil its early promise. Unfortunately it only looks at one side of the argument and assumes that the scientific approach is 'right'. The later comments are rather simplistic – a scientific approach can reduce risk but certainly cannot remove it.

Mark: Content 2/2, Application & Analysis 4/6, Evaluation 0/3. Total = 6

To what extent does a scientific approach to decision-making guarantee the right decision is reached?

(11 marks)

Student answer

Scientific decision-making is a logical process in which decision-makers gather data and look at it very carefully before making a decision. This makes sure they think before they do anything and that what they do has a basis in 'facts'. Research is done to collect data; this can be done internally using backdata or externally using field or desk research. Then it is analysed. For example, this may involve ratio analysis, correlation analysis or investment appraisal. Once this has been done the 'right' decision is made. But this does not mean that the firm never makes a mistake because the data can be wrong or out of date. By the time you have gathered the data the market conditions may have changed, especially in fast-changing markets such as computer software. So although data can help sometimes it is not enough because there is not always enough data to tell you everything. Sometimes intuition is needed because the data is not there (or we cannot afford it) or because some things are difficult to quantify, such as people's reactions to an idea.

Marker's comments

This is a strong answer which outlines the scientific process and explains the possible gains of this approach. At the same time it highlights a possible problem with the scientific method and gives a good example ('in fast-changing markets such as computer software'). This type of answer is to be encouraged!

Mark: Content 2/2, Application & Analysis 6/6, Evaluation 3/3. Total = 11

How important is decision-making in the management process?

(11 marks)

Student answer

Decision-making is very important in the management process, because if you do not make a decision then nothing gets done. If nothing gets done, nothing happens which is bad. To makes things happen you must decide what to do and that counts. Imagine if no-one made a decision – where would we be then? What would we do if no-one can decide? It is crucial for the firm to decide things if they want everything to be going smoothly and make lots of profits.

So decisions really count because they tell us what to do and when to do it. That keeps everything going fine and gets everything right. So, everyone is happy and knows what to do.

Marker's comments

This is a very weak answer full of assertions and with no development of the points made. Essentially, the candidate claims that decision-making is important but does not explain why. Candidates should also be using phrases such as 'going smoothly' and 'lots of profits' which are not very impressive.

Mark: Content 1/2, Application & Analysis 0/6, Evaluation 0/3. Total = 1

Information technology has made decision-making much easier. Discuss.

(11 marks)

Student answer

Information technology means spreadsheets, word processors, databases, emails and other equipment like computers which allow information to be kept and used. Information technology is very important to a firm because it can help a firm to be competitive. It can cut costs, help a firm to do things more quickly and improve communication. Information technology is very important these days because there is much more of it and it changes quickly. Firms which do not use information technology will fail because they cannot keep up. There is lots of information technology around and this helps speed things up and makes decisions easier and quicker so people can get on with things.

Marker's comments

Another weak answer which does not address the question which is asked. This answer feels as if it has been written before in response to a different question. At no time does the candidate refer to the relationship between information technology and decision-making or discuss whether IT has made the process easier or not.

The candidate makes the assertion that 'Firms which do not use information technology will fail because they cannot keep up.' This kind of statement is not helpful because it is not developed or discussed. Why will such firms fail? Is it inevitable? In this particular case, however, this was not even the issue – the candidate has wandered from the point.

Mark: Content 1/2, Application & Analysis 1/6, Evaluation 0/3. Total = 2

End of section questions

1 Analyse the possible value to decision-takers of using decision trees. (9 marks)

2 How useful is scientific decision-making? (9 marks)

3 Is information technology making decision-making easier? (9 marks)

4 Examine the problems which can occur when making a decision. (9 marks)

5 Discuss the factors which can influence the way in which a decision is made. (11 marks)

6 Examine the problems which can occur when using decision trees. (11 marks)

7 Analyse the value of intuition in the decision-making process. (9 marks)

8 To what extent should a manager base a decision on his or her experience? (11 marks)

9 Which is more useful in decision-making: gut feeling or data? (9 marks)

10 Consider the problems which can occur with scientific decision-making. (11 marks)

Essays

1 Is decision-making an art or science? (40 marks)

2 Is scientific decision-making better than using your intuition? (40 marks)

3 To what extent does effective decision-making determine a firm's success? (40 marks)

4 'The more decisions you make, the more likely you are to get them right.' Discuss this view. (40 marks)

5 'Making the decision means nothing. It is the implementation of a decision which determines its success.' Discuss this view. (40 marks)

Starting up and business formats

Starting a new business

The process of establishing a new business involves four main stages:

1. *Identifying an opportunity and generating ideas.* Before a business can be started, the owner must have an idea of what and to whom they are going to sell. This is likely to involve a certain amount of research, depending on the level of capital commitment that is needed to get the business up and running. The greater the start up costs, the more research is likely to be needed, because the greater the risks involved in starting up.
2. *Developing a business plan.* Traditionally, it has been thought that the main reason for writing a business plan has been to raise capital – banks will rarely lend without one. Recent surveys however, have suggested that more firms are seeing them as central to the ongoing survival of their business – 50% of small firm business plans now contain a long-term strategy compared with only 27% in 1994.
3. *Selecting an appropriate business format.* The main choice here is between unlimited liability (partnerships and sole traders) and limited liability (companies – private or public). The choice will depend partly on the type of business being run and partly on the risk involved – the riskier the venture, the more likely that limited liability will be sought. Hence, most manufacturing firms with a heavy investment in capital and a sensitivity to the trade cycle tend to have limited liability, whereas service sector firms with lower set-up costs are more likely to have unlimited liability.
4. *Surviving the early years.* The first few years are the hardest to survive, with 50% of new firms closing within 18 months, and only 33% making it past five years. Effective planning and raising finance from appropriate sources are two important steps that firms can take to enhance their survival chances.

A business plan is not only needed when a firm starts up; it should be regularly reviewed to provide the business with a sense of direction.

KEY TERM

A **business plan** sets out the firm's objectives and strategy, and provides relevant financial, marketing and human resource information.

FACT FILE

Ben Cohen and Jerry Greenfield, founders of Ben and Jerry's ice cream, first met at school in 1963. They met up again in 1977 and decided to set up in business together. They wanted to make bagels, but when they found out the equipment cost $40,000 they changed their minds and invested $5 in a course on how to make ice cream! They opened Ben and Jerry's Homemade Ice Cream Parlour in May 1978, in a renovated petrol station in Burlington Vermont. Their products were launched in the UK in 1994. In 1997, British customers were asked to come up with suggestions for their own flavour. 'Cool Britannia' was announced the winner, beating 'Jack the Rippler' and 'Cream Victoria'!

Protecting ideas

Before an entrepreneur can commence trading, he or she will need a viable idea for a product or service. Having created the idea, they must decide whether it needs legal protection.

KEY TERM

An **entrepreneur** is someone who takes business risks. He or she sees a business opportunity and takes advantage of this. Entrepreneurs exploit gaps which appear in markets, create new markets and innovate. They act as a dynamic force within the economy, pushing forward into new areas and developing new products and innovative processes.

What makes a business more likely to succeed?

The high failure rate for new businesses indicates that there are a number of key factors that have to be in a firm's favour if a new opportunity is to succeed.

The USP

One of the most important factors is that the idea itself is different – there should be a **Unique Selling Proposition (USP)**. If the new firm simply does the same as existing firms in the same way with the same prices and services, there will be little to attract new customers. Customers will probably stay with the tried and tested products that they already buy. The new firm might feel that it has to spend a great deal of money on advertising and promotional activities, which it may not be able to afford in its early stages.

KEY TERM

A **Unique Selling Proposition** is an aspect of a firm's activities which is distinctive and differentiates it from the competition, e.g. home delivery or the fact that only natural ingredients are used.

The market segment

The new firm's target market segment should be large enough to support the firm, and preferably growing quickly. This last point is important because it is far easier to win genuinely new customers than to convert those who already have a brand preference.

Research

The key to success regarding the USP and the market segment lies in effective research. If the firm thoroughly researches its market segment before starting up, then it should be able to identify whether the market is too small, whether there is too much competition, or whether demand is static. Although formal market research can be very expensive, and is beyond the means of most business start-ups, this does not mean that thorough secondary research and basic primary research cannot be carried out.

An example: Amazon.com

The example of Amazon.com highlights the importance of good research before entering a market. Amazon.com is a virtual bookstore which sells books on the Internet. Up until 1994 Mr Bezos, the founder, worked on Wall Street as a senior vice president of a fund management firm. Having read about the growth of the Internet itself and amazed by the growth rate of Internet usage (over 2000%) he decided to set up an Internet business for himself.

FACT FILE

Lynda Hays owns Done Me Wrong, a company which supplies gifts for people to send to those who have upset them or let them down. Its products are for 'those who have been mistreated in business, love or in life'. An example is a dozen black roses packaged in black paper.

Before choosing to start up as an Internet bookseller, Bezos analysed around 20 different possible products which he thought could be sold effectively on the Internet. Books were particularly appealing because there are so many titles (over 3 million titles are in print at present) and because no traditional bookstore could hope to carry all of these in its shops. The growth of mail order bookselling also proved that people were prepared to buy books by post. Bezos chose Seattle as his location because it has a large pool of people with the necessary technical ability (Microsoft is also based there). It is also near the largest book warehouse in the world.

Before beginning trading, Amazon.com developed unique order processing software which was tested by friends and family in a trial six week period before going live. Since then, the business has grown at an incredible rate (much faster than Bezos expected), probably because it had such a unique selling proposition. On its very first day, it was bigger than any established bookshop, offering over 1 million titles and it is now worth several billion dollars!

FACT FILE

In 1998 over 20,000 new products were launched in the US, many by well established firms. By 1999 only 4,000 remained on the shelves.

Venture capital

Another factor which influences the viability of an opportunity, is the funds required to get it running. In the UK, venture capital is usually restricted to firms that are already showing some success, so getting finance for new ideas that need a large amount of start up capital may not be realistic.

There have been new businesses that have succeeded in spite of little research or capital back-up. In the early 1980s Sir Clive Sinclair launched the ZX80 and Spectrum home computers, in spite of the fact that the chairman of IBM was on record saying that he thought the market for computers to use at home would never exceed a few dozen units. Sinclair struck an unforeseen market and overcame his lack of capital by getting customers to pay him before they received their products, in some cases several months in advance. Therefore, careful research and high levels of initial finance are not always necessary for a new idea to succeed. On the other hand, Sinclair's more recent ideas have been less successful, most notably the electric car launched in the late 1980s, which eventually forced his organisation into liquidation.

Whilst careful research and planning of finances can never guarantee success, they at least reduce the risks of what is a very difficult journey. The vast majority of new firms do fail and entrepreneurs should do everything they can to improve their chances. In fact, many successful entrepreneurs have previous business failures behind them. For example, the Oxford-based computer games firm, Rebellion, quoted in the 1998 White Paper on Competitiveness as a rapidly growing, long-term focused business, was once forced (in its previous incarnation) into liquidation – proof that even eventually successful ideas may have initial teething troubles.

PROGRESS CHECK

To what extent can effective research guarantee the success of a new business idea?

Legal protection of ideas

There are four main ways in which ideas may be protected – **patents**, **designs**, **trademarks** and **copyright**. A firm that has a new product or service will probably be looking for a patent or a design, which deals with the technical and functional aspects (patents) and the visual appearance (designs) of a product. A successful application will give protection for up to 20 or 14 years respectively.

KEY TERMS

Patent
the right to be the sole user of an invention of a new product or process.

Trademark
a logo or symbol used to distinguish a firm's brands; this can be legally protected by registering it at the Patent Office.

Copyright
legal protection for authors, composers and artists against having their work copied.

Whether it is worth a firm going through the lengthy procedure of getting a patent depends on whether the firm is a manufacturing or a service sector firm. If the firm is in the service sector, it is very difficult to file a patent application, because there is no technical specification for a product. The firm may be able to trademark its particular service, but it is very difficult to prevent another organisation providing essentially the same service. As a result, many firms with innovative service ideas have sought to expand as rapidly as possible, to saturate the market before competitors become established. Generally this has involved business format franchising: both Body Shop and Majestic Wine warehouses expanded in this way in the 1980s, so that although other firms have since copied their ideas, they are still major players in their sectors. In these cases, protection of their intellectual property, other than trademarking their names and logos, has proved unnecessary.

With an innovative product, the decision to patent may be clear. For a firm such as SmithKline Beecham (SKB), which spends around £200 m and 10–12 years to bring a new drug to the market, a patent is essential. Without a patent, competitors could produce generic copies of the drug without having to fund the research and development costs. This would make it very difficult for SKB to recoup their research costs.

KEY TERM

Venture capital
is risk finance provided for small and medium-sized organisations. The venture capitalist usually lends money to the organisation in return for interest and shares in the business.

For a smaller firm the costs of a patent, at a time when the firm may be uncertain about the success of their product, may be prohibitive. Even the early stages of filing a very straightforward idea are likely to cost £2000–3000. These costs will continue to rise during the patenting process and may eventually run into tens of thousands of pounds. And this is just for a patent in the UK. In the US there is a much greater use of corporate venturing in which a larger firm will assist a smaller one with the development costs of innovative products, making patent filing less of a burden for small firms.

FACT FILE

In 1983 Michael Dell was selling PCs out of his room at College. When his parents came to visit he had to hide them in his bathroom, so that they wouldn't think that he wasn't neglecting his studies. Two years later he was employing 250 people. Today he employs over 23,000 staff and has sales of over $16 bn.

Even if the firm does manage to obtain a patent, it may not be much of an advantage unless the design is difficult to adapt. In fact, some firms employ people to search through patent applications to see whether there are any ideas that they can adapt and re-register before the original inventor has really got going. This can act as a further deterrent against patenting to some firms. One of the problems facing Intel in the late 1980s and early 1990s was that as soon as they created new computer chips (the 386, 486 etc.) firms in South Korea and elsewhere copied the designs, adapting them slightly to get round patent descriptions. This forced Intel to develop a strategy of trademark strengthening, focusing on quality, rather than worrying about protecting its designs (hence the 'Pentium' was the successor to the 486, rather than the 586 that might have been expected).

Extending patent protection abroad is likely to cost several hundred pounds for each additional country. Without this protection, a UK patent by itself is not much use. One of the problems that faced Rubik, following the success of his cube in the early 1980s, was the huge influx of generic copies from the Pacific rim, which dramatically reduced his overall profitability.

Ultimately, the decision to seek patent protection is likely to be a difficult one. The more radical the product, the greater the likely commercial viability, and the more likely it is that a patent application will be worthwhile.

FACT FILE

James Dyson first marketed his distinctive yellow and grey vacuum cleaner in the UK in 1993 but success only came after years of hard work and struggle. The Dyson's cyclonic system represented the first real breakthrough in vacuum cleaner technology since H.C. Booth first patented an electronically powered suction machine with a filter bag in 1901. His initial finance came from selling his shares in another product he had designed: the ballbarrow. For over four years Dyson earned almost nothing as he worked on over 5000 prototypes of the Dyson cleaner.

PROGRESS CHECK

Analyse the factors a firm might take into account before taking out a patent on a new invention.

Arguments for and against patenting

The case against

There is a body of opinion that suggests that patents are strongly anti-competitive and consequently are not ethical. The argument is that, just because an organisation happens to discover or invent something, they should not automatically be allowed to exploit the public through high prices. For example, in the case of Beta-Interferon, a drug used to treat multiple sclerosis, the annual cost of treatment is over £10,000 per patient per year, partly because the drug is patented. This allows the drug company to charge a very high price for the drug and, because they are protected by a patent, other firms cannot produce cheaper substitutes.

KEY POINTS

A patent is more likely to be worthwhile:

- if the idea is a product rather than a service
- if the idea is 'novel and non-obvious'
- the more unusual the product is
- the larger the potential market.

The case in favour

The other side of the argument is that, without patent protection, drugs such as Beta-Interferon would never have been developed in the first place. SmithKline Beecham (SKB), the giant drugs multinational spends £600–700 m per year researching and developing new drugs. Without patent protection, competitors could simply copy their products, meaning that SKB would incur huge losses. As a result, businesses such as Beecham would be unwilling to engage in research and development at all.

FACT FILE

In 1997 164,500 firms deregistered themselves from VAT records, about 10% of the total, indicating that they were no longer trading.

A further argument relates to the competitiveness of the UK economy as a whole. It is already the case that UK firms invest far less as a percentage of sales than companies in other leading developed countries. Without patent protection, these research and design (R&D) levels would be likely to drop further, since R&D would be less profitable. This would further reduce the UK's competitiveness in international markets, already lower than ideal.

Therefore, although there are some unfortunate consequences of patent laws, the damage that would be done by abolishing them is probably greater than the damage done by their retention.

PROGRESS CHECK

1 A pharmaceutical company develops and patents a drug that prevents the spread of cancer. It markets this drug at a cost of £20,000 per patient per year 'to cover its research costs'. Taking account of the firm's responsibilities to its stakeholders, to what extent do you feel that the firm is acting in a socially responsible manner?
2 Discuss the view that the government should shorten the length of time a new product idea is protected under a patent.

KEY POINTS

A business opportunity is more likely to succeed if:

- the firm engages in research
- the niche is narrowly defined and consumers are easy to reach
- the firm has a USP
- the niche is growing quickly
- start-up costs are not too high.

FACT FILE

In 1999 a legal battle over a trademark between international drinks company Barcardi and the Cuban venture of France's Pernod Ricard threatened a US–Cuban trade war. In a US court it was decided that Bacardi was allowed to continue to use the disputed Havana Club name in America. Since 1994 Havana Club International has been selling the Havana Club brand of Cuban-produced rum around the world, excluding the US market, where sales are barred due to the US economic embargo against Cuba.

Business plans

A firm's business plan is a statement of intent, setting out its objectives, policies and strategy. At best, it can be a reference point for the firm to help in its decision-taking, containing detailed descriptions of its target markets, with forecasts of how those markets will change and a plan for how the firm will deal with those changes. The plan should also contain profit and cash flow forecasts, to allow the firm to assess its performance, as well as details about how the firm will cope with growth – details of departmentalisation for instance.

Why have a business plan?

Colin Barrow, editor of Sage Software's *Guide to Setting Up a New Business*, described the importance of a business plan in the following terms:

> '... Consider it like this. You have to cross the M1 [motorway] to pick up £100. You could run across randomly without looking and you'd probably get squished. Alternatively, you could make a plan – I'll go at 5 o'clock in the morning on a midsummer's day, look both ways, proceed to the central reservation and use the same process to cross the second carriageway. OK, you might still get squished, but in business to succeed planning is essential ...'

Raising finance

Whilst it is obviously possible to succeed without a formal business plan – many firms have done so in the past – it is becoming increasingly difficult to do so, simply because of the complexity and speed of change in today's marketplace. Apart from anything else, without a business plan, it is extremely unlikely that a bank would be prepared to lend the business any money.

Setting and monitoring objectives

Importantly, the business plan will set out the objectives of the organisation. If these are constructed effectively, this will allow the firm to compare its *actual* rate of progress with what it *projected*. This is a vital analytical tool for any firm.

FACT FILE

In 1934 Percy Shaw filed a patent for a device with two small, reflective chunks of glass in a rubber mounting, designed to sit in a metal frame embedded in the middle of the road. These 'cats eyes' as he called them, were to make his fortune, as no other firm was able to produce a design as effective as his patented one.

FACT FILE

Patent application GB2272154 is a ladder to enable spiders to climb out of a bath. It comprises a thin flexible latex rubber strip which follows the inner contours of the bath. A suction pad is attached to the top edge of the bath.

Furthermore, the creation of a business plan forces the firm to think about key aspects of the business, which may help prevent dreadful mistakes being made.

For example, an effective business plan may help the firm to avoid the classic mistake made by a very high proportion of new enterprises – underestimating the amount of start-up capital that is required. If the firm has produced an effective plan, has examined customers' demands for credit terms and has worked out how soon creditors will need to be paid, it is far more likely to judge correctly the amount of initial finance that will be needed. Going back to a bank 6 to 12 months after the business has started and asking for more money will not meet a favourable response: it shows that the firm is unable to plan and has weak management. Poor cash flow can pull a firm under when it may have survived if it had planned more effectively.

Making decisions

Plans which include a long-term strategy can provide a reference point for firms which are making difficult decisions; they can use the extent to which the decision fits in with the original vision to help decide what to do. The presence of a long-term strategy is likely to help the firm remain focused. In Tom Peters' *In Search of Excellence*, he highlights one of the key features of successful firms: they stick closely to their core values and business. The presence of a coherent plan makes this focus easier to achieve.

Research

Finally, an effective plan will have a major section on the firm's anticipated market – a profile of consumers and a cash flow forecast derived from likely sales. To generate this information, the firm will have to conduct market research. This act in itself should help to weed out unrealistic ideas, or at least force the firm to think about changing the nature of the product if there doesn't seem to be much interest. If the firm fails to engage in market research, it is unlikely to succeed – the firm will be entirely **product driven**. There will be no information on whether anyone wants the product, let alone what design is preferable or how much customers would be prepared to pay. The business plan is important, because it acts as a spur to the generation of this information.

Accuracy and flexibility

A business plan is rarely completely accurate. The entrepreneur writing the plan may have limited experience of the market they are planning to enter. In the case of an innovative product, it would be impossible to have such experience. Consequently, the firm's forecasts are likely to be inaccurate and the firm's plans must be subject to change. One potential danger of business plans, is that they can encourage firms to be inflexible in the face of changing circumstances. This could make failure *more* likely. Even so, attempting to see what the future *might* bring must be better than not thinking about it at all. Even a plan that has to be amended is a starting point for analysis. A firm with no plan at all will probably flounder even more than one with a plan when faced with unexpected changes.

The process of planning may be as important as the plan itself.

No guarantees

It is unlikely that Richard Branson had a detailed business plan when he started a record label out of nowhere, getting some friends to pretend to be a band for publicity photos. The same goes for Alan Sugar when he started moulding plastic tops for record players – but they both survived to become multi-millionaires. By comparison, many firms with highly detailed business plans have failed nonetheless, because of economic downturns or marketing mistakes. A business plan is neither essential to success nor a guarantee of it, but by forcing the firm to consider various contingencies, it does reduce the risk of failure. Therefore, the less experienced the entrepreneur is, the more worthwhile a business plan is likely to be.

FACT FILE

The Financial Mail Enterprise 2000 winner was the Helphire Group, an accident assistance firm in Bath. The company was started in 1992 and sells insurance policies that give extra help to drivers in the case of accidents which are not their fault. The company was praised for its vision, business planning and clear objectives which turned its team of founding investors into millionaires within 7 years of setting up the firm.

PROGRESS CHECK

Questions

1 Analyse the features of an effective business plan.
2 What problems might a firm with no business plan face?
3 What dangers are inherent in the creation of business plans?

Effective business planning

A small firm's business plan fulfils the same role as a mission statement for a giant corporation. Therefore, to have any real impact, it must be developed for *use* – not just as a way of raising finance. The problem with plans designed simply to raise finance is that they tend to be self-deceiving. However, if a plan has been carefully thought out, it will provide support and guide the company through difficult times.

FACT FILE

According to the British Chamber of Commerce 84% of small firms prepare a business plan (1997), 60% reviewing them on an annual basis. Over 50% of small business plans now contain a long-term corporate strategy, compared with only 27% in 1994.

There are elements that every effective plan must contain – market analysis based on market research and a cash flow forecast, for example. Analysis of the market will guide the firm in its initial marketing decisions, e.g. pricing and distribution channels. The cash flow forecast allows the firm to estimate effectively the level of start-up capital that it will need.

Similarly, the best plans will contain estimates of break-even and profit forecasts. Perhaps the most important aspect of an effective plan is a clear statement of **objectives**. What exactly is the firm trying to achieve by when? This is important because it will guide the firm in its decision-taking throughout the start up period and beyond.

Fred DeLuca, the founder of the Subway Sandwich organisation, always had clear goals in terms of the number of outlets he wanted open. His objective in his first business plan was to have 32 outlets open after the first 10 years. When he realised that this was not going to happen (he only had 16 outlets open at the beginning of the 10th year), he decided that the only way he could create the growth he wanted was through franchising. By the end of 1975 (the 11th year) he did have 32 open.

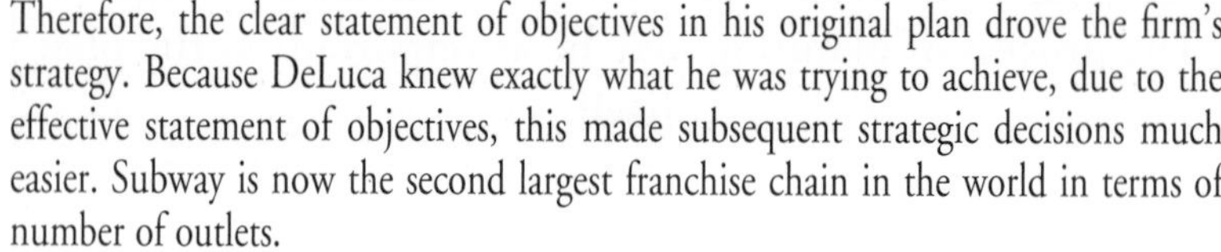

Therefore, the clear statement of objectives in his original plan drove the firm's strategy. Because DeLuca knew exactly what he was trying to achieve, due to the effective statement of objectives, this made subsequent strategic decisions much easier. Subway is now the second largest franchise chain in the world in terms of number of outlets.

FACT FILE

Although most commentators suggest that the main reason for the creation of business plans is to raise finance, a recent survey found that only 9% of small businesses claimed that this was a motivation. Almost 90% claimed that developing an effective strategy was their primary reason.

The planning process

However, the *existence* of these forecasts and analyses is not what makes the plan effective – it is the *process* through which they are created that matters. In other words, it is the effort the firm makes to generate the information and to ensure that the data is as accurate as possible that makes the difference. A firm that takes time to think about its market and to generate data before it starts trading is likely to be in a better position than a firm that takes less time. Managers will know more about the customers and will have an awareness of competitors in the market.

KEY POINTS

A business plan is more likely to be effective if:

- it is carefully researched
- it contains forecasts of profit, cash flow and break-even
- it has a detailed market analysis
- it is used as a reference point for decisions
- actual performance is compared with objectives, and objectives are regularly updated
- it evolves over time, to ensure that growth targets are realistic and challenging.

Keeping up to date

Plans need to be updated as time goes by if they are to remain effective. For example, Fred DeLuca continually set new and challenging objectives – at one point he even included his objective in the company's letterheads and business cards. A plan is not intended just to help the firm through its first years, it should be a constant guide throughout the organisation's life. Therefore, the plan needs to be regularly updated, with new forecasts, marketing information and details on strategy.

Measuring 'effectiveness'

As we have seen, the effectiveness of a business plan cannot be judged separately from the process through which it is created and the way in which it is used. If the plan is prepared carefully, with a great deal of research and is used subsequently as a reference point for key decisions in the organisation's growth, then it is more likely that the firm will succeed. In that sense the plan can be said to have been 'effective'.

Planning increases preparedness.

PROGRESS CHECK

To what extent do business plans guarantee the survival of a business?

Business formats

Limited and unlimited liability

When a firm sets out, the basic choice of format is either limited or unlimited liability. Unlimited liability means that, in the event of the liquidation of the business, all of

the owner's personal assets are at risk. Sole traders and partnerships are th
ness formats that have unlimited liability. With a few minor differences, t
similar formats in law. Any unincorporated business with more than o
automatically a partnership.

The decision to have limited or unlimited liability will depend on
business is. Many service sector businesses tend to keep unlimited li
they will probably not run up large debts: they are unlikely to nee
ment into heavy capital equipment and usually rent their premises
businesses are more likely to be limited companies because the con
ure tend to be more serious, mainly because of the large scale of

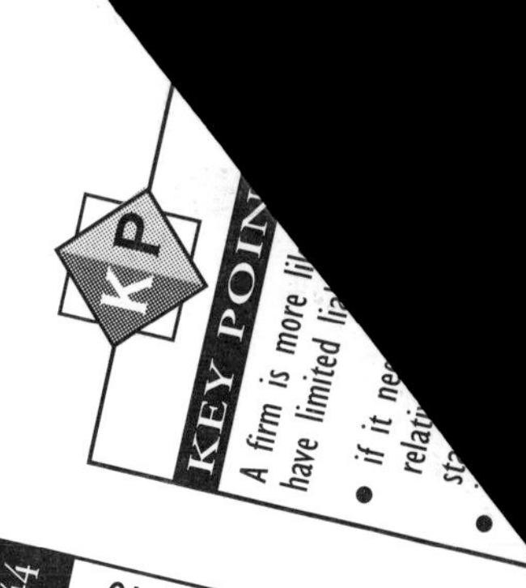

Advantages and disadvantages of different forma

Unlimited liability businesses do have advantages. They are simple to establish, requiring only that you inform the tax and national insurance agencies in the first instance. Similarly, they are not difficult to close down; the organisation can simply stop trading. Certainly, anyone considering running a business in their spare time would probably want to start an unlimited liability business.

unlimi... will operate as a sole trader or partnership.

Nevertheless, many small businesses do decide to opt for limited liability status. This tends to give the company more credibility. Even though they are relatively easy to set up, companies are often seen as more permanent than sole traders. An entrepreneur, anticipating difficulty negotiating contracts with suppliers and customers, might decide to go for limited liability status to give the impression that the business is permanent.

FACT FILE

When Nicky Harrison was a student in York, she wanted to supplement her income by making chocolate bars moulded in the shape of York Minster. She just started trading under her own name, and when she left college she simply stopped trading. All the time she had unlimited liability, but that didn't worry her: 'It was never a big deal because once I got started I just used the cash from sales to buy my next stock. Liability never really came into it.'

One reason that some entrepreneurs set up limited companies is that they believe that the limited liability will protect them in the event of failure. Whilst this is true to an extent, the idea that limited liability means that there are no risks to the owner is overstated. In the first few years of the company's life, suppliers, and especially banks, are likely to demand personal guarantees from the directors before credit will be extended. As a result, the consequences of failure may well be the same as if the firm had been a sole trader.

Company status (Ltd)

Opting for limited liability may be most appropriate when a large amount of start up capital is required. This is because private investors are less likely to provide the capital for a business if they are going to be held liable for any losses. Therefore, if a firm needs financial input from a number of backers who are not going to run the business, ltd status may be the only answer.

FACT FILE

Registering a company at Companies House only costs about £20. Alternatively, ready-to-trade 'shelf companies' can be bought through the Yellow Pages for £100–200.

PROGRESS CHECK

Questions

1. A group of five individuals want to start a computer solutions business together. They each have computing expertise and have sums ranging from £2,000 to £15,000 to invest. Consider whether a partnership or a company would be the better option in this case.
2. Discuss the possible value for a firm of acquiring limited liability status.

Converting to plc status – flotation

One of the main limitations on private limited companies is that they are unable to advertise their shares for sale to the general public. This means that sources of finance are limited to investors that know the business, venture capitalists and loan capital from banks. A firm seeking to expand rapidly might therefore 'go public'. Whilst this does not necessarily mean being quoted on the Stock Exchange (the majority of plcs are not), it is more difficult to sell shares to the general public if the company is not quoted. Investors worry whether they will be able to sell the shares that they have bought. Assuming that we are dealing with a company seeking to be quoted, a main market listing is unlikely, unless the firm has been trading for some time – a minimum market capitalisation of £700,000 is required. It is more likely that the first step for a firm will be to look for a quotation on the **Alternative Investment Market** (AIM). There are no real requirements for listing – the firm can sell only a small percentage of its shares if it wishes – but the vast majority of firms raised between £1 m and £10 m. So, even for this market, a firm needs to be quite substantial before a launch can be contemplated.

Really, only successful firms can take advantage of flotation. Firms with poor trading records or which need funds to cover debts, are unlikely to be successful in raising new equity finance simply because investors will not want to risk their funds in a failing organisation.

Many successful firms are not keen to convert to public status or even to issue shares because this involves investors who are unknown to the original owners. A British Chamber of Commerce survey in the 1990s found that only 33% of small firms would consider issuing shares to finance expansion. Of the firms not wanting to issue shares, 45% stated that the reason was that they did not wish to lose control of their business. Once an organisation is quoted, it is likely to attract institutional investors who may have aims which are different to those of the original shareholders. In particular, institutional investors (such as pension funds) usually have a fairly short-term horizon, meaning that they put pressure on firms for short-term profit and dividends. It was for these reasons that both Richard Branson and Alan Sugar sought to buy back their companies in the late 1980s and early 1990s.

Most of the world's largest firms are public limited companies. Many have been able to expand to the size that they are because they have been able to raise large quantities of equity finance from the general public. They have avoided both the slow rate of expansion suffered by firms which rely on retained profit and the risks taken by firms that expand through leverage (or high gearing). In 1997, over £14 bn of new equity finance was raised through the London Stock Exchange alone.

Essentially, the move to public status is likely to reduce the control that the management have over the organisation; they will be influenced in their decisions by the needs of external shareholders. If nothing else, major new investors will expect a place on the Board of Directors. This may force the organisation to fundamentally change the way it is managed or even change its objectives. In addition, Stock Exchange regulations mean that the amount of information public companies have to disclose is far more than is required of private companies. A business may have to disclose sensitive information that it would rather keep confidential.

...TS

...ely to ...bility:

- ...ds to raise ...vely high levels of ...rt-up capital
- if the owners believe it provides a better image
- the greater the risk of insolvency.

KEY TERMS

Public companies
are allowed to advertise their shares and have plc after their names.

Private companies
cannot advertise their shares and have ltd (for limited) after their name.

Stock Exchange
is a market for stocks and shares.

Market capitalisation
is the total value of a company's shares (share price × number of shares); it is the market value of a company.

FACT FILE

At the start of 1998 the UK companies quoted on the London Stock Exchange main market had a market value of over £1 trillion.

Consequently, launching a company on the Stock Exchange is something to be considered when large amounts of finance are needed to grow further, when the funds cannot be raised safely in any other way and when the original owners are not afraid of losing control.

FACT FILE

Tie Rack was one of the greatest success stories in 1980s niche retailing. When it was floated it was oversubscribed 85 times. In 1999 the company was sold to the Frangi scarf and tie manufacturer.

PROGRESS CHECK

Analyse the factors a firm might consider before changing from a private limited company to a public limited company.

Franchise opportunities

When setting up in business, one option is to buy a franchise. It is generally believed that purchasing a franchise operation greatly enhances the chances of a new business surviving the first few years. A variety of surveys suggest that non-franchise business start ups have a failure rate of 60–90% in the first three years, whereas around 95% of franchises are said to remain in business after 5 years. A recent Gallup poll of franchisees found that 94% of franchisees considered themselves successful, and that over 75% would buy their franchise again if they were starting from scratch.

FACT FILE

In May 1999, Goldman Sachs, the Wall Street investment bank, was floated on the New York Stock Exchange. Demand for the shares was so high that the share price rose 43% the minute the shares started to be traded. This put a value on the company of $35 bn. It also meant that the chief executive's shares were worth $311 m; the chief operating officers were worth around $230 m each. Goldman had tried to float in 1998 but had to pull out when the stock market crashed.

The advantages of franchising

One of the claimed advantages for franchised operations is that new business owners avoid the steep learning curve that others have to negotiate if they are to succeed. If someone sets up in business on their own, they have to build up a customer base and learn about bookkeeping, tax returns, cash flow management, marketing and a whole lot more, whilst also working very long hours. By purchasing a franchise, it is claimed, many of these problems can be substantially reduced, because the franchiser has faced these problems and can pass on his or her experience.

In the best franchise operations, support will be provided in almost all areas of the business. For example, initial advice may be provided to help franchisees find suitable premises, prepare their business plans and undertake their market research. Ongoing support might include promotional support in the form of national and local advertising (which a single outlet would be unable to afford by itself), stationery and other promotional and marketing materials. The franchiser may also help with training in specialist business-related skills (such as marketing and bookkeeping) and provide a legal advice service. Clearly with this level of support, a firm might be better managed than a sole trader going it alone for the first time.

KEY TERM

A **franchise** is a business format in which a franchiser sells the rights to use or sell its products or services to a franchisee.

Franchising may, therefore, be the answer to many small businesses' start up problems, but in some cases the advantages may not be as great as they seem. The franchiser may limit the activities the franchisee can undertake (e.g. by controlling the product range and promotional strategy) and a particular franchisee can suffer if the actions of another damage the brand image. Franchising also involves payment of an initial fee and giving over an ongoing percentage of turnover. This reduces the franchisee's profits. Furthermore, the reported high success rates of franchising are

FACT FILE

Australia's fastest growing franchise is called Hire A Hubby. It was set up by Richard Gray after he heard women complain that their husbands always went to the pub whenever there was a job to do around the house. Hire A Hubby provides rented spouses to do the jobs that husbands hate.

open to question; for example, owners classify only franchise units that have *closed* as failures. If a particular franchise outlet has failed and gone out of business, but then been resold, it may not be counted as a failure. This gives a false impression to would-be buyers.

Buying a franchise

It is clear that many franchise opportunities are genuinely successful. Few would claim that McDonalds is not a very profitable organisation. However, there are many very different types of franchise and some take a very different approach to McDonalds. Therefore, unless a potential franchisee is considering purchasing a well established franchise, care must be taken. Obvious precautions include getting an accountant and solicitor to check out the contracts and accounts, visiting franchisees and seeing how long they have been trading, finding out how many franchises have been sold, and where. By acting cautiously the franchisee should be able to derive the benefits of an existing reputation, as mentioned above. The important point is to realise that a franchise is not a guarantee of success – buying a poor one may be a guarantee of failure.

FACT FILE

The cost of buying a franchise varies enormously depending on the type of business. In 1998 the cost of a 'Molly Maids' franchise was £7800 plus equipment, whereas a McDonalds franchise would run into hundreds of thousands of pounds.

PROGRESS CHECK

Questions

1 **What features of a franchise format will make it more likely to succeed?**
2 **Do the costs of purchasing a franchise outweigh the benefits?**
3 **How beneficial is franchising for a franchiser?**

Surviving the first few years

What makes success more likely?

Cash flow

New business start ups face a very difficult task in getting themselves established in the market. Unless the business is a franchise, initially the firm will have a small or non-existent customer base, meaning that cash flow is likely to be weak. The firm will have to pay creditors for stocks and equipment before any funds have come in through sales. Furthermore, in order to attract new customers, the firm may need to offer generous credit terms or favourable prices (unless the product is highly original and innovative), potentially worsening the cash position. A further problem is that low initial sales may lead to low **capacity utilisation** and high **unit costs** (since **fixed costs** are only spread over a few units); this is likely to damage the profitability of the business. When this is combined with the fact that many new business owners are inexperienced, lacking basic financial and marketing skills, it is hardly surprising that the majority of new businesses fail.

KEY POINTS

Firms are more likely to sell a franchise if:

- there is a high level of interest from potential franchisees
- they are eager to grow rapidly
- they are willing to lose some control
- they want to raise revenue from the sales.

The business plan

As discussed earlier in this chapter, the creation of an effective business plan can go a long way in helping to avoid some of these difficulties. A business plan encourages the firm to research its market fully, to set clear and realistic objectives and to engage in financial forecasting.

KEY POINTS

Firms are more likely to become a plc if:

- they need to raise finance through share issue
- they are willing to lose some control
- they want the company to have a higher public profile
- they believe demand for their shares will be high.

A desirable product

Obviously having a product or service that consumers want to buy is one of the most important factors influencing success. However, even firms producing products which attract a large customer base may experience problems if cash flow management is poor. In the majority of cases, it is cash flow problems which lead to business closure. The better a firm's management of cash flow, the less likely a firm is to get into trouble.

Management of invoicing

Clearly, if a firm is unable to sell any units, cash flow difficulties are inevitable. Assuming, however, that it is selling products, effective management can mean the difference between success and failure. Even simple steps like sending invoices as soon as jobs are completed and making sure that customers know when payment is due can help. If the firm can afford to employ somebody to ensure that payment is collected in time and to negotiate payment terms with large clients, then cash flow is likely to be less of a problem.

Location

The location of a business can also be a vital factor in its success or failure. Apart from the obvious point that some locations are more expensive than others, an effective location can give the edge in terms of delivery times and, therefore, customer satisfaction and cash flow. A survey by Cranfield School of Management in the late 1990s found that those firms expressing themselves most satisfied with their location were also those reporting the fastest growth in sales and profits.

Finance

Finally, selecting an appropriate form of finance can be vital. A survey conducted by the Federation of Small Businesses in the 1990s found that 73% of firms had an overdraft on their business account. Of these, 17% were using the overdraft to finance long-term expansion. Since overdrafts attract extremely high interest rates and are repayable on demand, many firms are financing themselves in rather a risky way. Many firms failed in the recession of the early 1990s because their banks called in or reduced their overdraft facilities. The implication is that firms need to be aware of, and probably make use of, less risky forms of finance where possible. The same survey found that 74% of small businesses had little or no knowledge of the government's loan guarantee scheme, which exists specifically to help small firms finance expansion.

The economy

Sometimes, however, the key to success or failure lies outside the firm's control. The high interest rates around the time of the UK's entry into the Exchange Rate Mechanism in 1990 and the subsequent domestic recession, were responsible for putting a large number of relatively successful firms out of business. By comparison, the recent buoyancy in consumer spending has helped to support a number of firms that might otherwise have failed. Luck, or absence of it, can therefore have an impact on business success.

Clearly, there is nothing that individual firms can do to influence key macroeconomic variables, but this does not mean that the firm is completely helpless in the face of change. The more flexible the firm is in dealing with the unexpected, the better its financial management, and the stronger its negotiating and marketing skills, the more likely it is to survive adverse economic circumstances.

PROGRESS CHECK

Consider whether the success of a new business venture is out of the control of its managers.

Government input

Business start ups often need assistance because they lack the management skills required to survive and grow (especially financial management). Their very nature makes them weaker than most of the other businesses that they deal with, especially suppliers and customers. Some of the large supermarkets, in particular, have been criticised for their policies of delaying payment to small suppliers.

New legislation

As a result of this criticism, the New Labour government passed a bill in 1998 allowing firms a statutory right to interest (SRI), so that if invoices are not paid on time, the small firm can automatically demand compensation, unless their contract specifically excludes this. In principle this should encourage larger suppliers to pay more quickly. The cash flow advantage gained from not paying will be outweighed by the higher bill after interest. Therefore, small firms' cash flows should be improved as customers pay more quickly.

Early evidence suggests that this policy is not working as well as it might. It is clear that some firms are renegotiating their contracts to avoid attracting interest on late payments. Research from other countries where an SRI exists, suggests that the end result tends to be that large firms demand more generous credit terms. In France, for example, where an SRI exists, the standard contractual payment period is 60 days, whereas in 1999 in the UK it is 30 days. There is, therefore, a danger that the new legislation might actually make things worse for small firms.

Training

As far as training is concerned, there is quite a range of support already in existence. Local Training and Enterprise Councils (TECs), Business Links and Enterprise Agencies all provide low-cost access to training. Nevertheless, many firms feel that their competitiveness is reduced due to skills shortages, especially in Information and Communication Technology. This may be due to a lack of awareness of what training is available. Given that so many small firms fail because of lack of basic business skills, this is probably an area in which more could be done.

In the 1998 White Paper on Competitiveness, the government also acknowledged that more could be done to assist the financing of small firms:

> 'Too many small UK businesses with good ideas have problems finding appropriate, affordable finance. US entrepreneurs are backed by a strong venture capital industry. The UK venture capital industry is the largest in the EU and is growing. However, relatively little UK venture capital goes into early-stage and technology-based investments.'

Finance

The government has decided to address these problems by the creation over 3 years, in alliance with the private sector, of an Enterprise Fund worth £150 m. The aim of this fund is to support very early-stage, high-technology businesses. In addition, new regional venture capital funds will specialise in providing small-scale equity to businesses with growth potential. How effective this will be will probably depend on how well publicised the schemes are.

One of the most important elements of support that a government can provide is a stable and healthy economy. If small firms can be confident that the economy will remain reasonably stable, they can plan accordingly. This confidence also encourages more small firms to invest, both in new technology and research and development. Therefore, although all the forms of direct assistance mentioned above are important, the freedom to carry out business without sudden, unpredictable changes in economic variables like interest rates, the exchange rate, unemployment and inflation is probably the key support that most businesses would desire.

PROGRESS CHECK

Discuss whether the government should intervene to support small firms, or whether a more laissez-faire approach is appropriate.

Definitions of a small firm

Most business start ups are small firms. However, it is not absolutely clear what is meant by the term 'small' – at what stage does a firm cease being small and become 'medium' or 'large'?

KEY TERMS

Capacity utilisation
measures how much a firm is producing at present compared to how much it **could** produce given its existing resources, e.g. a capacity utilisation of 60% means the firm is only producing 60% of its maximum possible output.

Unit cost
measures the average cost or cost per unit, e.g. if the total costs are £200 and the output is 400, the unit cost is 50p.

Fixed costs
are costs which do not change with output, e.g. the rent of a building.

One of the best descriptions of the characteristics of a small firm is contained in the Bolton Committee 1971 Report on Small Firms. This stated that a small firm is an independent business, managed by its owner or part-owners and having a small market share. The Bolton Report adopted a number of different statistical measures of a small firm but recognised that a firm of a given size could be small in relation to one sector, where the market is large and there are many competitors, but large in another sector with fewer competitors. It may, therefore, be appropriate to use turnover as an indicator in one sector and number of employees in another sector.

For statistical purposes the Department of Trade and Industry uses the following measures:

- *micro firm* – 0 to 9 employees
- *small firm* – 10–49 employees (includes micro)
- *medium firm* – 50–249 employees
- *large firm* – over 250 employees.

Typical features of a small firm:

- often managed by their owners
- lack of specialist managerial expertise
- lack of a formal organisational structure
- high degree of informal interaction
- limited finance
- often lack long-term strategy.

How important are small firms to the economy?

It might be argued that small firms are relatively unimportant to the UK economy because the largest 0.1% of businesses employ 36.6% of the country's employees and account for 43.3% of turnover. So, the very biggest firms are responsible for a significant proportion of jobs and revenue in the UK. The failure of a single large business can have a serious impact on the economy. This may make such companies seem very important, especially to the government. By comparison, the failure (or even success) of a small firm has much less impact on the UK economy in terms of jobs and income.

Large firms also play a vital role in the competitiveness of the economy as a whole. An enquiry into international productivity in manufacturing in 1998 found that US firms had a major edge in productivity over UK firms simply because the average US firm was larger. The US firms, selling in a larger market, have longer production runs of each product type. This minimises down-time and enables the firm to benefit from economies of scale. In the UK, because the total market is generally smaller, production lines are often used for different product types, leading to wasted time and higher unit costs as the line is cleaned and reset.

NUMERICAL INVESTIGATION

Size by number of employees	Number of businesses (000s)	% of all businesses	Employment (000s of people)	Turnover (£ m)
0	2524	68.1	2866	86,706
1–4	803	21.7	2106	215,110
5–9	192	5.2	1396	112,403
10–19	107	2.9	1511	142,295
20–49	50	1.3	1539	152,559
50–99	15	0.4	1071	105,087
100–199	8	0.2	1121	112,913
200–249	2	–	352	38,550
250–499	3	0.1	1118	142,789
500+	3	0.1	7993	688,751
All	3708	100	21,073	1,797,164

Table 3.1 Number of businesses, employment and turnover by size in the UK at start of 1997

Using the table above answer the following questions.

a) What percentage of businesses have less than 200 employees?
b) What percentage of total employment is in firms of less than 200 people?
c) What percentage of total turnover in the UK is generated by firms with less than 200 employees?
d) What percentage of turnover in the UK is generated by firms with more than 500 employees?
e) Comment on your findings.

FACT FILE

According to a British Chamber of Commerce survey 83% of firms in 1997 thought that the government could do more to assist small firms' access to finance.

FACT FILE

In the UK, businesses with 0–9 employees form 94.4% of all businesses, and employ 28.2% of the UK's workforce.

In addition, small firms tend to be UK focused – the majority of the UK's export earnings come from large international and multinational firms. So, smaller firms make little contribution to the Balance of Payments.

Whilst the importance of large firms cannot be denied, it would be naive to conclude that the UK economy would be better off without smaller businesses. Small and medium-sized enterprises (SMEs) comprise 99.9% of the UK's businesses and employ about two-thirds of the UK's workforce. Without these firms, unemployment in the UK would be much higher and the level of competition in many markets would be lower, leading to a reduction in choice for consumers.

KEY TERMS

The **balance of payments** measures the difference between a country's earnings from its exports and its spending in imports. A balance of payments surplus means that a country earns more from its exports than it spends on imports.

The importance of small firms to the economy was highlighted in Gordon Brown's Budget speech in 1999:

> 'A dynamic and innovative business sector is vital to long term growth. SMEs have an important role to play as drivers of productivity and innovation in the wider economy. Small firms can help increase competitive intensity by introducing new products and through the pressures they put on existing firms to improve efficiency and compete on price ... to grow these companies need;

- entrepreneurs who have the energy and drive to create a company and the ambition to keep it growing

- access to finance to allow good ideas and innovations to be developed into saleable products. Such businesses often require significant start-up capital to develop products. Providing finance for such businesses is often perceived to be high risk and in many cases investment may be needed over the long term to realise significant returns. Bank or standard equity finance is often not available for such ventures

- key employees who are willing to join and stay with a small company to develop an idea, obtain finance, and see a product through to the market even though initial salaries may be low and job security is less than working for a large company.'

NUMERICAL INVESTIGATION

INDUSTRY	TOTAL NUMBER OF BUSINESSES (000s)	SME PERCENTAGE SHARE OF NUMBER OF BUSINESSES	SME PERCENTAGE SHARE OF EMPLOYMENT	SME PERCENTAGE SHARE OF TURNOVER
All industries*	3708	99.8	56.8	53.8
Manufacturing	322	99.2	49.7	46.4
Hotels and restaurants	149	99.8	57.7	56.8
Agriculture, forestry and fishing	221	100	98.3	96
Financial intermediation	52	99.3	22.5	19.2
Education	109	99.9	86.5	72.6

*finance sector excluded from turnover totals

Table 3.2 The contribution of Small and Medium-sized Enterprises in different industries in the UK
Source, DTI

a) All firms in the agriculture, forestry and fishing sector are small or medium enterprises rather than large. Explain why this might be the case.
b) Consider the contribution of small and medium firms to the UK economy.

FF

FACT FILE

Both Rowntree-Mackintosh (now part of Nestlé) and Sainsbury's began as corner shops in the late 19th century. Today they employ thousands of workers, and sell billions of pounds of products, in the UK and abroad. By fostering small firms, the government may be helping future world beaters – many of the present day success stories (e.g. The Carphone Warehouse, Virgin, Yahoo!) started small relatively few years ago.
Similarly Sage Software, a leading provider of business accountancy packages, began trading in 1981 with four employees, but invested heavily in marketing as the firm grew. Sage is now a major international company, employing over 2000 employees and with annual sales of over £150 m. In under 20 years, Sage has turned itself from a micro business into a major firm employing a substantial number of people, and generating large export earnings.

Provision of niche goods and services

Small firms may be essential in the provision of **niche** market goods and services that would be uneconomic for larger firms to produce. This helps to maintain the variety of goods on offer and allows smaller firms to *specialise*. Research in the United States has also suggested that smaller firms are more innovative – per $1 spent on research, they register far more patent applications than their larger counterparts, adding dynamism to the economy as a whole. Many of these ideas are subsequently bought and developed by larger firms, creating world-wide markets. Therefore small firms may play a significant, if indirect, role in the overall performance of the economy.

So, both large and small firms are important to the economy. Government policy reflects this. In April 1999, for example, the government announced the creation of a new £100 m Small Business Service to provide advice and support for small firms, whilst simultaneously paying over £200 m to BMW to help keep the Longbridge plant open.

PROGRESS CHECK

Questions

1 Should the government focus on supporting small or large firms?
2 Consider the value of small firms to the economy.

FACT FILE

When asked the key quality required of a successful start up entrepreneur, only 11% thought a firm understanding of the marketplace was essential. Whilst 29% thought determination to succeed was the key, only 1% thought that luck was important.
Source: NOP Start Up Survey, September 1998

Is business success due to luck?

Almost certainly! Ask any successful business person and there is likely to be some luck in their story. A lucky break with raising finance, a fortunate order at exactly the time when it was needed, a chance meeting with a would be partner could all be down to luck. Similarly, failure may be due to bad luck – an unexpected change in the economic climate, a fire at the suppliers or an important customer going bankrupt could all cause a business to fail. However, whilst there are always some factors which are beyond a firm's control, there is also some truth in the idea that winners make their own luck. A good manager will be better prepared for unexpected change than a bad one. An effective entrepreneur will turn a constraint into an opportunity. Success is, therefore, a combination of luck and skill. A skilful business person will exploit opportunities and protect his or her business against threats; it may look like luck, but it is often the result of careful thought, hard work and ability.

Success almost certainly depends on being prepared or at least being able to react quickly. Effective preparation involves being aware of market changes. The dangers of not being aware of developments in the environment are increasingly severe given the rate of change in modern business; miss the boat and it is getting harder and harder to catch up. One of the most famous examples of a company failing to identify market changes is IBM. IBM owned a mainframe computer business but was slow to see the development of the minicomputer market and so failed to exploit this opportunity. The minicomputer industry came to be dominated by Digital Equipment which then failed to spot the move towards smaller and cheaper personal computers!

KEY POINTS

A firm will be more likely to succeed:

- the more favourable the external environment
- the better its cash flow management
- the more appropriate its choice of finance
- the more attractive its product is to consumers
- the better its marketing and negotiating skills
- the more effective its business plan.

Similarly, Wang took the word processing market away from IBM, which had previously dominated with its Selectric Typewriters. Then Wang's stand alone word processors were beaten by word processing software systems such as WordPerfect and Word. Information Technology is an excellent example of an incredibly dynamic industry and it highlights how managers must continually scan their environment; if firms take their eye off the market, it may well have moved by the time they look back. However, success does not just come from identifying change; the firm must also be able to exploit the opportunities which are created. This means it must be flexible – old competencies and strengths may not be appropriate to changed conditions. Firms must be able to retrain, to invest and to completely restructure their approach when necessary.

KEY TERM

A **niche** is a relatively small market segment.

Success can involve a radical rethinking of approach – the ability to identify new ways of meeting customer requirements; the ability to identify new needs. A good example of innovative thinking is provided by the company, Philips. For more than 80 years General Electric (GE) dominated the US lighting industry

FACT FILE

One the most successful airlines in the world is SouthWest of the US. Its strategy is to focus on short haul flights with an average distance of 425 miles. It does not offer in-flight meals, designated seats, films or multiple seating classes – all the things which, traditionally, were thought to be indispensable. What they do offer is frequent flights at a substantial discount and a quick turnaround. It developed this strategy by looking at the substitute to flying as competition – namely, driving – rather than at existing airlines. What makes someone fly rather than drive? Not the food, not the films but the speed. So it offered quick and regular flights from local airports. Why would people choose to drive? Because it is cheaper. So SouthWest focuses on very low cost flights.

with more than 50% of the market. GE's approach was to sell direct to other companies' purchasing departments, listening to their needs and requirements. As a result, it produced commodity products where firms competed on price and brand. In 1995, Philips Lighting introduced the Alto, the first environmentally friendly light bulb which also offers big savings because it has low levels of toxic mercury and can just be thrown away (whereas most other lights have to be carefully disposed of). The Alto has severely damaged GE's position and has created a high margin, high growth market out of a low growth, low margin, commodity situation. Philips succeeded by ignoring conventional thinking and selling to the companies' financial officers, not the purchasing managers. The purchasing managers focused on the cost of buying; the finance managers focused on the *overall* cost including cost of disposal. By approaching a different department Philips identified a new set of needs. Similar, radical thinking enabled Canon to seize a large part of the copier market from Xerox and IBM, who sold mainly to corporate buyers wanting big machines which could be located centrally and handle large quantities. Canon approached the users of the copiers – the secretaries – who wanted smaller, lower capacity machines which they could use in their own offices. Today, Canon sells more copiers than any other company in the world.

Winning companies are the ones which are prepared to think how something could be done differently and better. The sale of books through book clubs, home delivery of food and e-commerce have all been successful innovations for companies willing to take a different approach.

Whilst the exact way in which firms succeed will vary from firm to firm and industry to industry, there are certain features in common: for example, successful firms are usually driven by passionate champions of change, have a high quality product or service, a commitment to customer satisfaction and a motivated workforce.

However, identifying the key requirements for success is a lot easier than actually putting them into practice! This may be because managers lack resources or because they do not have the necessary skills and experience. They may also face great resistance to change within the firm and have to deal with a culture which is not forward-thinking.

In addition, developing a winning company is an ongoing task. You cannot afford to leave a business standing still for any length of time.

KEY POINTS

According to the Department of Trade and Industry 'Winning companies':

- are led by visionary, enthusiastic champions
- know their customers
- unlock the potential of their people
- deliver products and services that exceed their customer expectations
- continually introduce differentiated products and services.

Business success is a mixture of good luck and good management.

PROGRESS CHECK

To what extent is business success due to luck?

Business failure

All organisations operate in a changing environment. Exchange rates rise and fall, competitors launch new products and customers' tastes change. Some firms succeed in this changing environment; others fail. The reasons for failure are many – a badly designed product, problems raising finance or external change. Ultimately, responsibility for failure must lie with management. Managers have control over a firm's resources and their role is to fulfil the owners' objectives. This inevitably involves risk and can, at times, be extremely difficult. But this is their job and is the challenge of management. In theory, failure is almost always avoidable – looking back, managers can usually see what they could have done differently. In practice, failure may be difficult to prevent. Imagine that interest rates suddenly double, a competitor unexpectedly launches a more effective product or scientific tests show that your product is dangerous. Some managers may have provided for such situations in their contingency plans or may be able to survive such changes by utilising resources or being flexible. Other managers would not be able to cope.

FACT FILE

Business success often involves risk-taking and the willingness to innovate. According to Bob Lutz, former vice chairman of Chrysler, 'it's just a question of getting people to accept that it's okay to step out of their comfort zone, which is the way they've always done it, and to be willing to take a risk on trying something new.'

PROGRESS CHECK

To what extent is the success or failure of a business due to factors beyond its control?

Summary chart

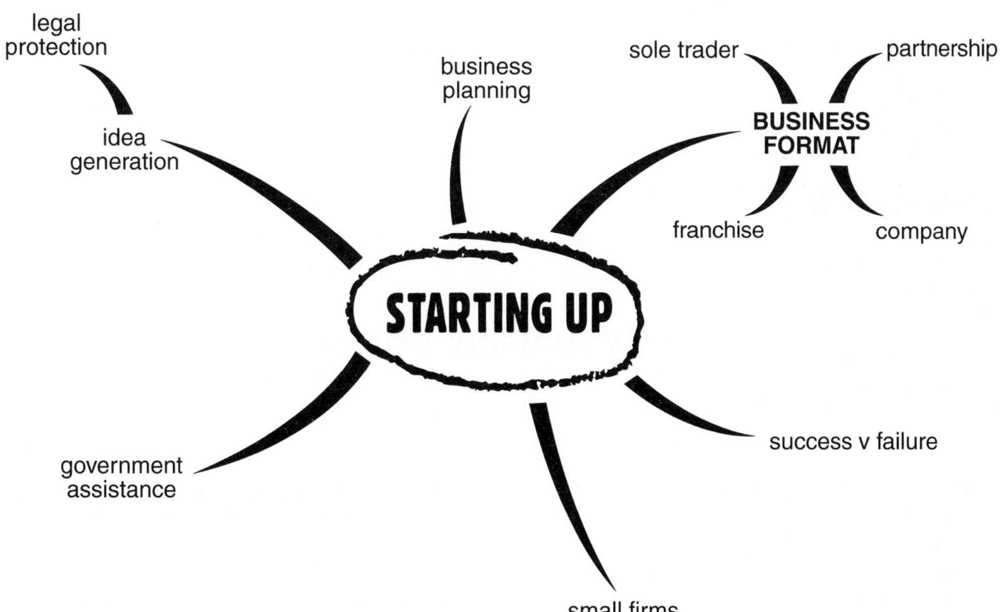

Figure 3.1

Approaching exam questions: Starting up and business formats

Consider whether the government should do more to help small businesses.

(11 marks)

The classic mistake here would be to list a well learned list of types of government support. Such an approach would score very poorly because the question does not ask *what* can be done, but *whether* the government should do more. As ever, it is important not to focus only on one part of the question, 'help small businesses', but to look at the question as a whole.

The other likely mistake would be to treat the question as if it were asking whether the government should help small businesses *at all*. Although such an answer would score better than the list-of-support style answer, it still misses the point: should the government be doing *more*? In other words, given what it is already doing, should the government take further action to support small firms.

Therefore, an effective answer might consider:

- what the government is already doing to help small firms
- whether that is adequate, given the government's own objectives
- what additional action could be taken, and whether it is likely to make a difference
- whether the costs of such action are likely to outweigh the benefits.

Only *after* some of these main points have been considered is it possible to evaluate whether the government should be doing more.

Analyse the reasons why so many firms fail within three years of starting up.

(9 marks)

A surprisingly large number of students would fail to score high marks on what is really quite a simple question. There are two main reasons for this. Firstly, with so many different points to choose from, some candidates would feel that they have to try and mention them all, giving only superficial detail. This would probably restrict the mark to about 2 out of 10.

Secondly, although many candidates would identify weaknesses of small firms, they would fail to link these weaknesses to the reasons why 'so many small firms fail within three years of starting up'. For example:

'As many small firms are started by inexperienced people, they lack many business skills like marketing and finance. This means that they might not know that much about the market or might get their cash flow wrong. Also the firm's customers may want generous credit terms, and their suppliers might want paying on demand because the firm is not well known.'

Although this answer is a reasonable attempt, it would not get the top level on this question because it does not link back to the question. In other words, it does not show why lack of management skills would be likely to lead to business failure. A better answer would be:

'As many small firms are started by inexperienced people, they lack many business skills like marketing and finance. This means that they might not know that much about the market or might get their cash flow wrong. If a cash flow forecast is inaccurate, a bank might not be prepared to extend further credit, especially if the reason is that the firm is not selling as much as expected. Therefore, the firm might find it impossible to meet its bills, eventually forcing it into liquidation. Generally, once three years have gone by, the firm will have overcome initial teething troubles, will have developed management skills, and will have a solid customer base – therefore, failure is less likely after that point.'

Evaluate the factors that a family-owned, private limited company would need to take into account when deciding whether to seek a Stock Exchange listing.

(11 marks)

The most common error with this type of question is to ignore the phrase 'family-owned'. Although it is possible to score a good mark by simply analysing key factors surrounding Stock Exchange launches, a top mark is only likely if the candidate considers all aspects of the question.

A family-owned business may have a different agenda from a non-family business – loss of control may be a more serious consideration in the family-run business and the overall business objectives are likely to be different. Many family-run businesses operate to employ members of the family. Therefore, even if the company is quite large, it might still prefer not to go public.

General points that might be included are:

- why the listing is being considered – is it essential for expansion purposes?
- the alternatives to listing
- the impact of institutional share ownership
- the impact on the family-run nature of the business – its employees and customers
- the importance of 'family ownership' to the current shareholders.

Consider what features of a start up business plan are most important in making it an effective plan.

(11 marks)

The main thing to avoid here is listing the features of a business plan. Even listing them and explaining why each is important will not score particularly highly. The question asks what features are *most important* in making the plan effective. The most important features are those that allow the plan's objectives to be achieved.

A good answer to this question will, therefore, set out what a business plan is designed to achieve. It will then consider various features and explain how they help the business to achieve the objectives set out in the plan. Finally, the answer will consider which of the features mentioned is *most* necessary for a business plan to do its job, and will explain why this conclusion has been reached.

Points to consider are:

- what the plan is designed to achieve – perhaps a survival guide for a firm's first few years?
- the need for effective research into the market
- the need for clear objectives
- the need for careful cash projections
- a conclusion which states which of these features is most important if the plan is to fulfil its purpose, with an explanation of why this feature is more important than the others.

Student answers

Discuss whether location is the critical factor in determining the success of a new business.

(11 marks)

Student answer

Business location is one of the most important decisions that a firm can take. If a firm locates in the wrong place, this can mean higher costs and longer delivery times, both disadvantages.

Costs could be higher than those incurred by other firms if the firm sets up in a high rent area, and its competitors are in low rent areas. Therefore, it might have to charge a higher price, which would mean that it would get less customers, and go out of business. Alternatively, it might charge the same price as other firms, and not be able to pay its costs, again leading to the firm going bust.

Longer delivery times again mean that other firms might get a competitive advantage. If a customer has a choice of getting their product today or tomorrow, they will pick today. Therefore, if the firm is located away from a motorway, this might put them at a disadvantage, because customers might go to firms that could deliver sooner. The firm might be restricted to a local market.

Overall, therefore, location is very important in determining business success.

Marker's comments

This answer is quite reasonable. The language is not very sophisticated, which detracts somewhat, but the candidate presents two main points which are analysed fairly well. The candidate makes sure that the points made are related back to the question of business success or failure, and comes to some conclusions ('the firm might be restricted to a local market'). Consequently, the answer will certainly be awarded marks in the 'analysis' level.

*Unfortunately, the candidate does not consider the full question – whether location is the '**critical** factor'. Because there is no attempt to weigh up location against other important factors such as cash flow, the answer cannot gain evaluation marks, and its analysis mark must also be limited.*

Mark: Content 2/2, Application & Analysis 3/6, Evaluation 0/3. Total = 5

Analyse the actions that a new business start up could take to safeguard its cash flow.

(9 marks)

Student answer

The first thing that a firm could do to improve its cash flow is to factor its debt. This involves getting an outside firm to give you 80% of the money you are owed, therefore improving cash flow. The money is then paid by the creditor to the other firm, who give you the other 20% when they've got all the cash, having subtracted its fee. This is good, but obviously costs because of the fee. Also, in the past, debt factoring was only used by firms in trouble, so it may damage the firm's image.

Secondly, the firm could use sale and leaseback. This means the firm sells off the assets that it's got to a specialist finance firm, who then rent them back. You get an immediate inflow of cash, improving cash flow, but in the long term you will have to pay back far more than the value of the asset, because otherwise there would be no profit in it for the leasing firm.

Marker's comments

This answer has two problems. The first is that the language is rather unsophisticated – use of 'you', 'they', and so on, damages the perceived quality of the answer. More importantly though, this answer does not really answer the question set.

The student has clearly learned the actions that a firm can take to improve cash flow, and has regurgitated that learning. By focusing too closely on the word 'cash flow', the student has neglected to notice the word 'safeguard'. The actions that a firm might take to ***safeguard*** *its cash flow will differ from those needed to* ***improve*** *it – safeguarding may well mean that cash flow is already acceptable, and that the firm simply needs to forecast any future difficulties.*

As a consequence, this answer would not make it to the top level of response.

Mark: Content 2/2, Application 2/4, Analysis 0/3. Total = 4

Consider how important government assistance is in determining the success or failure of a new business.

(11 marks)

Student answer

The government can and does make a big difference to the chances of a new business surviving, and it can do this both directly and indirectly.

Direct assistance comes in the form of finance from the Loan Guarantee Scheme, which helps firms without much collateral to get loans. This is very important because shortage of finance is one of the main reasons that small firms fail. Without this, many firms would have to finance themselves using overdrafts, which are much more expensive. This would damage a cash flow position that is already likely to be weak because of the firm's poor bargaining position with respect to both customers and suppliers. Therefore, financial assistance is important in determining the firm's success, as is other assistance in the form of subsidised training through TECs which can also help to improve cash flow management skills.

Indirect assistance comes in the form of economic management – if the government and the Bank of England can keep interest rates steady, and stop unemployment rising, then firms will be able to plan better and consumer confidence will probably be higher, resulting in more sales for most firms. This absence of difficult trading conditions will really help the firm's cash flow, as sales will be higher and customers/suppliers will be less worried about their own cash flows, meaning the firm will probably be able to negotiate better credit terms.

However, the key to success does not really rest with the government – the fate of new businesses usually rests in their own hands. If firms can plan effectively, and managers get the training that they need, they should have a clear idea of the market and their likely cash flows. Under these circumstances, they will look organised enough to negotiate a good finance package from a bank, and success will be more likely. Therefore, although the government is important, it can only do so much. If firms are organised, then they will probably survive.

Marker's comments

This is a top quality answer that scores very well on a number of fronts. Firstly, the answer is very well ***structured****. The candidate flags at the start what the main points are that they are going to make. Secondly, the candidate's choice of language is well considered: 'probably', 'usually', 'more likely' all crop up in the candidate's answer, generally indicative of an evaluative approach. Finally, the candidate thinks about the question and makes sure that he or she answers 'how important', converting the answer into an evaluative one.*

Mark: Content 2/2, Application & Analysis 6/6, Evaluation 3/3. Total = 11

Analyse the reasons why the divorce of ownership from control might hinder the performance of a public limited company.

(9 marks)

Student answer

Public limited companies are on the Stock Exchange and have loads of shareholders all over the place. Because of this they can get taken over easily and they don't have control over what the shareholders are doing. Because of this the company has to make loads of profit in the short term, meaning that they might not invest enough in research and development etc., so in the long term they might go bust. Therefore, their performance is hindered because the shareholders want different things from the firm.

Marker's comments

This answer is clearly very weak. It makes almost no reference to the divorce of ownership from control, and the answer quickly slips into a preprepared answer on Stock Exchange short termism. The candidate makes no attempt to link the two parts of the question, and consequently gains no marks for analysis. There is essentially no real explanation, certainly none that is relevant to the question set, so explanation or application has not been achieved either. Therefore, the examiner has to decide whether the answer is worth 0, 1 or 2 marks. The last sentence of the answer probably saves it from 0 marks, showing some awareness of the topic.

Mark: Content 1/2, Application & Analysis 0/4, Evaluation 0/3. Total = 1

End of section questions

1 Consider the most important factor that a firm should take into account when deciding on the viability of a new product idea.

(11 marks)

2 Discuss the factors determining whether or not a firm should patent a new product idea.

(11 marks)

3 Analyse the actions that a new business start up could take to safeguard its cash flow.

(9 marks)

4 Consider what is the most important factor in determining whether a small firm will survive its first few years.

(11 marks)

5 Analyse the advantages a firm can derive from using an effective business plan.

(9 marks)

6 Consider whether the costs arising from limited liability status outweigh the benefits.

(11 marks)

7 Discuss the arguments for and against buying a franchise rather than starting a completely new business.

(11 marks)

8 Analyse the reasons that a firm might decide to expand through selling franchises.

(9 marks)

9 Consider what is the most important contribution the government can make to the success of a small firm.

(11 marks)

10 Discuss the advantages and disadvantages to a new firm of setting up as a partnership.

(11 marks)

Essays

1 REM ltd has developed and patented a device for recording dreams. Discuss the factors that it might consider when deciding whether to float on the Alternative Investment Market.

(40 marks)

2 'Luck is more important than planning for most business start ups.' Discuss.

(40 marks)

3 Since large and medium-size firms generate 80% of sales in the UK and the majority of export earnings, consider whether the government should increase support to these firms at the expense of small businesses.

(40 marks)

4 'Patents are unethical and should therefore be abolished.' Discuss.

(40 marks)

5 Franchising has grown rapidly throughout the 1980s and 1990s. Consider the factors that will determine whether this rate of growth will continue unchecked into the 21st century.

(40 marks)

CHAPTER 4

Business mission, objectives and culture

Elements of success

An organisation's success will depend on its mission, its objectives and its culture and the extent to which these three elements are integrated in the business planning process. The mission defines the overall purpose of the organisation (its *raison d'être*); the objectives set out what the firm has to achieve and the culture influences all aspects of how it operates. The interaction of these three elements helps to determine the long-term success of an organisation.

FACT FILE

Johnson and Johnson comprises more than 188 companies based in 52 countries. Its products sell in over 175 countries and sales are over $20 bn. It has over 93,000 employees; more than 40,000 of these are in the US.

Mission statements

A mission statement is a statement of vision that defines both success and the ground rules by which success will be achieved. In other words, it develops the overall aims of the organisation and establishes the values by which it wishes to operate. At its best, it will be highly distinctive, and will form a set of guiding principles for all employees to refer to and apply to their actions, thus influencing the organisation's culture.

FACT FILE

The opening phrase of IBM's mission statement is 'I think therefore IBM'. Definitely distinctive.

How beneficial is a mission statement?

A mission statement provides a statement of intent to a number of different parties and, as such, provides a range of different benefits. The three major groups towards whom mission statements are directed are:

1 customers
2 investors and potential investors
3 employees.

FACT FILE

'Our purpose is to meet the everyday needs of people everywhere – to anticipate the aspirations of our consumers and customers and to respond creatively and competitively with branded products and services which raise the quality of life.'
Unilever Annual Report, 1998

Customers

An effective mission statement can make a lasting impression on the mind of the customer, because it contains the essence of what that company is. Consequently, it can have a longer lasting and more powerful impact than any advertising campaign. Part of Volvo's mission is safety. They have directed their company towards this with such consistency over the years, that the firm's name is almost synonymous with car safety. The humorous phrase 'Volvo driver' has entered the language, as a reference to someone who needs to pay little attention to others because they themselves are so safe. This type of publicity is the envy of many firms, but simply derives from defining a mission of providing safe cars and sticking to it.

FACT FILE

'We aim to be a dynamic, market driven, global provider of glass products, judged best in class by our customers, our people and our shareholders.' Pilkington Glass, Annual Report, 1998

Investors

For investors, a mission statement can provide a straightforward picture of the company and where it is going. Potential investors can view mission statements and see where the firm ranks the relative importance of different elements – the balance between profitability and social responsibility, for example – and use this to predict future behaviour. Provided the statement is a genuine declaration of intent, representing input from all parts of the organisation, it will help investors to find the type of firm that they are looking for. It also helps the firm to avoid investors whose aims conflict with the organisation's own. This latter point should help to avoid volatility in the firm's share price and should, therefore, reduce the likelihood of hostile take-over bids.

Employees

For employees, the mission statement can provide a guide towards the values of the organisation. This can assist employees when making difficult decisions: they will be aware of the values that the organisation considers to be of prime importance. This can, therefore, assist the firm in providing a uniform response from different staff members.

Employees guided by clear principles are more likely to react in a consistent manner than those who are not, and this can make a major impact on the organisation's image.

Nevertheless, mission statements can be little more than a public relations exercise. The Maxwell Corporation, guilty of misappropriating hundreds of millions of pounds of its pensioners' money and widely acknowledged to have a culture of bullying, had the following mission statement:

> 'We aim, by excellence of management and pre-eminence in technology to grasp the great opportunities created by the ever-increasing world-wide demand for information, prosperity and peace.'

In this case, the mission statement had little or no impact on the behaviour of senior management, nor was it widely believed by employees. Consequently, the statement had little real impact on the day-to-day running of the organisation. It seems to have been devised mainly to delude potential investors and consumers.

Mission statements – a waste of time?

Robert Fritz, a leading business writer, declares in his book *Corporate Tides*:

> 'Mission statements have usually trivialised the organisation's most meaningful concepts through weak, watered down, simplistic declarations.'

Fritz believes that mission statements are widely ignored in practice, because they are simply a compromise by the people who write them. As a consequence, they work against a true sense of vision, purpose and mission, because they have nothing meaningful to say. In his view, most mission statements are too vague and abstract to have any real impact on the behaviour of individuals within an organisation. As a consequence, mission statements may, in the long term, create little more than cynicism amongst employees. They may take the view that the aims and values that are lauded by the organisation are little more than a PR exercise. In these circumstances, the creation of a mission statement may prove to have been simply a waste of time and money.

FACT FILE

A survey of 429 managers of UK companies in 1992 found that 82% believed that properly implemented values contributed to profitability.
The same survey found that 6% of managers agreed that their organisation's values made little difference to their daily work behaviour. 53% said they partly made a difference, and 39% said that the values really did make a difference to their actions.
Source: Corporate Values, 'The bottom line contribution', December 1992

PROGRESS CHECK

Some employees may feel that the introduction of a mission statement is a waste of time. What arguments might you put forward as a Chief Executive Officer to persuade them otherwise?

What makes a mission statement worthwhile?

There are three key areas that an organisation should focus on if its mission statement is going to be effective. These are:

- the process of drawing up the statement
- the nature of the statement itself
- the way it is used.

Writing a mission statement

The process by which the mission statement is created is as important as the statement itself. This is because the point of a mission statement is to unite all employees to drive the organisation in the same direction – to have a positive impact on culture. Unless employees are consulted thoroughly during the creation of the statement, they will be unlikely to identify with it and it will not have the desired impact on organisational attitudes and behaviour. Nevertheless, it is important to avoid too much compromise, because this will make the statement too vague and too general to have anything meaningful to say.

The nature of the statement

The statement itself is likely to work best if it has a clear and stretching vision of where the organisation wants to be, a vision that all employees can identify with. This will provide a solid platform on which objectives can be based and from which employees can see the point of their goals. There is a balance to be struck between attainability, without which the statement is potentially demotivating, and durability. The point of the mission is to be long-standing, so that a consistent set of ideals and values can be built up.

FACT FILE

Over 80% of organisations now have some form of written value or mission statement.

In addition, a good statement will usually contain a set of clear values through which the organisation expects its mission to be achieved. If these values can be communicated effectively, they will have a positive impact on business culture, helping to ensure that all members of the organisation are pulling in the same direction. Effective statements tend to contain a clear picture of what the organisation is, does and stands for. This helps to make all employees aware of exactly who they work for, and what impact their organisation has on its environment.

How the statement is used

The way in which the statement is used is probably the key to whether or not it impacts on behaviour and culture. If the actions and expectations of senior managers conflict with the values contained in the mission statement, employees further down the chain of command will soon use the *actual* behaviour patterns as their guide, rather than the *values* of the mission statement. This links back to the creation of the statement in the first place – the more people that are involved in the design, the more they are likely to use the mission to guide their behaviour. Failure of management to match their actions to the organisation's stated values will dramatically slow any cultural shift that the mission statement was intended to promote.

PROGRESS CHECK

Discuss the case for including employees in the construction of the mission statement.

The process of producing the mission statement may be as important as the statement itself.

One company cited in a DTI survey on successful business practice, whilst attempting to change its culture through introducing a set of shared values, was set back months by a supervisor who, when an employee collapsed on the production line, rushed forward to restart the line before attending to the sick person. The employees viewed this action as a true reflection of the organisation, rather than the new values the company was trying to introduce. This sort of conflict between actual and stated behaviour can seriously undermine the faith of employees in management initiatives, especially if they were unreceptive to change in the first place. Similarly, unless the management team introduces programmes, structures and strategies to help ensure that the mission is achieved, any motivational impact is likely to be short-lived, because employees may feel that the senior managers do not really believe in the change.

Which firms need mission statements?

Large organisations

In principle, a mission statement can bring benefits to *any* business by clarifying its aims and communicating them to the organisation's key stakeholders. However, the larger and more complex an organisation is, the more important an effective mission statement becomes. This is because co-ordinating the actions of a wide number of diverse individuals is more difficult when the organisation is large. So, a set of clear guiding principles is helpful.

In general, the more employees in an organisation, the more useful a mission statement may be. If an organisation has only a handful of workers, then it should be possible for managers to communicate aims and objectives without the need for a formal mission statement.

KEY POINTS

A mission statement will be more effective if:

- staff from all areas of the business are involved in its development
- it presents a clear vision of where the business is and where it is going
- it states unambiguously the values the organisation believes to be important
- the actual actions of managers are aligned closely with the values contained in the statement
- structures are created to assist in its fulfilment.

Decentralised organisations

A mission statement may also be useful in a highly decentralised organisation. In this type of business there is a greater risk of inconsistency. If the organisation can develop a strong culture, based around core values in its mission statement, the danger of different approaches developing can be reduced. The decision-takers will have a firmly imbedded set of principles to use when taking decisions.

Multi-nationals

Similarly, the greater the geographical spread of an organisation, the greater the need there is for strong cultural values to be laid down. This is especially important when an organisation is spread over a number of different countries: national cultural patterns may take precedence over the organisation's own. For example, Nike was accused of exploiting labour in the developing world. Local managers were applying local values to the situation, but international commentators thought that Nike should have applied the values used elsewhere in the organisation. A strong mission statement, communicated effectively to all managers, can be useful in such circumstances.

FACT FILE

Even the Girl Guides have a mission statement, which is:
'To enable girls to mature into confident, capable and caring women determined, as individuals, to realise their potential in their career, homes and personal life, and willing, as citizens, to contribute to their community and the wider world.'
The Guides, which is a loose federation of groups across the world, therefore, has a set of core principles that all Guides, wherever they join, will be taught. This provides focus and direction for the movement as a whole.

Times of change

Mission statements may be particularly important in times of change as they can provide the necessary sense of direction. Growing firms, for example, may need to take on new values as the scale of production changes. A statement may be especially useful when two quite different organisations have merged, because there is a danger of culture clash. Following the merger of Carlsberg-Tetley in 1992, one problem was the loyalty of Ind Coope's staff to its own products. The parochial outlook of some staff made it more difficult for the organisation as a whole to change. This prompted Carlsberg-Tetley to develop a new mission and a culture which was prepared to embrace change.

Firms under pressure

Firms that are suffering in the market may also need a new direction, which can be expressed in the form of a mission statement. An example of this was Bisto Foods, which faced a declining market for gravy powder, but was locked into a traditional and risk-averse culture that prevented the company from moving into the booming convenience foods market. Bisto brought in outside consultants to help design a new overview for the organisation, which led in time to a cultural change towards

KEY POINTS

Mission statements are needed when an organisation is:

- large
- diverse
- located in different countries
- undergoing rapid change
- growing
- subject to new ownership
- failing.

'foodies' – employees with a passion for food. In the six months after the implementation of the full programme supporting the new mission (in early 1997), Bisto launched five new products, compared with only six in the previous decade. A change in mission, which then drove change throughout the organisation as a whole, was the key to success.

PROGRESS CHECK

Discuss the view that all organisations, regardless of size or sector, should have a mission statement.

Business objectives

Objectives are targets for an organisation and are usually focused on the medium to long term. They are usually quantified, allowing a firm to use them as a measurement of organisational effectiveness. If a firm's objective is to raise its share of a particular market to 25% by a certain year, for example, its managers can assess whether or not this has been achieved. Without such targets, the firm would be less able to assess its performance. Objectives are derived from an organisation's aims, values and culture; charitable organisations such as Oxfam are likely to have very different aims compared to defence industry firms such as Vickers or Marconi. These aims and values are generally contained in an organisation's mission statement.

FACT FILE

In 1995, Procter and Gamble, the world's biggest consumer group, set a goal of doubling its sales to $70 bn by 2006. Unfortunately, the company struggled to launch successful new products or to hit its sales targets. In 1999, it announced that several thousand job cuts were to be made over the next 5 years. It also announced a new aim of halving the time it took to bring new products to the market.

Types of objective

Objectives vary from time to time and from organisation to organisation. In fact, most firms have a range of quite diverse objectives that they hope to achieve simultaneously, both in the short term and long term. Objectives commonly focus on:

- sales
- profit
- customer awareness
- quality
- social responsibility
- productivity.

The precise nature of an objective depends on the nature of the organisation to which it applies. A main objective of the health service is to cut waiting lists, for example, whilst the Bank of England wants to hold down inflation and Friends of the Earth want to encourage recycling. These are all objectives and are just as valid as the profit-related ones set by public limited companies.

PROGRESS CHECK

Consider the similarities and differences in the likely objectives of two organisations such as an A Level examination board and a major industrial corporation like Cadbury-Schweppes.

FACT FILE

In the 1990s, ICI became a target for Hanson, the asset-stripping conglomerate. ICI had become a target because its heavy expenditure on research and development had restricted its dividend payments and short-term profitability. The share price fell to a level where Hanson thought it worth buying the organisation just to break it up. Although ICI successfully resisted the bid (partly through making voluntary divisions in the company), the case serves to illustrate that focusing solely on the long term can have its dangers.

Short and long-term objectives

Objectives are set to help achieve the agreed aims laid out in the mission statement. This means that a long-term focus is often considered to be important, since the ultimate aims of the organisation are usually couched in the long-term. Nevertheless, there are times when a more short-term focus may be necessary. In the UK, plcs are strongly influenced by their share price, due to the large amount of merger activity that has occurred over the last 20 years. If share prices fall too low, firms become an attractive target for take-over. Given this need to support share price, some UK firms have become vulnerable to pressure put on them by some pension funds and insurance companies (aiming to make maximum returns in the shortest period), and so have sacrificed research projects to boost dividends.

When trading conditions are difficult, firms are more likely to focus on short-term objectives, such as survival. This is often the case in a recession, or when market share is falling. At the very least, firms will often put ambitious expansion plans on hold and cancel purchases of corporate jets for example – which reflects a shift in emphasis away from the long term and towards the short-term. In early 1999, Sainsbury's used their 'value to shout about campaign' as a strategy to stop the steady decline in market share that it had experienced over the preceding few years. It focused on a very short-term objective (holding market share) while it regrouped. Finally, some organisations are inherently short-termist in their outlook. The most obvious cases are organisations such as Hanson, which identify organisations with an underperforming share price, buy them and then break them up for a profit. For such organisations, the long-term is simply a succession of short-terms.

FACT FILE

In 1999, Opel (the European arm of General Motors) announced that its profit margins were likely to be under pressure in the short run as the firm focused on launching new models and revitalising its brand. Its return on net assets had fallen from 12.5% to less than 10% and its share of the European markets had fallen from 17% in 1995 to 14.3% in 1998. The firm's plans included substantial investment in new products to try and lift market share by 1% a year. This long-term goal is likely to mean lower short-term profits.

Other firms may feel that they don't have the resources to be able to look to the long-term. Small firms with overworked bosses, for example, may have objectives which include meeting the next delivery on time.

There are dangers in having a very short-term focus as actions taken by a firm in the short term are likely to have longer-term ramifications. The problem arises when short-term objectives conflict directly with long-term ones. At its simplest, a firm that cuts back on its research and development spending is likely to have fewer new products to launch in the future. The firm may have made cut backs as a short-term reaction to a cash flow problem, arguing that it would soon be rectified and would cause no real long-term impact. However, by taking this course the firm may do intangible damage to the research staff's morale, causing the head of research to take a job elsewhere. Gradually, the rest of the team may leave, to join up with their former boss, leaving the original firm in a weak position for the long-term. Short-term actions must have an impact in the longer term and, if the firm ignores its long-term objectives for too long, it might undermine confidence in its whole mission, causing a cultural change within the organisation. Since building the original culture and mission takes a great deal of time and money, a firm needs to think carefully before sacrificing long-term aims for short-term reward.

FACT FILE

BBA Group plc is a heavy textiles producer from Yorkshire. They are clearly focused on the short term – their argument, successful so far, is that the long term is so unpredictable, there is no point in worrying about it. Short-term gains will lead to long-term success. Part of their mission statement, under 'money', is:

'(a) The longer run belongs to Oscar Wilde, who is dead.
(b) The key variables of our business are so dynamic that poker becomes more predictable than planning, and reactivity more profitable than rumination.'

Source: *101 Great Mission Statements*, Timothy R.V. Foster

FACT FILE

In the 1990s, BA was caught operating a 'dirty tricks' campaign against Virgin. This was essentially a short-term campaign to damage Virgin's image and market share. However, this short-term objective backfired when they were found out, tarnishing their reputation with the general public and damaging their longer-term goal of becoming 'The World's Favourite Airline'.

Do objectives matter?

Making decisions

Objective setting is the first stage of a scientific or structured decision-making process. The whole of the organisation's strategic planning and tactics should derive from the objectives. Therefore, objectives are both the driving force behind the actions an organisation makes and the way in which performance will be assessed. Clear objectives are the hallmark of an effective organisation. They help to co-ordinate the actions of diverse individuals in far flung parts of the organisation, meaning that the same decision would be taken by two different managers in different parts of the organisation. They also help to prevent conflict between different parts of the business. If the firm has a set of objectives that cascade from its mission statement, this should help to ensure that all different parts of the organisation are pulling in the same direction, helping to boost organisational effectiveness and profitability.

PROGRESS CHECK

How important are clear objectives to a structured decision-taking process?

Motivation

At an individual level, objectives may have a motivational impact. By setting out clearly what is expected from individual employees, workers know what is expected of them and can derive a sense of achievement when objectives are achieved. Also, by aligning the assessment of individuals to the objectives of the organisation as a whole, it is more likely that the efforts of individual employees will be of direct benefit to the organisation as a whole. The management technique in which individual workers' objectives are derived from the organisational objectives is known as management by objectives (MBO).

Strategy

At an organisational level, objectives are responsible for driving the strategy of firms. In this sense, objectives are crucial to a firm's survival, since they set the direction in which all of a firm's resources will be turned. If that direction is wrong, the firm will fail.

PROGRESS CHECK

To what extent is it important for an organisation to have written objectives?

What makes an objective effective?

Although clear objectives are generally desirable for an organisation, their usefulness can be undermined if they are not designed and implemented effectively.

SMART objectives

Many businesses use the acronym SMART to represent desirable features of objective setting. Objectives should be:

- *specific* – state exactly what is expected to avoid confusion
- *measurable* – include some sort of target so that performance can be assessed
- *achievable* – objectives should be challenging but achievable; unrealistic objectives can be demotivating
- *relevant* – objectives should be set that will actually help achieve overall aims
- *time limited* – deadlines need to be set, even if they have to be changed later, otherwise there is little pressure to achieve!

KEY POINTS

Effective objectives:

- are the key to a structured decision-making process
- co-ordinate actions
- prevent conflict
- motivate individuals
- provide a framework for strategy.

Specificity

Objectives such as 'to increase sales' are of little use; there is no way of assessing the extent to which the objective has been achieved. There is no timescale, no notion of whether we are talking about the organisation as a whole or a part of it. A more useful objective would be 'to increase the sales revenue of Brand A by 15% over the next 6 months in the US market'. The point of the objective is clear, it has a timescale, it is measurable or quantifiable and, provided it is achievable, it is likely to have a motivational impact. Furthermore, because it is specific, it will have an impact on the organisation's strategic and tactical planning.

FACT FILE

Both Marconi and BAe wanted to dominate the defence market in the 1990s but neither was able to do so, partly because of the presence of the other firm. This objective was partly what drove them to merge early in 1999, with major repercussions for each firm and the defence industry as a whole.

Objectives can be a double-edged sword. By setting expectations and targets, the firm opens itself up to attack if those targets are not reached. A very common cause of a fall in the share price is the failure of an organisation to hit its own profit targets. Although over-ambitious targets can make the firm look impressive in the short term, the longer-term losses from such actions are likely to be greater than any short-term gains: investors will cease to take the organisation seriously. On an individual level, unrealistic objectives can be demotivating, if an employee believes they are impossible to hit. It is partly this that drives the Japanese *kaizen* philosophy, in which small, achievable targets are set as stepping stones to larger gains.

Linking objectives to the mission

This is only part of the story, as it overlooks the fact that objectives should not be divorced from the overall picture. Unless an objective is based on the firm's mission, it is unlikely to be effective, however clearly it is stated. Failure to link objectives to the overall mission can lead to a conflict of objectives. If a target of increasing sales was given to the marketing department at the same time as the operations department was aiming to cut costs, the resulting conflict could mean that neither objective was achieved *and* create ill feeling in the process. The build-up of such ill feeling is a consequence of poor communication in an organisation.

FACT FILE

Following the integration of Guinness and Grand Metropolitan to form Diageo, the new Chief Executive set a clear target of doubling shareholder value by 2002. To achieve this managers were encouraged to set HATs – Hairy Audacious Targets. HATs are deliberately aggressive targets to force managers to think of every possible means of improving performance.

Even if objectives do derive from a firm's mission, they may still conflict with each other. Many firms' mission statements claim to put the interests of stakeholders first, which would imply a set of objectives designed to achieve this. The problem is that different stakeholder groups want different things, leading to potential conflict. Increasing quality, salaries and dividends may be possible when an organisation is growing rapidly, but if growth slows, these objectives may conflict directly with one another. Some objectives may have to be sacrificed or compromised, damaging the objectives-based culture of the organisation.

Communicating objectives

Finally, an objective cannot be considered to be effective unless it is communicated

KEY POINTS

Objectives are more likely to be effective if:

- they are SMART
- they have been agreed by all key players and derive from the firm's mission statement
- they are communicated effectively
- they do not conflict with one another.

effectively. If the human resource function in an organisation is unaware of a proposed expansion, it will be unable to meet the demand for more staff. Consequently, many organisations arrange organisation-wide team briefings which start at the very top and filter down throughout the workforce. The aim is to make sure all employees are aware of what else is happening in the organisation. This can help to increase understanding of how their own objectives fit in with those of the organisation as a whole, increasing motivation.

Management by Objectives (MBO)

KEY TERM

Management by objectives is a system of agreed target-setting designed to bring employees' actions in line with the overall corporate objectives.

One of the problems with establishing a clear mission and related objectives is that they need to be communicated effectively to employees, who then must be encouraged and motivated to act. MBO is a system of management that encapsulates all of the above. Proposed originally by Drucker, management by objectives states that the organisation's mission can only be achieved if the objectives of the corporation as a whole are cascaded down through the organisation into smaller divisional objectives, objectives for individual managers and targets for staff. Ultimately, every employee has objectives which have been derived from the objectives of the organisation as a whole, meaning that every employee is contributing to the organisation's mission. Generally, payment systems are also geared around MBO, so that individuals have an element of performance-related pay, based on achieving agreed targets.

KEY POINTS

MBO is more likely to work if the organisation:

- has an effective mission statement
- has clear objectives that do not conflict
- has consensus-based management
- sets achievable objectives
- keeps employees aware of the big picture.

MBO is more likely to work in organisations which have a clear mission and clear objectives. It is difficult to cascade objectives down through the organisation if there is no clear idea of what the organisation was attempting to achieve. Also, the greater the extent to which the objectives can be agreed, rather than imposed, the more likely (in Drucker's view) MBO is to work. If an employee understands why an objective is important, and has had an input into setting it, agreeing that it is reasonable, then he or she is far more likely to be motivated to achieve it. If, on the other hand, the employee is given an objective out of context and does not think that it is attainable (having had little opportunity to discuss it), they are unlikely to be motivated to achieve it.

One potential problem with MBO is that, in some organisations, it may lead to over-emphasis on the achievement of individual rather than corporate objectives. This means that objectives need to be carefully constructed so that they do not conflict, especially where the achievement of objectives is linked to pay. There is also a potential danger that MBO may encourage something of an isolationist view in which the 'big picture' becomes lost, with individuals concentrating on achieving their objectives but with only a limited idea of why they are doing so. To avoid this, regular team briefings are necessary to ensure that employees understand the importance of their task within the organisation, and also to ensure that employees are fully aware of developments in other areas that may affect their own objectives.

PROGRESS CHECK

Discuss the possible value for a firm of introducing a management by objectives system.

Business culture

An organisation's culture defines the way in which employees actually behave. An organisation may have all sorts of values, aims and objectives, but it is the attitude of the individual employees that makes the difference. If an organisation's culture differs substantially from its stated values, it is likely to run into difficulties. Its actions and direction will diverge increasingly from its stated mission and objectives. Business culture can be seen simply as 'the way we do things here'. Regardless of mission or objectives, it is culture that determines the actual response to a particular situation or decision. Consequently, the management of culture has been of great concern in recent years.

FACT FILE

The Stephen Lawrence case highlighted an example of the conflict of claimed objectives and actual practice. The Metropolitan Police has always claimed that its objective is to provide an equal and open service to all citizens, but the Macpherson Report found it guilty of institutional racism – a direct conflict between organisational culture, business objectives and mission.

Values and attitudes

The culture of an organisation depends on the attitude and values of its employees. In some organisations there is a strong work ethic – the best manager is always the last to leave. In other firms the employees spend half their time watching the clock to see when they can leave. There can also be major differences in employees' attitudes to customers. In some firms there is a strong, underlying belief that the customer always comes first and this is reflected in everything they do; employees go out of their way to make sure the customer receives excellent service. With other organisations (whatever their mission might say) customers seem to get in the way; walk into some shops and the assistants seem to resent the fact that you are taking up their time. Differences in culture are reflected in attitudes to:

FACT FILE

Dreamworks is a film and animation company established by Steven Spielberg in the mid 1990s. It has produced hit films such as *Prince of Egypt* and *Saving Private Ryan*. The culture at the company is quite unusual: office size is not determined by seniority but by practicality – artists who need room to work get more space than their supervisors. Dress is informal and you can walk into anyone's office for a chat. The company provides a free breakfast and lunch, but employees have to spend an hour a day in the cafeteria mixing with their colleagues.

- *Risk* – are employees encouraged to take risks, to try things out, to use their initiative? Is failure accepted on the grounds that at least it means you have tried to do something? Or are employees expected to follow the rulebook or training manual and no more? Are they discouraged from making decisions for themselves on the basis that managers know best?
- *Innovation* – this obviously links with the concept of risk. Does the firm encourage new ideas and processes or does it prefer to keep things the way they are? How many new products have been launched in the last couple of years? Are employees encouraged to suggest improvements?
- *Stakeholders* – how important are the stakeholders? Does the organisation put profit before stakeholders? How are suppliers treated? To what extent are they pressurised to lower the price or speed up delivery?
- *Customer service* – to what extent does the customer really come first? How seriously are customers' comments taken? To what extent is the organisation market or product-led?
- *People* – how important are people within the organisation? How well are people treated? How are they rewarded? If employees are struggling how does management react?

You usually get an immediate impression of the culture of an organisation as soon as you walk into the building. How is it decorated? How do people talk to each other? Does it feel active? New? Old? Dynamic? Tired?

FACT FILE

At International Telephone and Telegraph (ITT), Harold Geneen converted a medium-size communications business with sales of $765 m in 1959 into one of the world's largest conglomerates with revenues of almost $12 bn in 1978. Geneen created an intensely competitive atmosphere based on confrontation and intimidation. All managerial reports, decisions and business plans had to be based on 'unshakeable facts'. He developed a complete information system, a network of special task forces and a method of cross examination which allowed him to check virtually every statement put forward. His meetings have been described as 'show trials' and his intensive questioning forced many executives to break down. He was liable to call executives up at any time in the night to inquire about various facts. The message was clear: 'ITT executives are expected to be company men and women on top of their jobs all the time.'

What determines a firm's culture?

Culture is what is regarded as 'normal' behaviour by the majority of employees. A new employee picks up the culture from the actions of their fellow workers, regardless of what their previous cultural experiences were. The collective views of hundreds of individuals can create a powerful force which can be difficult to change.

The culture of a firm is likely to be influenced by the type of recruitment policy that it adopts. If it recruits innovative high-fliers, offering top-quartile salaries, for example, it will tend to create a more dynamic, forward-looking culture than if the firm pays below the industry average. A firm filled with top-quality graduates all aiming to make their mark is likely to have a quite different feel to one in which most employees are clock-watching.

If the firm's mission statement makes clear the aims and goals of the organisation, as well as the values that are expected, this is likely to have an impact on the prevailing culture. If this is further supported by clear objectives stemming from the mission and cascaded down through the organisation, and employees are rewarded for displaying the values that the organisation considers to be important, the impact will be even greater. Cultural impact is reduced if the actual attitudes that are encouraged are at variance with the organisation's mission. If the mission states that quality is the number one priority, but in practice employees are encouraged to cut corners to hit deadlines (whether deliberately, or simply by the structure of their payment system), the culture which develops will probably be one of corner-cutting. People tend to respond to the actual behaviour of their peers rather than to hypothetical statements of principle.

Does culture matter?

Culture and attitudes

Whether an organisation has a formal values statement or not, a culture will always develop – there will always be a way of doing things. This matters, because it is people that customers interact with. The first impression that customers get from staff will be based on the organisation's culture. Culture will also permeate the employees' attitude to work and the enthusiasm with which they deal with customers. It influences the way they respond to challenges, their attitude to progress and their desire to innovate. A culture which encourages employees to 'keep their heads down', to only use the established channels of communication, to keep to their own work area and to follow orders is likely to struggle in a rapidly changing environment. By comparison, a firm which encourages teamwork, multi-functional thinking, which rewards initiative and develops an attitude of 'let's try it' is more likely to be innovative. In Tom Peters' *In Search of Excellence* a 'can do' culture is highlighted as a major source of competitive advantage over rivals.

Culture and change

Culture is also likely to manifest itself in terms of attitude towards change and flexibility. A culture of openness to change will assist a firm in responding to the changing needs of the marketplace. This should lead to greater profitability in the longer term. On the other hand, a 'can't do' culture is likely to lead to high levels of absenteeism and lateness, imposing large costs on employers, and without employees really caring. In some organisations, theft of components is the norm, because the culture of the organisation believes that this is acceptable or one of the perks of the job. One of the major obstacles to successful mergers is the differences in culture between the two organisations. This prevents meaningful communication between employees in the two halves of the organisation and means that the business is unable to co-ordinate its actions effectively. In the majority of mergers in the UK, the profitability of the new entity is less, even in the medium to long term, than that of the two separate organisations. This reflects both the importance of culture to an organisation, and the difficulty that an ingrained culture can cause.

The impact of culture can be seen in employer–employee relations, the quality of the firm's work, labour turnover and the degree of innovation within a firm. When organisations are struggling, it is often because employees lack the desire to put things right. In many ways, therefore, culture is what the firm's mission and objectives are seeking to control. The way that an employee responds to a particular situation is vital to the organisation's success, and it is always likely to be culture that defines this. Unfortunately, whilst culture is a crucially important element of a firm's success it can be extremely difficult to control.

FACT FILE

Shell is often criticised for its bureaucratic culture which fails to encourage innovation or quick decision-making. Decision-making often happens in committees and is consensual; whilst this may have advantages, commentators say it has made the organisation slow to react to change and seize opportunities.

FACT FILE

The electrical giant Philips wishes to nurture an innovative culture, so that a stream of new products is continually hitting the market. They are careful to recruit high-fliers out of university, but they also promote this culture by allowing staff to have Friday afternoons to use the company's resources to work on their own projects, whether work-related or not. This has helped to reinforce the innovative culture of the organisation, because the actions of managers are aligned with their words.

PROGRESS CHECK

Questions

1 **Which do you think is more important to long-term organisational success – its mission, its objectives or its culture?**
2 **Discuss the ways in which a firm's culture might influence its success.**

Changing cultures

The main problem with attempting to control culture is that culture is non-quantifiable, is made up of the views of hundreds of people and is often self-reinforcing. Trying to change the culture of a small group of workers has been shown to be short lived, because they soon revert to the majority behaviour pattern. For change to occur, the *majority* of the workforce need to change *simultaneously*. This is difficult to achieve because of the degree of co-ordination and effort required. In many cases, the existing culture will have been ingrained for many years and will be deep-set in many employees and managers' minds. Therefore, there can be substantial resistance to change.

KEY TERMS

Values:
what the organisation says it stands for.

Culture:
what happens in practice.

FACT FILE

ICI had a very strong reputation as a paternalistic employer which looked after its employees well. However, competitive pressures forced it to examine its strategy (which has led to a move out of bulk chemicals) and cut costs. Cost cutting included the sale of the 19th century Wilson castle and estate, which had been used as a private hotel for executives, a conference venue and, until the 1970s, the main offices for its heavy organic chemicals business. Its assets included a golf club, a privately run nursery and four farms. The company also cut back on Christmas hampers for its staff.

FACT FILE

Virgin has a culture which is dynamic and which actively encourages people to enjoy their work. One of their criteria for any new project is: is it fun?

Change from the top

To effect change there has to be a change in attitude from the very top, so that employees can see that there is commitment to the change that is being implemented. When Rover attempted to change its culture to one of 'single status', one of the most effective actions was for the Board of Directors to wear overalls and eat in the staff canteen. The managers below them soon realised that it was incongruous for them to keep wearing suits and so, gradually, the process trickled down the organisation. Leading by example can have a major impact on culture, provided that it is sustained.

Changing personnel

In some cases, however, attitudes are so ingrained that leading from the top is not enough. A change in personnel at the top, or throughout the organisation, may be necessary. In other cases, a change in location, to break up existing cultural groups may be necessary.

Changing location

When the Ministry of Defence wanted to relocate its Defence Procurement Executive from 14 different sites around the country to a new HQ in Bristol, it was keen to use the opportunity to change the culture too. Previously, each regional function had tended to be elitist and hierarchical, which created a culture of non-communication. A major part of changing the culture was played by the design of the new HQ building, which was open plan with offices connected by indoor street areas to create a 'community feel'. The combination of culturally designed offices, plus a fresh start, has meant that the culture is now one of talking to people rather than behind-closed-doors elitism.

Ultimately, the key to a successful culture change is complete commitment from all managers. Since it is actions that influence culture, all managers have to force themselves to behave according to the new cultural values that they wish to implement. They also have to create structures, especially payment and reward systems, to match the new cultural values.

Bringing all the managers on board may not be possible. Change usually has both winners and losers. Often it is those who are entrenched in the old culture that stand to lose the most. This is why radical change, such as the introduction of a whole new management team or relocation to a new place of work, may be necessary before major cultural changes can be made. Not surprisingly, cultural change often occurs when a new manager comes in (or is brought in specifically for this purpose), fresh with ideas and energy, and not linked in to the old systems and processes. The newcomer often has a different perspective because he or she has worked elsewhere and has different experiences.

An example of dramatic cultural change brought about by a new Chief Executive can be see at Cadbury-Schweppes, where John Sunderland has transformed the way the group operated by introducing a programme known as Managing For Value (MFV). MFV's purpose is to show where and how most shareholder value can be created. The result has been a significant increase in shareholder value and double digit earnings. The first step of MFV involved an audit of Cadbury's top 150 managers. Following this assessment, nearly half of those audited were in different jobs or had left the company because they lacked the necessary qualities for the new approach. Part of the cultural change involved a realisation that the company was no longer a largely domestic group but a global player. Employees had to stop thinking of its competitors as United Biscuits and Associated British Foods and realise they were up against Coca Cola, Philip Morris and Nestlé. The drastic change in priorities at Cadbury-Schweppes can be seen in its Annual Reports:

> 'Our task is to build on our traditions of quality and value to provide brands, products, financial results and management performance that meets the interests of our shareholders, consumers, employees, customers, suppliers and the communities in which we operate.'
> Source: *Annual Report* (1996)
>
> 'Our primary objective is to grow the value of the business for our shareowners.
> Managing for Value is the business philosophy which unites all our activities in pursuit of this objective.
> The objective is quantified. We have set three financial targets to measure our progress:
>
> 1 to increase our earnings per share by at least 10% every year
> 2 to generate £150 m of free cash flow every year
> 3 to double the value of our shareowners' investment within 4 years.'
>
> Source: *Annual Report* (1999)

FACT FILE

Matsushita is a large Japanese conglomerate which owns brands such as National and Panasonic. *Basic business principles*: 'to recognise our responsibilities as industrialists, to foster progress, to promote the general welfare of society and to devote ourselves to the further development of work culture.' *Employees creed*: 'progress and development can be realised only through the combined efforts and co-operation of each member of our Company. Each of us, therefore, shall keep this idea constantly in mind as we devote ourselves to the continuous improvement of our Company.' The seven 'spiritual' values of the company are:

- national service through industry
- fairness
- harmony and co-operation
- struggle for betterment
- courtesy and humility
- adjustment and assimilation
- gratitude.

Summary chart

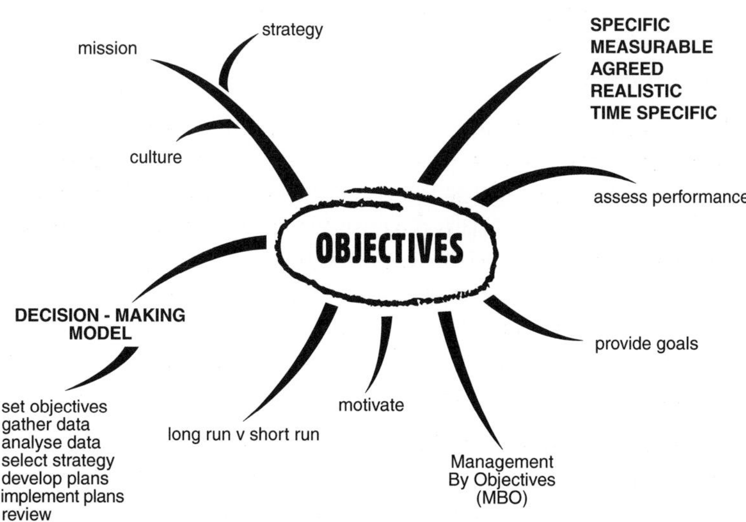

Figure 4.1

Approaching exam questions: Business mission, objectives and culture

Consider the circumstances in which a firm might wish to focus on short-term rather than long-term objectives.

(11 marks)

There is a classic weak answer to this type of question, which tends to miss the point and does not answer the actual question set. What often happens is that students learn a set of points about the advantages and disadvantages of long-term versus short-term objectives, and then apply them to any question on objectives. In this case, the approach fails because the question asks about the *circumstances* in which a firm might focus on each; not the advantages and disadvantages of doing so.

The second point to note is that the question refers to both long-term and short-term objectives. A strong answer will not lose sight of this, and will attempt to contrast the two. The answer might mention that in a recession, a focus on immediate cash flow might be more appropriate than continuing to invest heavily in research and development for the long term.

A weaker answer might make a similar point, but would not introduce the long-term element. The answer would be less evaluative, and less directly focused on the question.

Weak answers might also miss the word 'focus'; this implies a *balance* between short and long-term objectives. The question is looking at what might cause this balance to change. A good candidate would see that this does not mean abandoning long-term objectives, but rather prioritising short-term objectives. This shows that the candidate is aware that most firms have both short and long-term objectives.

Because the question is a 'consider' question for 9 marks, an evaluative approach is needed. Other ways of going about this question might involve identifying the *most* appropriate time for a focus on short-term objectives, i.e. look at a range of situations and then choose between them. This element of reasoned choice is a type of evaluation, and would be rewarded accordingly. An alternative approach might be to look at a range of possible circumstances, and then conclude that none of them really justify abandoning the long term.

The sort of points that might be looked at are:

- the nature of the firm – does it really have a long-term interest?
- the state of the external environment
- if the firm is suffering loss of market share
- if the firm has very short-term oriented investors
- if it is on the verge of liquidation.

The temptation to run through all of these in detail should be avoided, however. Two or three of these explained fully and then evaluated would easily be sufficient to score a top mark on this question.

Discuss how important business culture is to a firm's long-term success.

(11 marks)

Sometimes it can be hard to answer questions asking how important something is, especially if you think it is very important. A useful way of dealing with this can be to turn the question around, and say 'what would happen *without* this factor?'

Using this approach to answer the question, we might argue that 'without a favourable business culture, a firm can be at a serious disadvantage, especially if its competitors do have such a culture.'

The other main point here is that there is no such thing as 'a' business culture; every firm has its own culture, whether bureaucratic, innovative, lazy, customer-centred, or whatever. A strong candidate will make the point that only certain types of culture will be conducive to long-term success, and that the most appropriate culture may vary from industry to industry.

Finally, the natural temptation with such a question is to focus *only* on business culture. But a question that asks you to 'discuss how important' something is, implies that other things are also important. Therefore, an important part of answering this type of question is to compare business culture with the other ingredients that contribute to a firm's long-term success. These might include:

- brand loyalty
- liquidity
- the quality of the firm's products
- competition in the market.

A strong candidate though might argue that many of these factors will be influenced by a firm's culture and might, therefore, conclude that culture is the most important factor.

Consider the main reasons that a firm might decide to create a mission statement.

(11 marks)

The candidate will need to make sure they appreciate the significance of the word 'main'. This is an invitation to evaluate, i.e. to choose between the reasons given and to justify the selection of the main reason.

There are many reasons that a firm without a mission statement might want to introduce one, and candidates should avoid discussing too many – this would be a waste of time and may prevent development of other points to higher levels of response.

The sort of points that should be considered are:

- *Large diverse organisations* – a mission statement may help the different areas to pull in the same direction
- *Organisations with conflicting cultures* – a mission statement can be a step towards harmonising cultures, although it can achieve little by itself

- *Growing organisations* – a mission statement can help a growing organisation hold on to the central values that made it a success in the first place
- *Organisations that have new owners* – a mission statement can help set a new direction, and make it clear to employees what is expected of them.

To gain a top mark, it is necessary to *choose* between these factors, and to give a reason for the choice. For example, the candidate may state that it is most important for a growing organisation which is recruiting new staff who do not know what is expected of them or what the organisation stands for.

Discuss whether a firm should alter its objectives in the face of changing external conditions.

(11 marks)

This is a difficult question to answer, because it asks about the *nature* of objectives; to what extent are they enduring goals towards which the organisation should strive, or are they simply targets along the way to some bigger mission? An effective answer would need to make at least some reference to this debate, possibly making a distinction between short and long-term objectives.

Perhaps the best approach is to find a point which sounds superficially true, explain it and then use the remainder of the answer to disagree with it. This ensures that the answer is two-sided, and means it heads towards a conclusion.

For example, the candidate might state that, during a recession a company might change its objectives from investing heavily in R&D with a view to expansion to a more pragmatic objective concerned with cash flow. This would be a good opening, because it relates directly to the question, makes a valid point, looks at the short and long term, and provides a feed into the rest of the answer. This might be to discuss the problems of changing objectives too many times.

As usual, the answer has two basic arguments, allowing for evaluation. In this case, the conclusion is likely to be based on the nature of external change. The answer should examine the view that sometimes we should change and sometimes we shouldn't – the conclusion should try and decide what the key factor might be. If the external change was survival threatening, for example, this might suggest that a change in at least short-term objectives is necessary.

Student answers

JB ltd is a traditional, long-established steel manufacturing firm without an existing mission statement. Discuss whether it would be likely to benefit from introducing one.

(11 marks)

Student answer

A mission statement is a statement of a firm's goal and aspirations. Without a mission statement, the firm will have no real basis for setting objectives, which in turn will make it difficult for the firm to take strategic decisions. Without clear objectives set, it will be difficult for a firm to know whether to act or not.

In a manufacturing firm, there may be a lot of people employed. If they are all to work together to achieve the same thing, it will be difficult if they don't know what they are aiming for. There might, therefore, be a conflict of objectives, with Marketing wanting to expand but Production wanting to cut costs.

If, on the other hand, the firm had a mission statement, each department would have had related objectives that would not conflict. Therefore, when marketing got new customers, production would be able to meet the demand leading to an increase in sales and profit.

Marker's comments

This is a fair answer to the question. The language is a little simplistic in places. Although in itself this does not directly cost marks, using more sophisticated language often makes candidates write a more evaluative answer.

Generally, the answer is quite analytical. The candidate is aware of the dangers of a conflict of objectives, although he or she does not discuss how likely this might be. The main problem is that the answer is one-sided; he or she does not consider the fact that the company might not really need a mission statement. At the very least he or she should consider the possibility in a 'discuss' essay.

Consequently, the answer does not reach the highest level of response.

Mark: Content 2/2, Application & Analysis 4/6, Evaluation 0/3. Total = 6

Discuss whether the time and resources invested in setting corporate objectives are likely to justify the returns.

(11 marks)

Student answer

Corporate objectives are the aims of the organisation as a whole. A good objective is quantifiable, has a time scale and is achievable, because otherwise it can be demotivating. Corporate objectives are the 'stepping stone' between the mission statement and strategy – they come from the mission statement, and define the strategy. For example, if the objective is to increase sales by 25% then the strategy will have to do this.

Corporate objectives take a lot of time and resources to draw up. To make sure that everybody knows what they are can also take a lot of effort, and time is money. Therefore, it might not be worth it. However, objectives are important because they give a firm a sense of direction and stop different people trying to do different things. This means that it might be worth it after all, because staff within the organisation will all be pulling together.

In conclusion, setting corporate objectives has costs and benefits, and in evaluation the benefits are more than the costs.

Marker's comments

Although the candidate attempts to address both sides of the question and tries to come to a conclusion, the answer is not very strong. The main problem is that each of the paragraphs contains assertions that are not supported by subsequent analysis:

- *'Corporate objectives take a lot of time and resources to draw up' – why?*
- *'To make sure that everybody knows what they are can also take a lot of effort' – why?*
- *'They stop people trying to do different things' – how?*

In addition to the lack of analysis, the first paragraph simply gives facts about objectives that are unrelated to the title and, consequently, are not worth many marks. Had the candidate tried to explain why objectives are important, the information would have been relevant and would probably have boosted the mark.

The conclusion is obviously something that the candidate has been taught to do. There is no support for what the candidate is saying either in the final paragraph or in the body of his or her answer, so no marks would be awarded for evaluation. Overall a weak attempt.

Mark: Content 2/2, Application & Analysis 2/6, Evaluation 0/3. Total = 4

Discuss whether managers can change business culture.

(11 marks)

Student answer

Business culture refers to the overall set of attitudes prevalent in a firm. The ease with which they can be changed will depend partly on how deeply ingrained these attitudes are and partly on what those attitudes are.

If a set of attitudes or culture has been held in an organisation for a long time, it may be difficult to change. This is because the culture will be shared between a large number of different people. If change is going to happen, it will have to influence them all at the same time (otherwise a sub-group will soon acquire the behaviour of the dominant group). This means that a very major change is required and, generally, the bigger the change, the more resistance there will be to it, because of the increased disruption to work patterns that will arise.

This might be less of a problem if the prevailing culture is forward looking and receptive to change. The desire for a change in culture does not necessarily imply that the existing culture is poor – it might simply need amending slightly due to changing social or legal attitudes, generally. Obviously, if the culture is one of resistance to change and distrust of management, then the task will be less easy!

The final factor will be the way in which the management go about attempting to implement the change. If they consult widely, involve external advisers and base the changes around a clear mission and set of objectives, the employees will know where they stand. If they act autocratically with poor communication, the change in culture will be more difficult to achieve. Overall, change should always be possible in the end, given determination and persistence. The above factors really determine how long the process will take – if they are really adverse it could be a long time.

Marker's comments

This answer is thoughtful and well structured. It immediately relates to the question, identifying a number of key points that are then explored further in the next two paragraphs. The second paragraph is almost a model of what is needed. The candidate makes a point, follows it with 'this is because...' and then further down says 'this means that...' and explains it. This approach is almost guaranteed to generate analysis marks if implemented properly.

The third paragraph then looks at the other side of the argument. The candidate is aware that the question is a 'discuss' type and, therefore, makes the point that there are different types of culture. Then, importantly, he or she goes on to explain why this is so. It is very easy to say 'but there are many types of business' or 'it depends on the external environment', but marks will only be generated if the candidate explains ***why*** *it matters.*

Mark: Content 2/2, Application & Analysis 6/6, Evaluation 3/3. Total = 11

To what extent should the objectives of plcs be to maximise profits?

(11 marks)

Student answer

Without profits, firms cannot survive in the long run, so plcs have to make profits if they are going to be there in the end. If they don't, they will go bankrupt, meaning that their shares become worthless and jobs will be lost. On the other hand, some firms like charities, get by without profits. So sometimes profits aren't needed to keep going, meaning that they're not as important.

Profits are the main money for about 90% of UK firms. Without profits, these firms wouldn't be able to expand. In conclusion, it's very important to make as much profit as possible, because otherwise the firm will go bust.

Marker's comments

This answer is very weak, containing mostly unsupported assertions about profit maximisation. The answer contains some relevant facts, but never really closes in on the key which is not profits but profit maximisation. An effective answer would need to look at what profit maximisation means and whether it is generally appropriate to maximise profits in the short run, given the needs of other stakeholders.

Given that the answer does not really look in depth at any of the points made few marks would be awarded.

Mark: Content 2/2, Application & Analysis 1/6, Evaluation 0/3. Total = 3

End of section questions

1 Discuss whether the benefits of introducing a mission statement are likely to outweigh the costs.

(11 marks)

2 Consider whether long-term objectives are more important than short-term ones in determining business success.

(11 marks)

3 Analyse the main steps an organisation would have to take to engineer a culture change.

(9 marks)

4 Discuss whether management by objectives is likely to have any real impact on organisational behaviour.

(11 marks)

5 Consider the extent to which long-term and short-term objectives are likely to conflict.

(11 marks)

6 Analyse the composition of an effective objective.

(9 marks)

7 Consider the factors which are likely to determine a firm's objectives.

(11 marks)

8 Analyse the steps an organisation might need to take to introduce an effective management by objectives programme.

(9 marks)

9 Analyse the steps an organisation might take to minimise the danger of conflicting objectives.

(9 marks)

10 Consider the circumstances in which a firm might change its corporate objectives.

(11 marks)

Essays

1 'Since mission statements are inevitably a compromise between the interests of different senior managers, they will be too watered down to have any real impact on organisational behaviour.' Discuss how far you believe this to be true.

(40 marks)

2 A stakeholder-driven firm faces an inherent conflict of objectives, forced on it by the different needs of its stakeholder groups. Consider the circumstances under which it might be possible for such an organisation to meet all its objectives simultaneously.

(40 marks)

3 An organisation is considering the introduction of a system of management by objectives. Discuss the likely costs and benefits of such a move.

(40 marks)

4 'Poor business culture is simply caused by poor management.' Discuss.

(40 marks)

5 'Since the objective of all public limited companies is to maximise profits, mission statements are at best an irrelevance and at worst a substantial drain on resources.' Consider the extent to which this view is true.

(40 marks)

CHAPTER 5

Business strategy

Introduction

A firm's strategy is the way in which it fulfils its objectives. If the objective is to increase profits, the firm may decide to do this by reducing costs or by increasing sales. These would both be different strategies to achieve the same overall target. It may even decide to do a combination of the two. A strategy is a long-term plan. It usually involves a large scale commitment of resources and, once a decision is taken, it is difficult to reverse. Getting the strategy right is, therefore, critical.

In some ways setting the objective is the easy part – it simply sets out a destination. It is deciding the strategy which often proves more challenging. How will the firm get to where it wants to go? What is the best route? If the plan is inappropriate, regardless of how hard people work, it is unlikely to be successful. A decision to move into the large-sized car market, when customers are switching towards smaller cars, would be an inappropriate strategic decision.

Strategy is the match between internal capabilities and the external environment. It involves a choice of business, markets and activities.

FACT FILE

The objective of Bacardi is to become the world's leading spirits group (and thereby move away from its dependence on white rum). This is being achieved through a strategy of acquisition. In 1993 it acquired Martini and Rossi which added drinks to its portfolio and gave it access to a significant European distribution network. In 1997, the company bought Dewar's Scotch Whisky and Bombay Sapphire Gin from Diageo for about £1.5 bn.

Types of strategy

One of the most influential writers on business strategy is Michael Porter of the Harvard Business School. Porter identifies two main types of strategy which a firm can successfully pursue:

1 low-cost strategy
2 differentiation strategy.

A low-cost producer seeks to reduce the unit cost, so that it can offer the same benefits as its competitors at the same or lower price but still be more profitable. This type of strategy would focus heavily on rationalising production, reducing wastage and achieving economies of scale. The giant American retailer Wal-Mart (which took over Asda in 1999) is a good example of a company which uses a low-cost strategy. Wal-Mart typically undercuts its rivals by 10 to 15% but can sustain these prices due to the sheer scale of its operations.

FACT FILE

According to best-selling writers Gary Hamel and C.K. Prahalad, a firm's strategy should be based around its core competencies. They define core competencies as 'the skills that enable a firm to deliver a fundamental customer benefit'.

A differentiated strategy seeks to offer more benefits than the competition enabling

FACT FILE

In their best selling book *Competing for the Future*, Hamel and Prahalad argue that the most important form of competition is the battle to create and dominate emerging opportunities. Traditional strategists look on companies as a collection of products and business units; Hamel and Prahalad look on them as a collection of skills. Traditional strategists try to position their business effectively on existing markets; Hamel and Prahalad argue that a company should try to reinvent a whole industry by following a vision. You win by establishing a monopoly (for however short a time), e.g Chrysler with minivans and Sony with Walkmans, or by setting a standard, e.g. Microsoft with DOS, or by establishing the rules of the game, e.g. Wal-Mart with out of town hypermarkets.

it to charge a higher price. This strategy may include providing a tailor-made product or brand building. Harrod's is not a cheap store but it is very successful because the benefits of shopping there (both actual and psychological) seem to justify the higher price.

Firms often run into problems when their strategy lacks a clear focus; for example, if their offerings are not particularly cheap and do not have sufficient benefits to justify a relatively high price. When companies such as Sainsbury's and Marks and Spencer had disappointing performances in the late 1990s, it was said to be due to a lack of strategic focus. The benefits they provided were not distinctive enough relative to the price they charged.

PROGRESS CHECK

Explain the difference between a low cost and a differentiation strategy, with examples.

As well as deciding whether to aim for a differentiation or a low cost strategy, firms must also choose which *sectors* of the market they want to compete in. A niche strategy focuses on a small segment of the market. This may have the advantage of requiring less resources (because of the small scale of production) and may enable a firm to gain control of a sector of the market in which the larger firms do not compete. On the other hand, a niche strategy may be risky in that, if the segment becomes profitable, the larger, more powerful producers may decide to enter. Niche producers may also be more vulnerable because they may rely on a few customers. By comparison a mass market strategy may involve more stable demand (in that the loss of one customer may be less significant) but may require much more investment to begin mass production. Entering the mass market may also bring a firm into head-on collision with existing producers.

The decision about whether to compete in a niche market or in the mass market will depend on the firm's resources, the existing and future predicted competition and the expected rewards and risks of both. To be successful a strategic plan has to be dynamic. Firms must be prepared to change their plans as the environment changes. Imagine you are the manager of a football team and you set out a plan to win the league. The success or otherwise of this plan is not totally under your control and it may have to change if the other teams do not play the style of football that you expected. The appropriateness of the strategy will also depend on how other teams do against each other. If Manchester United are way ahead in the league, you may need to alter your strategy to try and catch up. Strategic planners must, therefore, monitor the environment at all times to identify trends and to ensure the plan is appropriate to the times and conditions.

KEY POINTS

Strategic planning is more likely to be successful if:

- it is based on the firm's strengths
- the firm has the necessary resources
- it matches the market opportunities.

What determines strategy?

When drawing up a strategy, a firm tries to match its own strengths to opportunities in the market. An effective strategy takes into account what the firm is good at in relation to what possibilities exist – this could involve extending the brand name, using its management skills in new markets or building on its distribution channels. A strategic match occurs when there is a fit between the firm's strengths and market opportunities. A strategic misfit occurs when a firm ends up attempting to execute a plan which does not fit with its abilities or the market possibilities. The strategy of a firm will be influenced by:

- *Underlying policies* – a firm may, for example, be unwilling to borrow significantly or attract outside investors. The Bacardi company, for example, is owned by around 500 descendants of Facundo Bacardi who founded the company in Cuba in 1862. Although the company has been eager to pursue a growth strategy in the 1990s, it has been unwilling to sell shares to the general public to raise funds since this would involve a loss of control.
- *Culture* – in a risk-taking culture managers may be more willing to enter unproven markets.

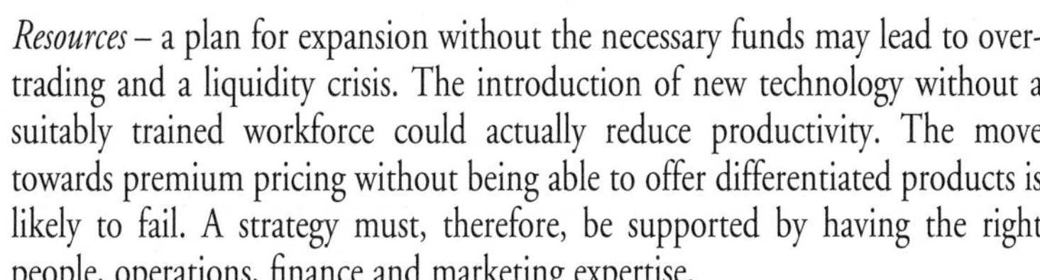

- *Resources* – a plan for expansion without the necessary funds may lead to overtrading and a liquidity crisis. The introduction of new technology without a suitably trained workforce could actually reduce productivity. The move towards premium pricing without being able to offer differentiated products is likely to fail. A strategy must, therefore, be supported by having the right people, operations, finance and marketing expertise.
- *External factors* – these include a competitor's behaviour. If a competitor has already entered one segment of the market, for example, it may be more profitable for a firm to enter another one, rather than fight it out in a head to head battle. If competitors are strong in one region, it may make more sense to focus on other regions. This will depend, however, on the extent to which a firm is concerned about competing in the same market as the competition. In a growing market it may not be a major issue.

A strategy cannot be determined in isolation from the organisation itself; it must arise out of its strengths.

PROGRESS CHECK

Analyse the factors which might influence a firm's strategy.

Strategic planning

SWOT analysis

As discussed, effective strategic planning is based on an examination of the firm's capabilities and its external environment. Decision-makers must be clear about what makes the firm distinctive, where its skills lie and what its abilities are compared to what is happening in its markets. This involves a detailed examination of the market and the organisation's position within it. For example, managers need to assess the size of the market, buyers' behav-

FACT FILE

The main supermarkets in the UK, Sainsbury's, Tesco, Asda and Safeway, have been accused by many commentators of making excessive profits. They have avoided price wars as this would probably reduce each of their profits. Competition has focused on services such as in-store bakeries, delicatessen counters and a better range of products. However, the arrival of the hugely successful American discount retailer Wal-Mart may force the UK stores to radically change their strategies. Discount stores do exist already (Aldi and Netto) but have limited product ranges. Tesco superstores stock around 36,000 product lines; most discount stores stock about 700. Wal-Mart stocks 100,000!

iour, the position and strengths of competitors and forecasts of the future trends.

To do this managers should undertake a **SWOT analysis**. This is an examination of an organisation's Strengths, Weaknesses, Opportunities and Threats. SWOT analysis considers all aspects of a firm, to identify its existing position and possible future external changes in its market. Having undertaken this analysis, managers should be able to develop a suitable strategy. An effective strategy will aim to exploit market opportunities by building on the organisation's strengths; it may also seek to protect the firm against future threats or make changes to improve on its weaknesses. The strengths and weaknesses of an organisation are related to its *internal* situation. A strength might be its low level of capital gearing or its positive working capital. A weakness might be a poor distribution network or a lack of research and development skills. Opportunities and threats refer to *external* factors. An opportunity could include new markets opening up due to the liberalisation of trade or the possibility of reducing unit costs through new technology; threats could be unwelcome changes in legislation or new entrants into the market.

Strengths and weaknesses are internal; opportunities and threats are external.

SWOT analysis is not a complicated concept and forms a natural stage in the planning process. There is no point planning what you are going to do next if you have not first examined where you are now. Nevertheless, many firms often engage in plans without considering whether they are actually appropriate in relation to internal and external factors.

PROGRESS CHECK

1 **Analyse the possible advantages of using SWOT analysis.**
2 **Produce a SWOT analysis for Virgin Cola.**

Undertaking a SWOT analysis simply examines the situation – it is up to the managers to decide what the resulting strategy should be. It is perfectly possible to undertake an effective SWOT analysis, identifying all of the relevant factors and still make the wrong decision. SWOT analysis makes managers think about the firm's existing position and possible developments in the future, but they also have to link the two in the form of an effective strategy.

The effectiveness of SWOT analysis also depends on how it is carried out. If it is undertaken by those directly involved in a project, they may be unwilling to confront some of the firm's weaknesses or may not be able to identify its strengths. Sometimes, managers can be too close to a product or business to assess its position and potential effectively. For SWOT analysis to be valuable, objectivity and honesty are required; this is why businesses sometimes bring in outside consultants to undertake the analysis. Having said this, the managers are the ones who really know the market and so, if consultants are brought in, they usually work closely with the firm's own staff.

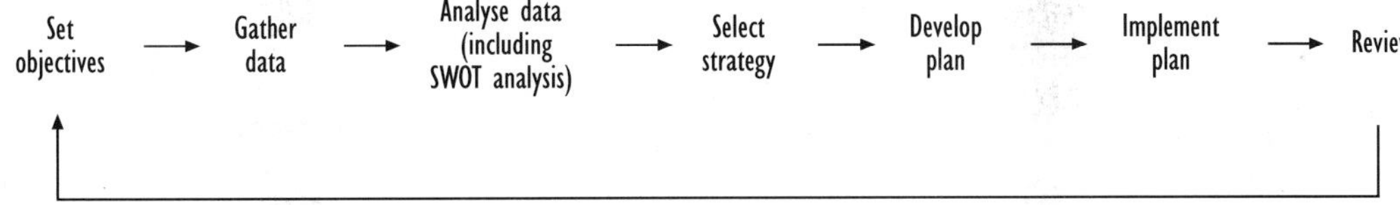

Figure 5.1 The strategic planning process

Ansoff Matrix

One highly influential model of strategic planning was developed by Igor Ansoff. Ansoff wrote one of the leading books in this area called, appropriately, *Corporate Strategy* in which he highlights the importance of a systematic planning process. He identified four corporate strategies which organisations might pursue. These are:

1. *Market penetration* – this aims to increase sales of the firm's existing products to existing customers. It may involve adjustments to the marketing mix to increase the usage of the product on particular occasions, the number of occasions when it is used or the number of users. Market penetration is a relatively safe strategy since it deals with products and customer groups which are already known.
2. *Market development* – this strategy focuses on increasing sales to new customers. This may involve offering the product to new segments or new regions. Switching from industrial users to households or selling the product abroad are examples of this type of strategy. Tobacco companies have focused on markets in the developing world in recent years as the Western markets have matured and legislation makes them a relatively unfavourable climate. Market development may be appropriate if competition within the existing segment is fierce or this sector of the market is felt to be saturated.
3. *New product development* – this strategy aims to develop new products for existing customers. In markets such as soap powders, toothpaste and personal computers firms are always trying to develop the latest, improved model to keep ahead of the competition. Success with this strategy relies on the ability of a firm to innovate and meet (or even anticipate) customer needs.
4. *Diversification* – this strategy involves becoming involved in markets and products which are new to the firm. This is the riskiest strategy of the four, since it involves less familiar products and customers. It is most appropriate if the firm wants to diversify to spread risk, the original market has become too competitive or is in decline.

The right strategy for a firm (e.g. market penetration compared to new product development) will depend on its existing situation, its skills and its objectives. Faced with several opportunities in its present market, for example, market penetration may make sense. If, on the other hand, a firm is under attack in its market, it may seek out new segments and pursue market development. Alternatively, if its research and development department is particularly strong, a strategy of regular product innovation may be appropriate.

FACT FILE

Kingfisher, the UK retail conglomerate, set out its strategy to develop in Europe. The Chief Executive, Sir Geoffrey Mulcahy, described 1998 to 1999 as a 'milestone in strategic development' and said Kingfisher intended to use its do-it-yourself and electricals businesses to expand in European markets other than France and the UK. It has already merged its B&Q home improvements chain with Castorama of France, meaning that 40% of group sales are derived outside of the UK.

FACT FILE

In 1999, Unilever, the AngloDutch consumer goods group, bought Mountain Cream, the leading ice cream brand in Shanghai and the second biggest in Hong King and southern China. This is part of a long-term strategy of expanding its food businesses in China, where the company has concentrated on healthcare, beauty and domestic products. The purchase also reinforces the group's commitments to its 14 product categories. Market share is the priority and the company expects to wait for several years before generating any profit.

NUMERICAL INVESTIGATION

Age	Profile of UK cinema audience (%)	Profile of total population (%)
15–17	10	4
18–24	31	11
25–34	29	20
35–44	16	17
45+	14	48
Social grade		
AB	33	21
C1	35	28
C2	16	22
DE	16	29

Table 5.1 Profile of UK cinema audience (age 15+). Source, National Readership Survey (1996)

Frequency	%
once a week or more often	0.7
2 or 3 times a month	4.4
once a month	6.3
once every 2–3 months	11.4
2–3 times a year	15.3
less often	15.4
never go these days	46.4

Table 5.2 Frequency of cinema going (% of all adults). Source, Target Group Index (1997)

Country	Attendances
Austria	1.5
Belgium	2.1
Finland	1.1
France	2.4
Germany	1.6
Netherlands	1.1
Spain	2.5
UK	2.1
US	5
Average EU	1.9

Table 5.3 UK Cinema market compared with Europe and US (attendances per head). Source, *Trade Sources* (1996)

Year	£M
1997	490
1998	540
1999	589
2000	636
2001	700

Table 5.4 UK cinema revenues. Source, Key Note Forecasts

a) What percentage of the UK cinema audience is aged between 15 and 24?
b) What percentage of the UK cinema audience belongs to socio-economic group C2DE?
c) What percentage of the UK adult population visit a cinema less than 2–3 times a year?

		Product	
		Existing	New
Market	Existing	Market penetration	New product development
	New	Market development	Diversification

Figure 5.2 The Ansoff Matrix

FACT FILE

3M is well known for its culture of innovation. Individuals are actively encouraged to try things out and fail! Only by trying will breakthroughs occur. Part of employees' budget is free for them to do with as they want to develop their own ideas.

PROGRESS CHECK

Consider the possible value of the Ansoff matrix to a firm.

FACT FILE

John Timpson is chairman of the Timpson high street chain which has grown successfully through a strategy of diversification. Under Timpson the family firm moved out of selling shoes and into shoe repair. When that market declined he diversified into key cutting and engraving. Now that business seems to have peaked he has moved the firm into watch repair. Timpson has 315 outlets and only about 37% of its £42 m sales is now from shoe repair.

Selecting a strategy

Similar companies; different strategies

The way in which companies can adopt different strategies, even if they have the same final objective, can be seen in the case of Caterpillar and Cummins, major players in the engine market. Caterpillar is best known as the world's leading maker of earth-moving equipment, but actually gains nearly a quarter of its turnover from sales of diesel engines. These are sold direct to customers in power generation, shipbuilding, truck and industrial machinery manufacture. Cummins focuses far more on engines and derives nearly all of its $6 bn annual revenues from these products, which are sold to customers who are similar to Caterpillar's. Although the two companies operate in the same markets they have very different growth strategies, especially when it comes to moving into new markets. In the past decade, Cummins has formulated a strategy based on joint ventures with outside groups, including its customers and competitors; for example, it has partnerships with Fiat and even Komatsu, which is a large engine builder in its own right. Caterpillar meanwhile goes it alone, preferring to stay in complete control; it acquires other companies rather than getting involved in joint ventures. For example, it bought MaK of Germany and Perkins of the UK. Caterpillar likes to keep complete control partly to protect its specialist knowledge. This has a direct impact on the engines it makes and uses for its own construction equipment.

KEY TERM

A **venture** occurs when two or more firms share ideas and resources on a particular business project.

Cummins takes a more flexible stance – it has a smaller financial base and so is not able to make acquisitions. The managerial style and culture is also biased more towards collaboration. Virtually all its sales are built around some kind of partnership with customers who buy engines for fitting into their own products. Both

KEY POINTS

A strategy is more likely to be effective if:

- it builds on a firm's strengths
- it exploits opportunities in the external environment
- it is realistic
- employees agree with it.

FACT FILE

In 1999, BOC announced a new strategy called 'Project Renew'. The plan involved over £120 m of cost cutting, 5000 redundancies, reorganisation along global, rather than regional lines, and the reselection of hundreds of managers. The company has now abandoned its traditional organisation in which top executives were responsible for continents and a local manager was in charge of all operations with a country. The company is now organised on four global lines of business (LOB) made up of business units. The managers of these 19 units, rather than the LOB chiefs, are responsible for day-to-day operations. The overall group is committed to a return on assets of 16%.

strategies have been successful because they match the individual organisation's particular strengths and circumstances.

The value of a strategy

The process of strategic planning is valuable because it brings together senior management in an attempt to identify external opportunities and the firm's own strengths. This requires interdepartmental and interfunctional discussion. Any activity which makes different parts of the organisation collaborate and examine where they are going in the future is likely to be useful. It is remarkably easy for people within the same organisation to act in different ways. Even within relatively small organisations, individuals working very close to each other may have surprisingly different views of the organisation's goals and how it intends to achieve them. By defining the firm's objectives and its strategy, individuals gain a common sense of direction and route. The strategy should, therefore, motivate employees and clarify their role and their own targets.

A strategy is only valuable if it relates to the firm's strengths and the external opportunities. If it does not build on the firm's competencies and real market analysis, it is unlikely to be successful. A strategy must also have the backing of the employees, because it can only be effective if it is implemented. Too often strategies are never put into practice. Putting the strategy into effect can prove to be difficult. People may resist a change because they do not agree with it or because it is easier to carry on doing things as they are.

PROGRESS CHECK

To what extent does having a strategy help a firm to be successful?

Strategic change

Strategies cannot be developed and used in the same form for ever more. As the external environment changes and the firm's own internal resources vary, the strategy must change and move forward. To continue with the old plan in a changed situation is a dangerous policy.

A good example of the need for strategic change can be seen in the example of Sony in the late 1990s. In 1999, Sony announced a major restructuring which, according to the chairman and chief executive Norio Ohga, was not just a reorganisation but the only way for the Sony group to remain 'young and active'. In spite of its vast technological wealth, its software assets, extremely strong marketing expertise and unparalleled brand recognition, Sony had missed an opportunity. It failed to exploit the possibilities of the Internet. Its new strategy aims to achieve a strong competitive position within the software and Internet markets. Sony has realised the need to transform itself into a business which is in tune with the new age.

Microsoft also underwent a major strategic change in the 1990s when it saw the opportunities created by the Internet (albeit at an earlier stage than Sony). It decided to diversify out of the PC software market. This strategy change has helped to turn it into one of the most successful firms that has ever existed. What is most striking about Microsoft's present strategy is its breadth: 'The mission I see Microsoft focused on today … is taking the Internet, combining it with great software and turning that into the most powerful tool of all time, the most empowering tool that people ever have had. The most revolutionary tool that will change how we do business, how we learn, how we entertain ourselves and how we communicate' says its founder Bill Gates. Mr Gates speaks of the 'web lifestyle', a term he has coined to describe the use of the Internet for daily activities, ranging from checking share prices to buying groceries, and 'web workstyle' which puts the Internet at the centre of business communications and collaborations, enabling retailers to deal direct with their customers and all businesses to interact with their suppliers and customers. Microsoft aims to be a crucial part of the web workstyle and lifestyle that will be an integral part of our lives.

KEY POINTS

People are more likely to resist a new strategy if:

- they lose out personally (e.g. loss of jobs)
- they disagree with the new strategy
- they do not see the need for change.

Mattel also exhibited strategic change in the late 1990s when it announced a diversification from toy maker to 'global children's products company'. As part of the strategy, it bought The Learning Company, the biggest US maker of educational software, for £2.3 bn. This strategy change reflects the fact that the traditional children's toy market has now matured in the West. Despite an annual craze for must-have products, such as Furby, overall toy sales only grow by about 3–5% per annum, even in good years. This statistic goes against logic to some extent, in that grandparents are richer and living longer and rising divorce rates mean children often belong to more than one family (more potential givers!). But children are increasingly switching to computers and video games, leading to a decline in the traditional toy market. Hasbro, one of Mattel's leading competitors, has also moved into software and has acquired Microrise and Tiger Electronics. Even Barbie now has her own website (www.barbie.com) and Monopoly is available on CD-Rom!

FACT FILE

Body Shop International underwent a major restructuring which involved moving out of manufacturing and an overhaul of its franchises. Instead of producing its own products, the company decided to outsource to third parties. This decision involved the sale of its Littlehampton manufacturing operations. The firm also decided to work more closely with some franchisees and to buy back others. The company also reorganised into a smaller headquarters and four regional businesses. The aim was to speed up the time it took to turn ideas into products and to focus more on its retail business. The founder, Anita Roddick, announced that it would allow the company to make a '180 degree shift' away from the 'manufacturing-obsessed' business the group had become, to return to its roots as a fast moving entrepreneur.

As the world changes so must your strategy.

Tactics

The tactics of a firm are used to implement the strategy. Using a football analogy, the tactics are the way in which each match is played. The *overall strategy* may be to play attacking football, but for each match a team must be selected, a formation chosen and a specific plan (the *tactics*) developed for the game.

In marketing terms, the *strategy* may be to aim at the upper end of the market; this must then be implemented using *tactics*: for example, an appropriate marketing mix might include a high price, a well-designed, quality product, exclusive distribution and suitable promotion for the target audience. In operations management the *strategy* may be one of cost reduction; the *tactics* used to achieve this may involve better quality assurance procedures and better training. Clearly, the tactics must fit with the strategy. You do not offer 30% off the price if the aim to is to build an exclusive brand.

FACT FILE

Marks and Spencer was one of the UK's most successful and most respected organisations until the 1990s, when it ran into trouble. Part of the problem seemed to be its marketing strategy, which focused on its own brand – St Michael – and did not include advertising the company on television. In the 1990s, there was a management reshuffle in which 25% of the senior managers were removed. As part of its strategic rethink, the company considered selling designer labels in its stores. It also altered its production strategy by switching to using cheaper overseas suppliers rather than UK firms.

The place of tactics in planning

Senior managers will determine why the organisation exists (its mission), what it is trying to achieve (its objectives) and how it will achieve its goals (the strategy). It is then the role of more junior managers to devise the tactics to carry out the strategy and ensure it is implemented effectively.

PROGRESS CHECK

Explain the difference between strategic and tactical decisions.

How do strategic and tactical decisions differ?

Strategic decisions are long-term, high risk and difficult to reverse. They determine the whole direction in which the firm is moving and are likely to involve significant investment in capital equipment and people. Once decided, the firm may be committed to this course of action for many years. By comparison tactics are short-term decisions. They are easier to change and do not involve the same commitment of resources. Although the tactics must be right to carry out the strategy, the strategy itself must be right for the firm to succeed.

So, the decision to enter a new market is a strategic decision. The decision on the specifications of a product is a tactical decision.

STRATEGIC DECISIONS	TACTICAL OR OPERATIONAL DECISIONS
longer term	shorter term
complex	simpler
non-routine	more routine
difficult to reverse	easier to reverse
significant use of resources	less use of resources

Table 5.5 A comparison of strategic and tactical decisions

If the strategic decisions are wrong the tactics won't save you.

Making strategic and tactical decisions

The precise way in which people make decisions varies according to their personality and the decision itself (see chapter 2). There are three main elements involved in decision-making:

- *Experience* – what the manager already knows, how often they have made this type of decision before.

- *Intuition* – what the manager feels is right.
- *Logic* – what fits with the data.

A strategic decision is likely to involve a high level of risk and managers are less likely to have made the same decision before. If they are considering launching a product, diversifying or acquiring a competitor, for example, the decisions will involve unique factors. In this situation, the managers may have little direct experience and may be wary of using intuition. They will probably want to base the decision on hard evidence.

When making a tactical decision managers may feel more comfortable relying on experience. When choosing a supplier, they will consider the data but will also take into account any past dealings with this firm and their experience of what type of relationship has worked well in the past.

KEY TERM

Gap analysis – this was a phrase coined by Ansoff which describes the gap between where you are now and where you want to be.

FACT FILE

In 1999, Psion launched a strategic review of its business centred on the Symbian wireless technology venture (with Nokia, Motorola and Ericsson) when it became clear that its traditional palm top computer market was stagnating. Symbian is developing an operating standard for wireless devices using Psion's operating system but this has involved heavy investment costs. At the same time, the success of the Palm Pilot organiser had caused a 16% decline in Psion palm top sales. Psion's new chief executive claimed that Psion's future 'lay in solutions' through partnerships. This would involve acquisitions and organic growth.

Financial Times 4 March 1999

Do firms need a strategic plan?

Some firms, particularly smaller enterprises, appear to survive without any clear strategic plan. In some cases, this is simply because they are so focused on immediate matters and the short term that any long-term planning gets put to one side. In other cases, they do not see the need for any long-term view; if they are doing all right now, why bother changing anything? In theory, it is possible to survive by concentrating on the near future. However, the existence of a strategic plan does help people to work towards the same goal and to ensure their efforts support, rather than conflict against each other. This does not mean that there has to be a formal document which lays out every step of the way – the strategy may well be inside the manager's head. However, it usually takes someone with a vision of the future, a well defined set of goals and a clear sense of how these can be achieved to drive forward a business.

How useful is formal strategic planning?

In the traditional view of business planning and decision-taking, a strategy is arrived at in a logical and calculating manner. Managers examine the business environment and their own firm's situation and find a perfect match. In reality, it is more likely that many organisations feel their way towards a strategy, rather than pursuing a formal planning system. Certainly small organisations may not have any formal strategic planning process at all; in some cases they may not even be able to clearly state what their strategy is!

Although the logic of strategic planning may be appealing, managers do not always adopt this approach. The work of Henry Mintzberg highlights the fact that many managers focus on the immediate term rather than engaging in long-term planning. According to Mintzberg, intuition is the 'soft underbelly of management' and strategic planning suggests a uniformity and formality which does not exist. He emphasises the creative, right side of the brain approach to management decision-making. His book, *The Nature of Managerial Work,* showed that managers are regularly interrupted throughout the day and only have a few minutes to focus on a particu-

FACT FILE

When Honda decided to break into the American motorbike market, it sent over executives to launch a series of powerful, large bikes. To get around the city the executives used small 50cc bikes. The sales staff got many enquiries from sports shops and other retailers about these small bikes (not from motorbike shops). There was little interest in the big bikes. Honda dropped its existing strategy and switched to promoting the small bikes. This was the turning point in its attack on America and highlights the need to be flexible.

KEY POINTS

Strategic planning is less likely to be desirable if:

- it is inflexible
- the market is changing rapidly
- it is highly time consuming
- it prevents initiative.

lar issue. Managers seem to spend most of their time fire-fighting, solving immediate problems, rather than long-term planning. To Mintzberg, a firm's strategy is more likely to emerge from within the organisation rather than being carefully crafted by strategic planning. It evolves rather than being formalised in some clear-cut process.

In fact, following a formal planning process can be dangerous. The planners may be too far from the action, too distant from the market to really know what is happening. Strategic planning may also be too inflexible if the market and conditions are changing rapidly. It may be better to simply state the overall objectives, ensure that employees are properly trained and let them decide for themselves what to do in a particular situation.

NUMERICAL INVESTIGATION

ICI has undergone a transformation over the last 20 years. Its high technology businesses, such as drugs and agrochemicals, were split off in 1993 to form a new company, Zeneca. Then it started selling off its bulk chemicals sections. ICI consists mainly of some speciality chemical businesses acquired from Unilever. In 1990, ICI undertook a study of the chemical industry's future, concluding that it was not an attractive long-term proposition, due to rising costs, slow growth and shorter lived gains from innovation.

	1979	1998
Total turnover	**£5.7 bn**	**£7.3 bn**
Fibres	£470 m	–
Organics	£520 m	–
Pharmaceuticals	£320 m	–
Oil	£560 m	–
Industrial chemicals	£2.1 b	£1.3 bn
Agriculture	£990 m	–
Plastics	£750 m	–
Speciality products	–	£3.3 bn
Materials	–	£480 m
Coatings	–	£1.9 bn

Table 5.6 ICI contribution to turnover from different sections of the business

a) Calculate the percentage increase in the firm's turnover from 1979 to 1998.
b) Calculate the contribution of industrial chemicals to total turnover in 1979 and in 1998.
c) Consider the problems ICI may have faced bringing about this strategic change.

Summary chart

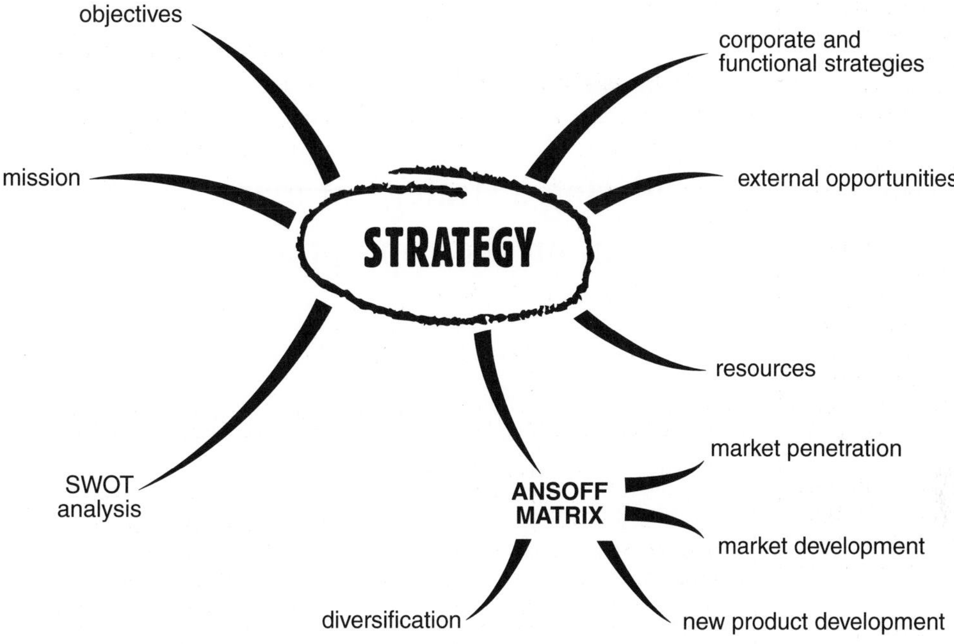

Figure 5.3

Approaching exam questions: Business strategy

Pennings plc is considering a strategy of market penetration. Advise them on the appropriateness of this strategy.

(11 marks)

A good answer to this question would have to demonstrate an understanding of market penetration and consider the options open to the firm. Under what circumstances is market penetration likely to be most suitable? What other strategies might be chosen?

Answers might discuss the fact that market penetration involves increasing sales of existing products and services to existing clients. Compared to other strategies it is relatively low risk in that it involves both markets and customers that the firm already knows. Diversification is a much riskier strategy.

The suitability of this strategy would depend on a range of factors such as:

- whether the market is growing
- whether the strategy matches the firm's competencies
- the potential risks and gains of other options (such as market development)
- the firm's objectives (e.g. is it trying to spread risks by diversifying?)
- competitors' likely reactions
- the opportunity cost.

The suitability of the strategy would depend on the match between the firm's internal capabilities and the external environment. For example, if it has lost its competitive advantage in its existing market it may, for example, be better to move out of this market.

Given that we know very little about Pennings plc or its circumstances, an answer can simply make recommendations subject to various conditions.

How useful is strategic planning to a large business?

(11 marks)

A good answer to this question will discuss the advantages and disadvantages of strategic planning. The benefits might include:

- the value of having a clear plan
- the value of the process of planning, i.e. forcing discussion and thinking about the future.

The disadvantages might include:

- the dangers of having a plan which is too rigid
- the time and resources consumed in the planning process.

The value of planning will depend on the strategy which is decided, how appropriate it is and how easy it is to implement it. Does it fit with the resources and culture of the firm?

If the trading conditions are changing rapidly and if the future is difficult to predict, long-term strategic planning may lock the firm into a plan which will soon be out of date.

A good answer would also refer to the fact that the company is large. This may mean there is a greater need for a formal strategy to tie the company together and unify all the various parts. In a small business a strategy still has considerable value but devising it may be a less formal process.

Consider how a firm's culture could influence its strategy.

(9 marks)

The culture of a firm is reflected in employee attitudes and beliefs. This in turn will influence their behaviour and decision-making, and will have an impact on the strategy which is chosen.

Culture may influence decision-making in terms of:

- the risk the firm is willing to take (it may prefer internal to external growth, for example)
- its attitude to collaboration (it may actively seek partnerships or deliberately avoid them)
- its view of profit, compared to social responsibility, for example
- whether it adopts a strategy for short-term to long-term profitability.

A good answer will stress the vital role culture has in strategic planning and how this helps explain why firms' strategies differ so widely. At the same time, other factors must also contribute and these could be usefully explored (for example, the market and the firm's strengths).

Is market penetration a better strategy than diversification?

(11 marks)

This is a provocative question which may lead some candidates to agree. In fact, it wants you to argue the case for *and* against. Whether one strategy is 'better' than another depends on the organisation and its circumstances. For a risk-averse business wishing to increase sales of its existing products or services, market penetration makes sense. For a firm willing to take the risk of moving into new markets, diversification may be more appropriate. A good answer would outline what these strategies are and discuss when they are more or less likely to be appropriate. It is possible that one firm could adopt both strategies at different stages in its life; it might even adopt both at the same time for different business units within the organisation as a whole. Both strategies can be good or bad depending on their suitability at the time and how well implemented they are.

Student answers

Examine the factors which might determine a firm's corporate strategy.

(9 marks)

Student answer

A firm's strategy is its plan. This depends on what it wants to do. It also depends on whether it has the money or the people. If a firm has lots of money it can do more things than if it has no money, and with lots of money it should be successful because it can buy the things it needs to succeed. If you have money, most things are possible. It also depends on whether the firm can do what it plans. This depends on its skills. Without the right skills it will not succeed. And the motivation of people because if they don't want to do it, they won't and the plan will not work. Competitors are also important because what they do can affect what this firm wants to do. The government can also affect a plan by changing the law and tax and things like that.

Marker's comment

This answer adopts a list approach. It comes up with many ideas which could be relevant and turned into a good answer. Unfortunately, it does not actually do anything with them. The ideas are left undeveloped and so the candidate struggles to get high marks. It would have been better to have taken a couple of ideas and developed them in more depth. The style is also rather weak; phrases such as 'lots of money' should be avoided. The candidate also needs to avoid assertions such as 'if you have money most things are possible'; ideas need to be justified.

Mark: Content 2/2, Application 2/4, Analysis 0/3. Total = 4

How useful is Ansoff's matrix?

(11 marks)

Student answer

The Ansoff Matrix outlines four possible strategies for a firm. One option is market penetration – this involves attempting to sell more of the existing products to the same market. This could be by lowering the price. Another option is to develop new products. Or sell into new markets (market development) or to sell new products into new markets (diversification). These are four options for a firm and it is useful to be able to think logically about the possibilities. However, in itself the Ansoff Matrix does not 'do' anything. It simply shows options. It is up to the manager to decide which one(s) to choose and then to actually implement the plan. Whether the right plan is chosen depends on the skills and experience of the manager and the information which is available. It guarantees nothing. The plan shows us options and this in itself may help managers to think clearly about things. However, the selection of the 'right' strategy will depend on the firm's existing situation and its objectives and strengths. Diversifying, for example, is quite a risky strategy unless the managers are good enough to cope with new markets and products.

Marker's comment

This is quite a good answer which outlines the matrix successfully and then shows real judgement. The candidate is right to comment that the matrix does not make the decision for the manager and that all it really does is show options. This type of critical approach is to be encouraged.

Mark: Content 2/2, Application & Analysis 5/6, Evaluation 3/3. Total = 11

Discuss why employees often resist strategic change.

(11 marks)

Student answer

Strategic change occurs when a firm alters its long-term plans. This can have significant implications for a business. It may lead to new approaches to marketing and operations and this may mean retraining or even redundancies. This is why people may resist such change – they may be worse off as a result. They may have to learn difficult new skills, they may get moved or lose their jobs. It might also mean that they lose their status because what they do becomes less important. They might also disagree with the plan and think it is wrong. However, not all employees will disagree – some may like it because they may be better off (e.g. promotion, chance to gain new skills); it depends a bit on what the change is.

Marker's comment

This is a fairly strong answer which highlights the reasons why an employee might resist a change of strategy. It also suggests that some people might welcome the change. However, it fails to develop the other side of the argument effectively. Why might some people welcome the strategic change? Also what makes the change more or less likely to be resisted? Why does it depend on what the change is?

Mark: Content 2/2, Application & Analysis 5/6, Evaluation 1/3. Total = 8

Analyse the factors which might cause a firm to change its strategy.

(9 marks)

Student answer

A firm may change its strategy because of a change in objectives. If a firm decided it wanted to become an international organisation, the strategy might have to change to incorporate expansion into overseas markets. If the firm decided more short-term profits were required, it might switch away from some of its longer-term projects, such as new product development, and adopt short-term strategies, such as sales promotion. Strategic change may also be caused by developments in the market. The rise of the Internet has caused some firms to re-examine their operations; it may even lead to the decline of some more traditional markets (such as high street banking). To survive, firms have to change how they operate. A final factor which may bring about a change in strategy is the firm's resources. If, for example, cash flow became limited (e.g. limited working capital) this might prevent strategies requiring heavy investment. In conclusion, strategies must adapt with the market, resources and the external environment.

Marker's comments

An excellent answer. It covers the points well, developing the ideas and making them relevant. It then sums up effectively, highlighting the dynamic changing nature of strategic planning.

Mark: Content 2/2, Application 4/4, Analysis 2/3. Total = 8

End of section questions

1 Analyse the factors which might influence a firm's strategy.
(9 marks)

2 Examine the possible value of strategic planning to an organisation.
(9 marks)

3 Consider the value of SWOT analysis to a firm.
(9 marks)

4 Examine the factors which might cause a firm to change its strategy.
(9 marks)

5 Consider the possible problems of introducing strategic change.
(9 marks)

6 Discuss the possible implications of a move from a low cost strategy to a differentiated strategy for a firm.
(11 marks)

7 Examine the issues which might be involved in a major strategic change.
(9 marks)

8 Discuss the importance of choosing the 'right' strategy in determining a firm's success.
(11 marks)

9 Analyse the differences between strategic and tactical decisions.
(9 marks)

10 Consider how market conditions can affect a firm's strategy.
(9 marks)

Essays

1 'An effective strategy is the key to long run success.' Discuss.
(40 marks)

2 To what extent does strategic planning help a firm's performance?
(40 marks)

3 'Given the rapid change in markets nowadays, strategic planning is likely to limit a firm's success.' Discuss.
(40 marks)

4 Is a firm's strategy more important than its objectives?
(40 marks)

5 Do firms need a strategic plan to survive?
(40 marks)

CHAPTER 6

Managing growth

Growth is one of the main objectives of many organisations. Growth brings with it greater power, potentially greater rewards for all stakeholders and personal satisfaction for those involved in pushing the business forward. The incredible growth of organisations such as Virgin, the Body Shop, the Carphone Warehouse, Microsoft and Intel show how much can be achieved in a short time. However, growth brings with it many challenges and to expand successfully requires very effective management and the ability to manage a constantly changing organisation. In this chapter, we look at some of the key issues relating to the size of a firm and the problems and opportunities created through expansion.

FACT FILE

Martin Dawes started out renting televisions in Warrington before moving into cellular phones in 1985. Martin Dawes Telecommunications now has over 800,000 customers and an annual turnover of several hundred million pounds. In 1999, Cellnet paid over £130 m for an 80% stake in the business, £70 m of which went to Martin Dawes personally.

Growth as an objective

Growth is a common objective for firms because it can put the business in a stronger position by gaining a cost advantage and by gaining more power in the market. Expansion can lead to economies of scale. It also makes suppliers and distributors more dependent on a firm and more likely to give favourable terms. Growth is appealing for many managers because it increases their personal power and their salaries are often linked to the size of the firm; as the business grows so do their earnings! It can be personally satisfying to work in a growing business, since this creates promotion opportunities and can satisfy an individual's esteem and self-actualisation needs. In many cases, the growth strategies of organisations can be traced back to personal ambition as much as to any commercial logic. For the owners, growth brings a bigger business which should be worth more, increasing their personal wealth.

PROGRESS CHECK

Many organisations set growth as a main objective. Consider why this might be the case.

Problems with growth

Organisations must be aware of the problems involved in growth – both in terms of managing the people within the firm and controlling its activities. More products, more markets and more people inevitably make decision-making more demanding. These problems can be reduced by the effective use of information technology, relevant training and effective planning, but the management of a large business is still likely to be a major challenge. The hands-on management style of a small scale entrepreneur has to be replaced by an effective system which controls behaviour, but at the same time creates an environment in which people can develop; this is no easy task.

FACT FILE

1990	1998
Nippon Telegraph and Telephone 119	Microsoft 318
IBM 69	General Electric 295
Industrial Bank of Japan 68	Intel 194
Royal Dutch/ Shell 67	Merck 188
General Electric 63	Exxon 174
Exxon 60	Coca Cola 170
Sumitomo Bank 56	Wal Mart Stores 165
Fuji Bank 53	IBM 152
Toyota Motor 50	Royal Dutch/Shell 149
Mitsui Taiyo Kobe Bank 50	Pfizer 146

Table 6.2 Top 10 companies by market capitalisation ($ bn), 1990 and 1998.
Source: *Financial Times*, 4 December 1998

NUMERICAL INVESTIGATION

	MARKET CAP. (£M)	TURNOVER (£M)	PROFIT (£M)	*ROCE	EMPLOYEES (%)
GlaxoWellcome	62,546.5	7,980	2,686	51.1	53,068
British Petroleum	52,692.7	43,460	3,646	17.1	55,650
British Telecom	51,215.5	15,640	3,219	22.9	129,200

Table 6.3 The largest three UK companies 1998 (* = return on capital employed)
Source, *Financial Times* January 1999

a) What is meant by market capitalisation?
b) Which of the above companies is the biggest? Explain your answer.
c) Calculate the sales per employee and the profit per employee for each company. Comment on your findings.
d) Consider how firms can improve these ratios.

Managers need to examine ability to keep effective control and maintain a growing business which is personally satisfying and meets the investors' objectives. A bigger business does not automatically generate higher rates of return and is not necessarily a better investment.

Investment in machinery, premises and people all cost money and profits may actually fall. Managers also need to consider the potential reaction of competitors. The growth of a firm may suddenly pose a perceived threat to other organisations and lead to an aggressive reaction. In the 1970s Laker Airways, which had previously concentrated on segments which were not especially attractive to established airlines, began to attack their main business. In retaliation, a number of the large airlines started a price war to remove Laker as a competitor. (They were later fined for this behaviour.)

Too much growth may attract the unwanted attention of potential bidders or lead to more entrants to the market. The success of niche producers such as Sock Shop and Tie Rack in the 1980s led to many of the major clothing producers launching their own sock and tie product lines. Body Shop's success in 'cause marketing' and products free from animal testing has led to many imitators.

Government regulation

Government intervention may occur if a firm becomes too big. Any firm with more than 25% of the market in the UK can be investigated by the Competition Commission (formerly the Monopolies and Mergers Commission). The Commission looks to see if the firm is operating against the public interest. Although monopolies are not assumed automatically to be bad in the UK, the government reserves the right to study their activities and decide whether or not they are abusing their power.

Growth and stakeholders

The desirability of growth as an objective can also be examined from the point of view of different stakeholder groups. For consumers it may bring lower prices as a direct consequence of larger scale production. On the other hand, it may lead to monopoly power and a reduction in the quality and choice of goods available. From the point of view of employees, growth may create job opportunities and may mean greater security. At the same time, it may place additional demands on employees to increase productivity or to acquire new skills. This can place tremendous stress on people. The implications for suppliers can also be positive or negative. The growth of a firm may mean that suppliers have the chance to win new contracts and expand for themselves (and even gain from economies of scale). However, it may also place the buyer in a stronger position. The growth of the major food retailers, for example, has meant that many suppliers are heavily dependent on firms such as Sainsbury's and Asda for their orders. They can be pressurised to lower their prices whilst being asked to increase their quality.

KEY POINTS

Some of the problems of growth may be reduced by control mechanisms such as:

- budgeting
- management by objectives
- appraisals.

PROGRESS CHECK

To what extent is growth desirable?

FACT FILE

Sophie Mirman and Richard Ross founded Sock Shop in 1982. Their stake was worth £50 million within 4 years. However, in 1990 the company went into receivership. Mirman and Ross now run Trotters childrenswear shops.

Growth and people

Increased size almost inevitably brings with it potential difficulties for management: for example, larger scale organisations usually have more employees and more levels of hierarchy, which makes communication more difficult.

Communication

In a small business it is possible to have face-to-face conversations with everyone involved; problems can be sorted quickly and any confusion or uncertainties should be easier to deal with. To get their message across to larger numbers of employees, managers may have to resort to one-way methods of communication, such as noticeboards, corporate videos and newsletters. This may mean that managers miss out on valuable ideas and information from staff.

KEY TERM

A **stakeholder** is any individual or group which affects and is affected by an organisation's activities.

With poor communication within a large firm employees are more likely to become frustrated, alienated and demotivated. This in turn can lead to lower productivity, poorer quality production, higher labour turnover and absenteeism.

Culture and growth

Partly because the chances of seeing people face-to-face in a larger organisation are reduced, different parts of the organisation may develop their own culture. With segments of the business focusing on their own goals (which may not coincide with those of the organisation as a whole), business performance is likely to suffer. Even with improvements in information technology, it is difficult to make sure that everyone is kept well informed or has the opportunity to contribute. British Telecom has over 120,000 employees, for example; imagine how difficult it is to

FACT FILE

Vodafone was established in the mid-1980s. It floated in 1988 at less than 60p per share which valued it at £1.7 bn. After that the shares soared. By early 1999, they were valued at over £10.62, outperforming the FTSE 100 index by more than 500% and increasing the market value to £32.9 bn. Vodaphone's price:earnings ratio was 65, compared to a FTSE average (excluding financials) of 24. In 1999, it grew even bigger due to a merger with AirTouch, the American operator, creating a world leader in the telecommunications business.

KEY POINTS

Communication in small-scale organisations is likely to be more effective because:

- there are less people involved in the process
- two-way, face-to-face communication is more likely
- employees are likely to feel more involved
- employees are likely to be part of a common corporate culture.

communicate with these people, to let them know the corporate objectives and to keep them on track, in terms of aiming for the same things, believing in the same approaches and behaving in a similar fashion.

PROGRESS CHECK

Outline the possible communication problems which may occur as a firm grows.

Communication mechanisms

To overcome some of the problems of large size, an effective two-way communication system is required. This allows individuals to contribute and to feel part of the business as a whole. This is absolutely crucial to keep people interested and excited in what they are doing and to maintain the 'buzz' which characterises any prospering business. Communication mechanisms can take many forms from newsletters, team briefings to works councils. Whatever systems they are using, companies need to check regularly they are listening and learning from their people and that employees believe they are genuinely involved. To ensure this is happening, the firm may use staff surveys to assess employee's opinion. Every firm needs to be aware of the importance of communication and should seek ways to develop a dialogue between people and between different functions.

Growth and finance

Working capital v loans

As well as requiring good communication mechanisms, successful growth involves effective financial control. To finance expansion, a firm may use either its own funds or borrowed money. Using its own funds avoids interest payments but reduces the firm's working capital and may place a strain on cash flow. It can also mean that growth is rather slow, because expansion can only occur when enough funds have been accumulated. Relying on internal funds may, therefore, limit a firm's opportunities: if profits are relatively low the business may not be able to afford to undertake an investment even if it is potentially very profitable. To avoid such problems a firm may borrow. By taking out a loan, firms can afford large items of expenditure and be able to pay for them in the future when the profits come in. However, the business may struggle with the interest payments if its performance turns out to be poor.

High gearing is not in itself undesirable, provided the firm can use the borrowed money to generate a higher return than the cost of borrowing it. (If a firm borrows at 5%, for example, but is able to earn 8% through growth, this is a profitable use of the borrowed funds.) The ability of a firm to borrow will depend on factors such as its track record in meeting repayments, its collateral, the expected returns of the project and the confidence that the lender has in the ability of the management to achieve these returns. A firm with limited collateral, a poor track record and unconvincing management may struggle to find lenders. If, on the other hand a firm has low gearing and high expected profits, borrowing may be relatively straightforward to arrange.

Investment

Another way of financing growth is to bring in outside investors. For example, a firm may sell more shares. This reduces the control of the existing owners and may lead to conflicts in decision-making. On the other hand the firm will not have interest payments and should be able to delay dividends if performance is disappointing; this should mean that raising money through share capital is less risky than borrowing.

Venture capital

Another option which is often used by smaller companies wishing to expand is known as 'venture capital'. A venture capital company is a financial institution which specialises in lending to relatively high-risk projects, such as new businesses. If it is interested in a project, a venture capitalist will usually take shares in the business as well as lending to it. This means that, unlike a bank, a venture capitalist takes a direct interest in the running of the business. (A bank will be interested in the firm's ability to repay, but not in how the money is being used.) One advantage of using a venture capitalist is that the firm can benefit from their advice and experience, as well as the finance they provide. The disadvantage is that some control is lost and, if the business fails to hit various targets, the venture capitalists often set up the deal so that more and more of the company is gradually transferred to them in the form of shares.

INTERNAL FINANCE	EXTERNAL FINANCE
do not have to pay interest	may enable quicker expansion
reduces working capital	may incur interest rate charges
growth may be slow	

Table 6.4 A comparison of external and internal finance

Raising finance can be a major problem for firms wanting to expand. Entrepreneurs and managers may have what they believe to be an incredibly profitable idea and yet struggle to find others willing to take the risk. Even very successful business people such as James Dyson have, in their early careers, struggled to convince financial institutions that their ideas made commercial sense. Dyson was told on numerous occasions that he was a designer not a manufacturer and not capable of running a business. This seems to be a particular problem in the UK where financial institutions are often criticised for being short-termist and risk-averse. It is claimed that they look for quick and safe rewards (meaning that more unusual projects may, therefore, be difficult to finance) and that small firms wanting to expand may be of less interest to them than an already established large business.

The appropriate mix of finance for a growing business depends on what the managers themselves want and what funds are actually available. Firms often use several different sources of finance together and it is a question of what combination works best for a particular project, rather than there being any fixed rules. The right bal-

FACT FILE

At the 1998 UK Innovation Lecture organised by the DTI, Richard Branson was asked, 'What is the most vital skill needed for building a small business into a big one?'
'It just comes round and round and round again to finding the right people. Looking after those people, motivating those people, making sure that the person who runs the switchboard is treated as well as your deputy managing director. If you've got the right people then look for a gap in the market, try to be bold and do it better than others are doing it. And maybe try to stand out from the crowd, sometimes you have to make a fool of yourself in order to make sure your company gets known.'

KEY TERM

Gearing measures the proportion of long-term funds which is borrowed. (Gearing = long-term liabilities/ capital employed) × 100

ance between the different options may change at different points in the organisation's development. When presented with low interest rates and a deal which is expected to generate a high rate of return, a company which had previously had low gearing might borrow heavily to finance the deal, for example.

FACT FILE

In 1999, Nissan, the Japanese vehicle maker, reported its 6th year of losses out the past seven. It had managed to reduce its debt but still owed Y2,900 bn (about £15 bn)! In the years before, the Japanese group had been shedding its non-core assets and businesses – partly through sales to western companies – in an attempt to cut its debts and return to profitability, but it still remained highly geared.

PROGRESS CHECK

1 Fallini Ltd is a family owned toy company. It is considering expanding overseas but would need to raise several million pounds to do this. Consider how it might raise the necessary funds for this expansion.
2 Analyse the ways in which a firm might finance its growth.

Managing cash

Raising the capital is not the only financial problem concerned with growth; another major issue is the control of the finance during the expansion. Many projects have failed, not because they were unprofitable, but because they became illiquid during the growth process. The restaurant chain Pierre Victoire, for example, became insolvent in the 1990s, not because it was unpopular, but because, if anything, it was too successful – it grew too fast! As it was expanding, money was put into new restaurants and new facilities; this took cash out of the business and left it with a shortage of day-to-day funds, leaving it vulnerable to any downturn in sales. This is a common problem with fast-growing businesses and the phenomenon is called 'overtrading'. Eager to expand, firms rush out to buy new equipment, new materials and use up valuable cash; the trouble is that the actual sales may occur weeks, months or even years later. Even then, the cash may take longer to follow. This is illustrated by the 'death valley curve' diagram below. As sales begin to increase, to prepare for further growth the management may order an expansion of capacity and purchase more materials. The result is that more cash may be leaving the firm than is coming in (because sales have not yet increased). The firm may simply run out of cash. Successful growth will, therefore, involve the effective management of cash.

FACT FILE

Andrew Palmer had the idea for New Covent Garden Soups whilst having a bath. He then spent six months researching the market and 2 years finding out how to perfect the soup's shelf life. Harrods was the first company to stock it in 1988. Palmer put in £130,000 of savings and raised the same amount from the Business Enterprise Scheme and 30 private individuals. To finance further expansion, he brought in a venture capital company which initially took 30% for £900,000; the cash was used to build two factories. Palmer's control was reduced when there was a rights issue. In 1998 he ended all connection with the company, selling his remaining shares for £2.5 m. A year later the venture capital company sold the business for £20 m to S. Daniels, a food group.

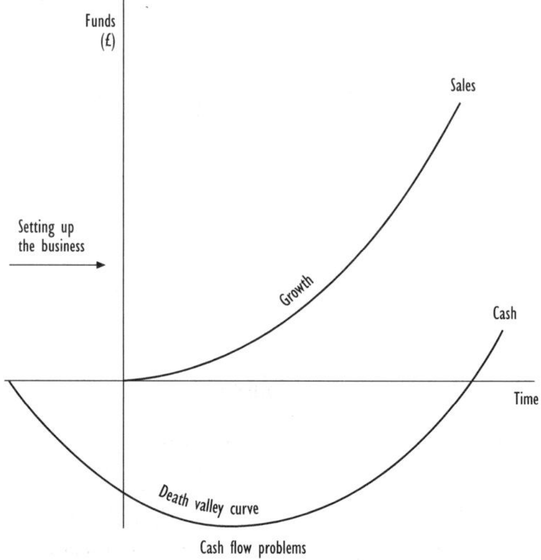

Figure 6.1 Cash flow when setting up a business

To manage cash flow effectively it may be better to grow at a slower rate than might at first seem attractive or possible. It is not always wise to take any and all orders which come along, because of the impact on cash flow in the short term.

The danger of liquidity problems highlights the need for managers to assess the impact on cash flow of every project, not just to focus on profitability.

To prevent overtrading a firm must keep close control over the cash outflows in relation to inflows. It must monitor, not just the amount of cash coming in and going out over a given period, but also the timings of these payments. Cash must be there when it is needed. To improve its cash flow position a firm may:

- attempt to reduce its debtor days by chasing up outstanding debts or by offering less credit in future
- raise finance from a debt factor using its debtors as assets
- monitor its outflow of cash to creditors and/or delay these payments (increasing creditor days)
- reduce its stock levels so that it avoids tying up too much money in a relatively illiquid asset.

All the policies mentioned above have potential problems. For example, chasing debtors may ruin relations with these customers. Delaying payment to suppliers may mean that they do not supply to the firm in future. Reducing stock levels may mean that the firm is out of stock when customers place orders. Debt factors charge interest. Firms must, therefore, consider the consequences of these actions carefully before undertaking them.

FACT FILE

In the late 1990s, the government set up a national network to connect business angels with unquoted companies seeking share capital. Angels are business people who invest between £50,000 and £100,000 in unquoted companies. They provide finance at a level which does not interest most venture capitalists. The new National Business Angels Network aims to link up angels and firms seeking funds.

PROGRESS CHECK

After college Andy Tirell set up his own catering business. In the first few years, the business did better than even he expected, but he is struggling to control its working capital effectively. Advise Andy on how the working capital of the business might be managed more successfully.

KEY POINTS

Borrowing is more likely when:

- the firm's existing gearing is low
- interest rates are low
- the expected rate of return on the project is greater than the cost of borrowing
- the owners want to keep control.

The changing role of managers during growth

Many businesses are established by individuals who have a particular idea and decide to set up on their own. These entrepreneurs or sole traders set up on their own because:

- they want to be their own boss
- they cannot find employment elsewhere
- they cannot get support for their idea from others
- they see this as a way of making more money than working for someone else.

KEY TERM

Overtrading occurs when a firm expands too rapidly and has liquidity problems because money is tied up in stocks and equipment.

FACT FILE

Screwfix Direct is a rapidly expanding mail order company. However, unlike most growing businesses it does not have cash flow problems because 95% of its orders are paid for in advance and nearly 80% are settled by credit cards over the phone. With no borrowings, not even an overdraft, it reinvests heavily in the business.

Often these firms specialise in niche markets, which the larger firms do not bother with, such as trekking holidays to the Himalayas, specialist computer services or homemade foods. In the early stages of the business, the founder is often responsible for all the firm's activities; life is generally hectic, stimulating and stressful. The individual has the exhilaration of being his or her own boss, but also the pressure of knowing that, if anything goes wrong, they are personally responsible.

Taking on staff

Over time the business may be successful and the owner may have to recruit staff to help run the business. The owner is now responsible for others and has to manage their activities. This will involve delegation, target-setting and ensuring that people are working effectively. By this stage, the owner may start to lose direct contact with customers as he or she starts to take more of a co-ordinating role. If the business continues to grow and the firm enters into more markets, the process of management inevitably becomes more complex. The owner has to give subordinates even more authority in order to get work done. The business is likely to need restructuring to ensure it functions effectively and that people have a clear idea of what they are supposed to do. In the early years of an organisation, individuals tend to define their own roles – in some cases jobs may overlap and some things may only get done when someone has the time to do them; the process is haphazard, often relying on goodwill and co-operation to get things done. However, with more people involved and less face-to-face contact, each individual's role has to be more clearly defined and a more formal structure established. This may involve drawing up job descriptions for the first time and considering issues such as training and development plans. Typically, the structure of an organisation will also change from being functionally organised (e.g. based on marketing, finance, and operations) to being product, customer or regionally focused.

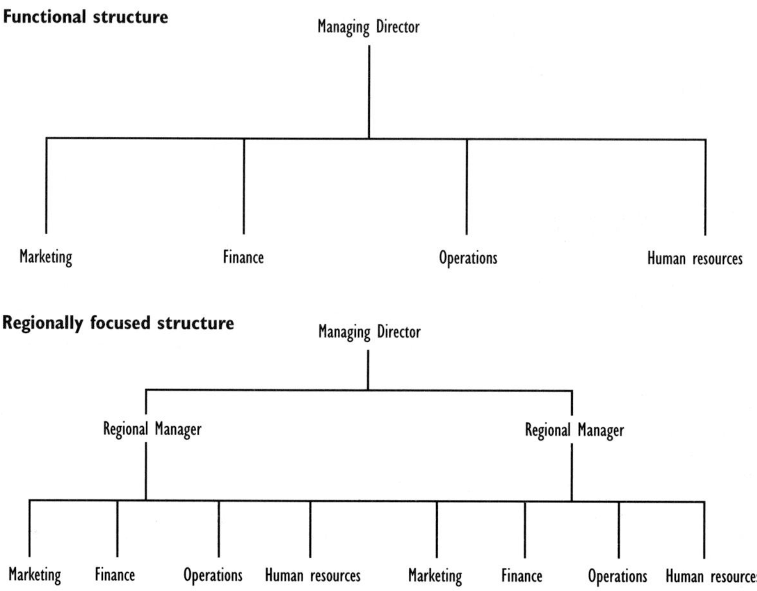

Figure 6.2 Managing for growth

Implementing systems

Growth is likely to require more control systems to ensure the activities of the firm are co-ordinated and that each individual's effort contributes to the organisational goal. Typically firms will introduce budgeting systems, formal appraisals and management by objectives to help co-ordinate and control their activities. The bigger the firm gets the more the founder's role becomes that of manager of the business. This means relying on others, motivating them, directing them, guiding them towards the organisational goals, but then letting them do the same with their own subordinates. Time is now likely to be taken up with meeting senior staff and making strategic decisions, rather than dealing directly with customers and day-to-day issues.

For some people, this change in role can be difficult to cope with. Although it offers new responsibilities, it may mean that the job that the entrepreneur ends up doing is very different from the one he or she started out doing; in some cases it could be less enjoyable and less fulfilling. Some individuals may also lack the skills needed to control a larger business effectively. Some entrepreneurs continue to interfere and this actually acts as a barrier to further growth. If the 'boss' decides to hold on to power, subordinates do not develop the skills necessary to take on responsibilities in the future. The result is that the organisation becomes very reliant on one or two people and may not be in a particularly strong position for the long term.

FACT FILE

In March 1999, Planet 24, the independent production company which makes The Big Breakfast for Channel Four, was bought by Carlton Communications for £15 m. Bob Geldof, the former pop star from The Boomtown Rats, and his partners, Charlie Parsons and Waheed Ali, sold their shares earning them £5 m each. Planet 24 employs around 250 people and makes around 600 hours of programmes for UK television.

PROGRESS CHECK

Questions

1 **Distinguish between the role of a boss and a manager.**
2 **Why do you think many managers fail to delegate properly?**
3 **Analyse the problems involved in managing a business as it grows.**

Growth and resources

Production

Growth sometimes occurs too fast for the productive capacity of the firm. If demand rises quickly, a firm may find that it cannot supply enough products. In the short run it can ask employees to work extra shifts or work overtime, or can bring in additional labour, but if demand keeps increasing it may not be able to fulfil its orders. This is a crucial moment in a firm's development – should it invest in new capacity or stay with its existing resources? Expansion creates new opportunities but involves a high risk. It requires investment and relies on demand staying at the new higher level. Maintaining the existing capacity may be safer but it may also mean that orders are turned away (unless the firm contracts the orders out – the problem with this is that it may lose control of the quality and this can be more expensive than producing the goods internally).

KEY TERM

The **capacity** of a firm is the maximum it can produce with its existing resources.

Staff

Expansion also places new demands on a firm's human resources. Employees may have to cope with higher workloads which can be stressful. They may also need

FACT FILE

Each year *The Sunday Times* produces a list of the fastest growing companies in the UK called 'Fast Track 100'. In 1998 the fastest growing company was a recruitment agency called 'Progressive Computer' which has grown at an annual compound rate of 197.78%. Between 1994 and 1997, for example, sales increased from £1 m to over £26 m. The company was set up in 1990 by Sunil Wickremeratne. It has grown so fast that it has had to move offices five times. Its headquarters are in Wimbledon and it has regional offices in Birmingham, Manchester, Reading and Glasgow.

KEY TERMS

Increasing capacity utilisation occurs when a firm produces more within an existing capacity level.

Increasing the scale of production occurs when the firm changes its capacity level.

KEY TERMS

Economies of scale are reductions in unit costs due to an increase in the scale of production.

Diseconomies of scale are increases in unit costs due to an increase in the scale of production.

training in new skills or new technology to cope with the changes necessary to increase output. The firm might also have to recruit more staff. This will involve recruitment costs and may prove difficult if the jobs are highly skilled or there are labour shortages. To attract additional employees, the firm may have to increase the rewards on offer which could increase its costs. Difficulties finding the right people can constrain a firm's growth. This is most likely to be the case in businesses which require particular skills that are in short supply. Over time it is likely to be easier to find employees – more time means the firm can train people and can spend longer on the recruitment process. In periods of rapid growth time may be short. Even if labour is available, firms may be reluctant to hire new staff in case demand falls in the future. They may not want to commit to employing more people, if they do not think they will be able to employ them in the long term. This is why, in the short run, firms often ask their existing staff to work more hours, rather than recruit.

Costs and size

The capacity of a firm is the maximum amount it can produce with its given resources. If a firm is operating *below* capacity its unit costs are likely to be *high* because the fixed costs are not spread over many units. As it expands its output (i.e. increases its capacity utilisation) this can lead to a reduction in unit costs, since the fixed costs can be allocated to more units. Once firms reach the limit of their existing capacity, they may consider changing the scale of their production. This means investing in people or capital to increase their capacity. By changing the scale of production, a firm may benefit from economies of scale; if it expands too much, however, it may suffer from diseconomies of scale. Typically economies of scale arise due to:

- *Discounts arising through buying-in bulk* – this can occur for a range of items.
- *Ability to have managers who specialise in certain areas as the organisation grows* – this means that instead of a sole trader trying to do all the jobs, different managers can focus on specific areas such as marketing and finance.
- *Ability to use mass production techniques as output increases* – the existence of this type of economy of scale will depend on the product. Mass production techniques do not usually apply in services, for example, which rely more on dealing with an individual customer's needs. Having said this, some service industries, such as insurance processing, have adopted many mass production techniques.
- *Ability to borrow at a relatively low interest rate* – due to the larger firm's size/collateral.

Diseconomies of scale usually involve the problems of managing a larger organisation and employing more staff. They include the difficulties of co-ordinating more people, more departments, more products and more divisions and the increased communication problems which occur between different locations and different layers of hierarchy. Unit costs can also increase because of motivational problems. These can occur in large businesses as individuals lose a sense of belonging (Maslow's social needs) and do not feel they are important.

What is the optimum size of a firm?

There is no one best size for a firm. It will depend on a number of factors such as: Size of the market – the market for cars is worth much more than the market for cufflinks i.e. firms have the opportunity to get bigger in the car industry; Economies and diseconomies of scale – the greater the economies of scale, the more incentive there is for a firm to expand and benefit from lower unit costs. In this situation, smaller firms may struggle to compete unless they have some USP as they will have a cost disadvantage. If, however, diseconomies occur at relatively low levels of output, firms are less likely to expand significantly; Competitors' reactions – if competitors are likely to react aggressively to growth, a firm is less likely to expand; Owners' and managers' personal objectives – to what extent do these groups see larger size as desirable? Government – in some countries the government actively encourages large scale production and even protects its industries to help them expand.

NUMERICAL INVESTIGATION

Although consumer goods sectors such as food, tobacco and soft drinks are dominated by a few firms selling brands worldwide the brewing industry remains fragmented. The top 20 brewers produce less than half the world's beer and there are few really global brands such as Guinness and Heineken. However, gradually firms are consolidating to achieve economies of scale and distribution.

COUNTRY	SIZE OF MARKET (MILLION HECTOLITRES)
US	223.9
China	186.1
Germany	107.6
Brazil	82.4
Japan	67.9
UK	60

Table 6.5 Top worldwide beer markets (million hectolitres)

BRAND	BREWER	MARKET SHARE (MILLION HECTOLITRES)
Budweiser	Anheuser Busch	50.1
Bud Light	Anheuser Busch	27.3
Brahma Chopp	Brahma	21.9
Asahi Super Dry	Asahi	21.7
Corona Extra	Modelo	19.5

Table 6.6 Top worldwide brands' market shares

BREWER	HEADQUARTERS	(MILLION HECTOLITRES)
Anheuser Busch	US	121.3
Heineken	Netherlands	73.8
Miller (Philip Morris)	US	52.9
South African Breweries	UK	43.0
Brahma	Brazil	41.3

Table 6.7 Top worldwide brewers' market shares (million hectolitres). Source, Impact Databank

a) What is the combined size of the top five beer markets in the world?
b) How big is the US market in relation to the UK market?
c) If a brand had a 5% share of the UK market how much would its sales be?
d) If a brand had a 5% share of the US market how much would its sales be?
e) What is the combined sales of the top five worldwide brands?
f) What is the combined sales of the top five worldwide brewers?
g) What percentage of Anheuser Busch's sales is Budweiser?
h) Why might the brewing market be relatively fragmented?

PROGRESS CHECK

Analyse the factors which determine the optimum size of a business.

Is large scale becoming more important?

With fewer trade barriers, more deregulation and more overseas competition, there are now more firms fighting for market share in a whole range of industries. In areas such as telecommunications, energy and transport, for example, there have been tremendous changes which have generated much more competition than in the past. This has led to a major restructuring as firms seek the benefits of large size. In the airline industry, for example, organisations such as British Airways have sought to take-over or develop alliances with other firms to provide a global service. In the car industry, the high level of excess capacity has led to mergers and take-overs (such as BMW and Rover, and Ford and Volvo) as firms seek to develop a complete product range and share resources such as research and development. In telecommunications, British Telecommunications has undertaken a large number of alliances and take-overs to build up a global presence as previously protected markets open up and create global opportunities. Similar changes have occurred in insurance, accounting, chemicals and pharmaceuticals. In these sectors there are world-wide markets and, to compete internationally, UK firms are seeking to ally or acquire other firms.

Obviously, these pressures are stronger in some industries than in others. The defence industry, for example, is traditionally protected by governments, but even here protectionism has been declining. This is creating opportunities for large UK firms with the right mix of skills and scale of production. By comparison, markets such as interior decorating and restaurants remain locally important and there is still plenty of scope for small producers to exist.

Why do so many firms remain small?

Owner preference

Although most media coverage focuses on large companies, it is important to remember that most businesses in the UK are actually very small. They are sole traders or employ less than 200 employees. Their small size is due, in many cases, to the personal ambitions and objectives of the individuals involved. They may have reached a stage in their career where they are happy. They may not want the additional stress of trying to make the business bigger. For example, they may not want to take on additional debt to finance expansion; they may not want to have to deal with more employees; they may actually prefer keeping the business small so they can keep an eye on everything. Some people set out to create the world's largest, most successful, most profitable business but they often find that they end up with other priorities in life, such as their family and their hobbies. They make a decision about the extent to which they want the business to dominate their lives and thoughts. They may also find that the business, however small, provides more than enough challenge!

Few economies of scale

Growth does not always offer significant cost advantages. In hairdressing and newsagencies, for example, there are hundreds of thousands of shops around the country serving local markets. Large economies of scale do not occur and this enables small firms to continue to exist. The same is true for taxi firms, plumbers, florists and garages. Although a few small producers do continue to exist in large scale, mass markets (e.g. small specialist producers in the car industry, such as Morgan) they usually have to serve a niche which enables them to charge a higher price to cover higher unit costs.

FACT FILE

In 1999, the government introduced a number of new employment laws under the title of 'Fairness at Work'. These provide new rights for employees. The Forum of Private Businesses estimated that these measures will cost small firms at least £3.5 bn and drive some into bankruptcy.

Other factors

There are also many factors which prevent growth, even if the owners wanted to expand. Finance, for example, is a major problem for small firms which often lack the necessary collateral to borrow and struggle to find willing investors. The government is also attacked for making it difficult for firms to expand; in particular they are criticised for having too much paperwork and too many rules and regulations which take up so much time that people cannot actually run their businesses properly!

KEY POINTS

Small firms are more likely to survive where:

- the market is local, e.g. taxi firms
- significant economies of scale do not exist
- several niche markets exist, e.g. holidays, fashion, music.

Individuals may lack the experience and ability to cope with a growing organisation; even if they wanted to grow they may not be able to control it effectively. The limitations to growth are, therefore, a combination of internal and external factors. Internally the firm may lack the retained profits, the capacity or the experience to expand. Externally it may lack the market or fear the government's or competitors' reactions.

PROGRESS CHECK

The majority of organisations in the UK are relatively small. Examine the factors which might prevent their growth.

The advantages of a small scale

Small size has many benefits. In particular, it may mean that managers are close to their customers and their markets and are sensitive to changes as they occur. In large organisations, the senior management may spend so much of their time managing that they lose touch with what is actually happening in the market place. Decision-making can be much faster than in bigger firms. In large organisations ideas may have to be approved by various committees and there is a danger of too much talk and not enough action. By comparison, a small firm can usually make decisions quite rapidly because managers can get to see each other more easily and are more likely to be able sort things out face to face. This may enable a quicker response to new opportunities in the market.

Cross-functional decision-making is also more likely in small firms; people from different areas of the business with different perspectives are more likely to be able to meet to exchange ideas and to contribute to each other's decisions. This may lead

FACT FILE

There were an estimated 3.7 million active businesses in the UK at the start of 1997. Small businesses, including those without employees, accounted for over 99% of businesses, 45% of non-government employment and (excluding the finance sector) 40% of turnover.

to more co-ordinated decision-making and a greater sense of working towards a common goal. By comparison, in larger firms individual departments and divisions are more likely to develop their own cultures and communication between functions may be poor.

PROGRESS CHECK

Consider the advantages of operating as a small scale business.

From big to small

A noticeable trend in recent years has been for firms to get smaller, rather than bigger. Although at one time the prevailing wisdom was that 'bigger is better' (due to the benefits of economies of scale and the power that large size can bring) many firms have found that the complexities of running a bigger organisation overwhelming. As a result, several firms have sold off parts of their business to enable them to concentrate on what they regard as the key areas. Operating in many different markets with a wide product range can make it difficult to keep people in the organisation focused. In this situation it may be better to focus on the core businesses; in the words of Tom Peters, firms may want to 'stick to the knitting'. According to the Pareto rule, 80% of a firm's profits are likely to come from about 20% of their products. It may be worth focusing on these 20% and give up the other 80% which generate relatively low returns.

Delayering

One way in which firms have made themselves smaller is through a policy of delayering. One of the problems of large size is communication between top and bottom, leading to slow decision-making. To overcome this and at the same time to cut overhead costs, firms may decide to remove layers of hierarchy. This places extra challenges (and burdens) on subordinates who are now given greater responsibility for their own work. It also means that the remaining managers have larger spans of control; this can be stimulating and motivating for the individuals involved – it can also be stressful. However, with fewer levels of hierarchy there may be less sense of 'us' and 'them' between senior managers and employees.

Breaking down

Firms can also reduce the scale of their operations by selling off parts of their business to focus on their central activities. This raises finance and can improve direction for the resulting firms. The sell off may be part of a demerger, whereby firms are separated into separate companies to compete independently in their own markets. For example, ICI split into ICI and Zeneca in the 1990s in the belief that the two firms would perform better independently than they did as part of a more diversified whole.

Re-engineering

Another trend which often leads to firms reducing the size of their activities is that of re-engineering (or business process re-engineering). When firms re-engineer their processes, they examine what they do from first principles. Instead of trying to adjust what they do at the moment, these firms ask the most basic question: if we started again how would we do it? It is often quite difficult to take this overview when you are heavily involved in an ongoing business. However, re-engineering tries to avoid narrow thinking by examining the whole process and comparing the existing system with the way it would be if it were designed from scratch. This can lead to major changes, and is often associated with large scale redundancies and a reduction in operations to focus on key activities.

PROGRESS CHECK

Discuss the possible impact of re-engineering on an organisation.

The decision to make the business smaller (sometimes known as 'retrenchment') may be a positive one – if it is part of a deliberate programme to refocus effort and energy – or it may be forced on a firm by circumstances. Poor economic conditions or the actions of competitors may make some business activities unprofitable or unattractive, and this may lead to a sale.

Big and small?

Decentralisation

The trade off between the cost and power advantages of large size and the flexibility gains of small size is one which is faced by many organisations. One way of balancing the two is to decentralise so that each division or subsidiary within the overall organisation is given a considerable amount of freedom. The different business units are able to benefit from the size advantages of the parent organisation (e.g. through lower costs of borrowing) whilst keeping the speed of reaction and the focus associated with smaller firms.

An example of this big and yet small approach is seen in the 'Virgin' empire. Although we see the name Virgin around us daily – Virgin cola, Virgin trains, Virgin airlines, Virgin Vie cosmetics, Virgin brides – this is simply a brand which has been extended to many products and services with relatively little central corporate structure. Each firm operates as a relatively autonomous business unit; its management is able to benefit from the brand awareness and the skills of Richard Branson and his corporate strategy team but is expected to act independently in its own business area.

Branson explained his approach at the DTI Innovation Lecture in 1998:

> 'I am still a great believer that "small is beautiful" and I think the skill of building a company is to try and keep remembering that philosophy. I could give an example about record companies – when we got to about 50

In 1987, Percy Barnevik announced what was then the world's largest cross border merger between a Swedish engineering company and a Swiss company, Brown Boveri. Since then ABB has acquired over 70 more companies. Barnevik identifies a small number of key executives, has a very small head office and has a matrix structure with over 5000 profit centres. Within a large overall business each unit is, therefore, kept relatively small.

or 60 people in one building many years ago, I went and asked to see the deputy managing director, the deputy sales director and the deputy marketing manager and said, "you are now the managing director, the marketing manager, the sales manager of a new company and you have got to go and find another building." When they got to 50 people in their building we did the same again ... In the end we had about 30 different record companies around the Notting Hill Gate area ... With Virgin Express, instead of just forming part of Virgin Atlantic and listening to accountants who had said, "look, you might as well share accounting, switchboards, and offices", we have separated it completely, and so there is no synergistic overlap at all. I think that is one way you can become quite a large company but at the same time remain small.'

Summary chart

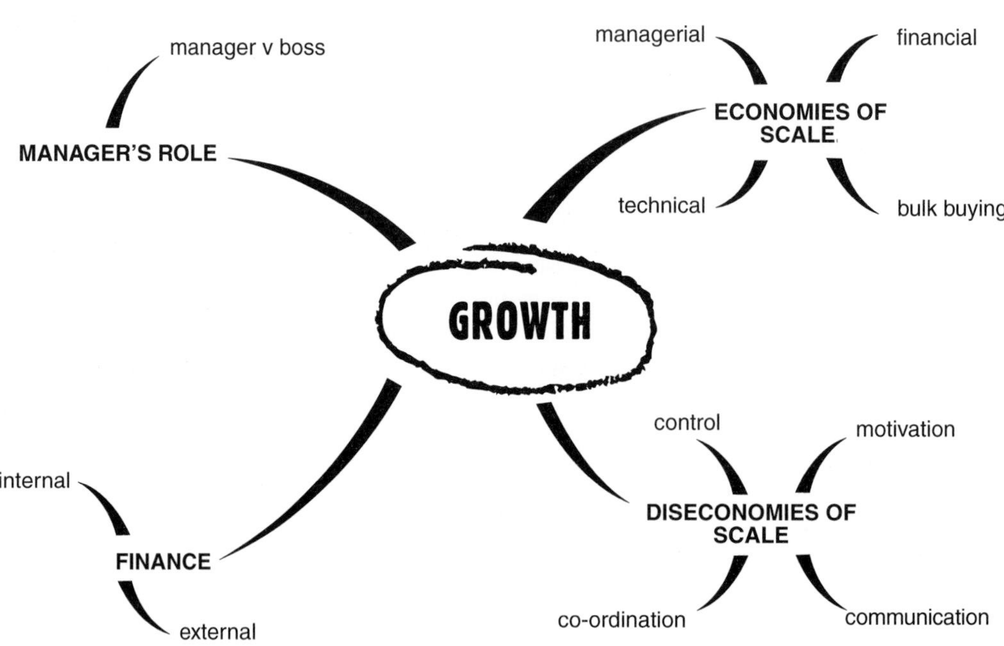

Figure 6.3

Approaching exam questions: Managing growth

Consider the problems facing the managers of a fast growing business.

(9 marks)

A good answer to this question will outline the typical problems facing a growing firm and discuss what factors would make them more or less significant. For example, communication is often a problem when firms expand; to overcome this firms try to devise effective communication mechanisms and design a structure which encourages a two-way flow of information. If the organisation ends up with many layers of hierarchy and relying on a one-way flow, such as noticeboards, communication is likely to be a major problem. If, however, communication is managed effectively (treating information as an important resource), this need not be a significant issue. The extent to which communication is a problem depends, therefore, on how it is managed. The same is true with other factors such as motivation, control and co-ordination. These issues should be highlighted and explained but they need to be developed. For example, to overcome the co-ordination problems, the firm may introduce a management by objectives system.

It is also important to refer to the fact that the firm in the question is a fast growing business. A strong answer will consider the additional problems this may present. Managers may lack the experience to cope with quick growth and not have the time needed to gain suitable experience. Rapid growth may exaggerate the typical problems of expansion because the difficulties may arise in quick succession. Before one problem is solved another challenge comes along.

'Growth presents more benefits than problems.' Discuss.

(40 marks)

This question has two clear sides: the benefits of growth and the problems it provides. Having discussed these issues the candidate needs to cover the factors which determine whether the growth presents more or less opportunities in relation to the problems. The possible benefits include potential economies of scale, greater market power and promotion opportunities. Problems could include the difficulties of managing a larger organisation or competitor reaction.

The key to this question is what determines whether benefits exceed problems. This will vary from firm to firm. For example, it depends on the extent to which economies of scale exist – in industries with high fixed costs, they are likely to be more substantial than firms with low fixed costs. It also depends on how the firm manages the growth – if jobs are defined appropriately, effective communication mechanisms developed and suitable training undertaken, the problems will be less than if managers were unprepared. Slow, planned growth may be easier to control; fast, unexpected growth may cause more managerial problems as appropriate structures may not be in place.

'Big is beautiful. All firms should seek to expand.' Discuss this statement.

(40 marks)

This is a fairly provocative and extreme statement and you should be prepared to argue against it. A good answer will explain the logic behind the statement (e.g. large scale can lead to economies of scale and more market power). At the same time the arguments against expansion must be explored. For example:

- the owners' personal objectives
- diseconomies of scale
- legislation
- market size.

The use of the word 'all' should certainly be challenged – some firms may want to expand but surely not all. Whether a firm wants to expand will depend on a range of factors such as the managers' ability to keep control, the ability to raise finance and the owners' wishes. These issues need to be discussed.

'Financing growth through borrowing is far too risky. Firms should avoid debt and rely on retained profits.' Discuss.

(40 marks)

This is a fairly strong set of assertions which should be challenged. Whilst it is true that debt can bring risk, this is not always the case. It certainly does not follow that firms should rely on retained profit. Areas which could be examined are:

- the debt involved – what is the rate of interest compared to the expected return from the growth?
- the problems of relying on retained profits, e.g. slow growth
- other sources of finance, e.g. share issue.

Whether retained profit is the 'right' form of finance depends on issues such as the interest rate, the willingness of the owners to lose control, the availability of profits as a source of finance and the strength of the desire for growth. It may be that a combination of sources is required.

Student answers

Discuss the factors which might determine the optimal size of a firm.

(9 marks)

Student answer

The size of a firm can be measured in many ways: employees, assets and turnover. The different methods can lead to very different results. The optimal size means the 'best' size; the size a firm should aim for. The optimal size depends on the extent to which the firm benefits from economies of scale and can avoid diseconomies of scale. The optimum in terms of cost per unit is the point at which the firm has benefited from all economies of scale without experiencing diseconomies. Economies of scale can be technical, purchasing, financial and managerial. Diseconomies can be managerial, motivational and communication-based. In industries such as telecommunications there are high fixed costs; these sectors are capital intensive. There is an incentive in these industries to expand and spread these fixed costs over more units.

The optimum size will also depend on what the owners and managers themselves want. If they want to maintain a close control, they may deliberately choose to keep the firm small, even if it could get bigger. Ultimately, the size will be constrained by the demand for the firm's products or services. Whatever economies of scale exist or however big the firm wants to get, expansion is only feasible if there is the demand to sustain production – there is no point producing without selling.

Marker's comments

This is a good answer which shows a sound knowledge of some of the issues involved such as economies and diseconomies of scale. The candidate also brings in the idea of personal motives which is an important and relevant factor. The answer highlights how size can be measured but does little with this. However, once the candidate gets going he or she discusses some factors intelligently.

Mark: Content 2/2, Application 4/4, Analysis 3/3. Total = 9

Discuss the ways in which unexpected growth might affect a firm.

(9 marks)

Student answer

With more growth, the firm will have to make more products. This means it needs to hire more people. This will mean recruiting more people. So costs will be higher. The firm needs to buy more supplies and store them somewhere. But when it sells these items it will make more profit because it is selling more goods. Growth also means the managers will be busy, which means they may not be able to do their job properly.

With more profit the firm can pay people more and invest more, which is a good thing.

Marker's comments

This answer highlights some of the issues involved in growth but does not develop them very much. In particular, the candidate does not really discuss the issues involved. Will the firm have to recruit or can it use its existing workforce? Just because the firm is selling more does not necessarily mean it will make more profit – this will depend on what has happened in terms of costs and revenues. Will managers necessarily be too busy or can they delegate tasks to their subordinates?

The candidate also fails to discuss the significance of 'unexpected growth'. A strong answer would have considered how this would have impacted on the firm.

Mark: Content 2/2, Application 2/4, Analysis 0/3. Total = 4

Analyse how a firm might ease the problems of growth.

(9 marks)

Student answer

Growth can cause communication problems. People do not get to see each other face-to-face as much. People have to rely more on written communication, such as memos and letters and these are not as effective as two-way communication. To overcome this, firms can try and manage information effectively; this may involve effective use of information technology (such as e-mail), ensuring there are regular meetings and that information is cascaded from the top of the organisation and back again. Nevertheless, as the firm gets bigger there will be more information, more messages, more channels and more opportunities for the message to be distorted. Communication also becomes difficult as individuals and groups form their own cultures (with their own values and attitudes). This can cause conflicts and difficulties understanding or co-operating with each other. To overcome this, the senior managers have to try and develop a corporate culture based on corporate values and attitudes. This could be done by developing a mission statement which reflects the aim of the organisation. Culture clashes could also be reduced by setting up multifunctional teams and committees, which encourage employees to appreciate the problems and issues facing other functions. These also provide an opportunity for ideas to be exchanged.

Growth can also cause diseconomies of scale which can reduce profits.

Marker's comments

This is a very unbalanced answer. The discussion of communication is good and examines a number of points effectively. However, the candidate does not cover any other areas well. It raises the idea of diseconomies of scale but does not develop this or discuss how these problems can be overcome.

Mark: Content 2/2, Application 2/4, Analysis 2/3. Total = 6

'Most organisations would be more successful if they were smaller.' Discuss.

(11 marks)

Student answer

Small-scale organisations are more flexible and can get things done more quickly. The owners or managers can make decisions rapidly and so they are more responsive to the market. This can make them more successful.

Also, people in small organisations are more likely to be motivated because they know each other and can talk all day. This should make communication easier which helps to swap ideas. If firms got smaller they would probably find it more friendly and make it easier to do things.

Marker's comments

This answer contains some valid ideas about the advantages of small scale organisations, but these are not expressed very well. Also it is a one-sided answer which fails to consider the benefits of operating on a large scale. It lacks any evaluation (small scale may be more desirable when … may be less desirable when …), so would not score very highly. A good answer to this question would examine the case for and against small scale, would examine the transition from large to small and would challenge the idea of 'most' organisations.

Mark: Content 2/2, Application & Analysis 2/6, Evaluation 0/3. Total = 11

End of section questions

1 Analyse the possible problems which a firm might encounter when it is growing rapidly.

(9 marks)

2 Consider whether internal or external growth is more desirable for a firm.

(11 marks)

3 Examine the possible reasons why so many firms in the UK are small rather than large.

(9 marks)

4 Discuss the ways in which a firm might finance its growth.

(9 marks)

5 To what extent should a firm finance its growth by borrowing?

(11 marks)

6 The government may intervene to prevent a firm growing 'too big'. Analyse the factors which the government may take into account when deciding whether or not to prevent further growth.

(9 marks)

7 Should firms aim to grow internally or externally?

(11 marks)

8 Analyse the reasons why firms may decide to become smaller rather than larger.

(9 marks)

9 Examine the possible benefits of re-engineering for an organisation.

(9 marks)

10 Consider the view that small firms are more important to the economy than large firms.

(11 marks)

Essays

1 'With the rapid liberalisation of markets only large firms are likely to survive in the long term.' Critically assess this view.

(40 marks)

2 To what extent should growth be the main aim of a business?

(40 marks)

3 There have been large numbers of take-overs and mergers in the last few years, leading to a few firms dominating in several markets. Critically assess the view that the government should intervene more to reduce the size of firms.

(40 marks)

4 'Small firms remain small because they cannot raise the money they need to finance growth.' Critically assess this view.

(40 marks)

5 'The effective management of finances is the key to successful growth.' Discuss.

(40 marks)

CHAPTER 7

Change in ownership: Mergers, take-overs, ventures, alliances and management buy outs

Organisations are dynamic. They are constantly changing shape and form as their objectives and resources alter and the environment they operate in changes. With developments in technology, in the behaviour of competitors or the economy, for example, firms may expand, join or seek partners. In this section we consider examining the ways in which the shape of organisations can change.

Take-overs and mergers

Mergers and take-overs involve a change in the ownership of a business. In a merger two or more organisations join together. The previously separate companies form one new business; if you owned shares in one of the companies before, you will now own shares in the newly merged organisation. The merged company will often take its name from elements of the names of the two organisations involved. For example, Commercial Union and General Accident merged in 1998 to form CGU.

By comparison, in a take-over situation one firm gains control of another. A bidder buys up the shares of the target company. If the take-over is *voluntary*, the directors of the target company recommend that their shareholders sell to the bidder. In a *hostile* take-over, the directors of the target company recommend that their shareholders do not sell to the bidder. Hostile take-overs tend to get a high level of publicity as the bidder tries to gain control of the victim company. Mergers and take-overs can be described as 'integration'.

Why would firms want to integrate?

The reasons for integration vary from one deal to the next, but the most common reasons include:

FACT FILE

Companies	Combined value $bn
Exxon/Mobil	86.4
Travelers/Citicorp	72.6
SBC/Ameritech	72.4
Bell Atlantic/GTE	71.3
AT&T/TCI	69.9

Table 7.1 Top five mergers, 1998

Source: *The Economist*, 2 January 1999

KEY TERMS

Integration
occurs when two or more firms join together; this could be either in the form of a merger or a takeover

Vertical integration
occurs when firms at different stages of the same production process join together

Horizontal integration
occurs when firms at the same stage of the same production process join together.

- *To share resources* – by integrating, firms can share resources such as customer databases, distribution channels and salesforces. This not only provides the opportunity for cost savings, but also means that firms can use each other's resources to improve their competitive position. For example, when Cadbury bought up Dr Pepper it was able to use the latter's strengths in the US to distribute its products there, whilst in Europe it used its own distribution to increase sales of Dr Pepper.
- *To gain access to the market or control of supplies* – through *vertical integration* firms can gain more control over the distribution system. The need to provide high quality goods as quickly as possible, whilst minimising stock levels, has meant that much more emphasis is now being placed on managing the whole supply and distribution chain. Also, with consumer groups increasingly investigating where and how products are produced, there is growing pressure on firms to ensure their supplies meet consumer expectations and, in some cases, this can best be achieved through integration.
- *To ensure their products are promoted and sold effectively* – this is why most tour operators have bought up travel agents (e.g. Thomson bought Lunn Poly) to generate business for themselves.
- *To access a market* – with the opening of markets in Eastern Europe and Asia, acquisitions have been one way of entering these markets quickly. Western firms have been able to gain from contacts and local knowledge, whilst bringing investment and marketing expertise.
- *Economies of scale* – by combining two firms, the new organisation has the advantage of larger size. This may mean it can borrow more cheaply (because it has more assets) and it will almost certainly give the firm more bargaining power with suppliers and distributors. By combining their marketing, firms can also achieve cost savings in this area and there may also be production economies of scale (particularly in the case of *horizontal integration*).
- *To spread risks* – although conglomerate integration is somewhat out of fashion at the moment, buying up or joining with companies in different markets does help organisations to spread their risk. If a firm is in a saturated or declining market, conglomerate integration provides an opportunity for growth.
- *Personal motives* – in a number of cases, mergers and take-overs have occurred to boost the reputation and egos of senior managers. Eager to make their mark and to control a larger firm, they have seen external growth as a means of increasing their power (and often their rewards).
- *To utilise existing management skills* – some firms specialise in developing a management system which can then be applied to a number of different business areas. Companies such as Hanson had an effective financial control system which could turn around companies in many different business sectors. The Hanson approach (in the past) sought to make use of its management resources by buying underperforming and undervalued companies.

- *To rationalise* – if there is substantial overcapacity in an industry, mergers and take-overs are part of the restructuring necessary to reduce the number of firms in the industry.

PROGRESS CHECK

Discuss the possible reasons why a firm might want to expand.

NUMERICAL INVESTIGATION

In the 1990s, Lloyds Bank acquired the Cheltenham and Gloucester building society. It then merged with the TSB to form Lloyds TSB. In 1999, it bought the Scottish Widows insurance company.

	Lloyds TSB	Scottish Widows
New business	159	116
Existing business	213	125
Investment earnings	25	165
Distribution costs	(81)	(96)
Total	**316**	**426**

Table 7.2 Profit/loss of Lloyds TSB and Scottish Widows after tax, 1998 (£m), *Financial Times*, 24 June 1999

Long-term insurance market share:

- Total net premium income in 1997 = £74.85 bn
- Scottish Widows premium income in 1997 = £1.93 bn

a) Calculate Scottish Widows' share of the long-term insurance market in 1997.
b) What percentage of total profit is from new business for i) Lloyds TSB and ii) Scottish Widows?
c) Why might it be important for potential investors to calculate this figure?
d) Explain possible reasons for this deal.

FACT FILE

In the 1990s, Dr Pepper/Seven Up (DPSU), the US soft drinks subsidiary of Cadbury-Schweppes relied on the bottling networks of its main rivals, Pepsi and Coca Cola. Pepsi distributed two-thirds of Dr Pepper. Coke distributed more than 40% of Dr Pepper and Canada Dry soda. This caused problems as these bottlers and distributors became fussier about distributing a rival product; the more successful Dr Pepper/Seven Up became the more difficult it was to get products distributed! For example, Coca Cola and Pepsi stopped distributing brands like A&W root beer and Sunkist orange. DPSU's reaction was to build an independent distribution system to ensure it could get to the market. At present this system relies mainly on small family businesses which are more expensive to use than the big cola bottlers. DPSU has, therefore, been eager to buy into these firms and get them to consolidate. Further vertical integration is likely if it wants to be certain of access to the market.

How does a take-over occur?

To take over another company, the aggressor must gain control of the majority of the shares. This involves bidding for the shares and buying them up. In many cases, the take-over is agreed and the directors of the victim company urge their shareholders to sell. This is because they think the price they have been offered is high compared to their perception of the value of the business and/or because they think the new owners will be good for the company. In some cases, however, the directors of the victim company may not believe the deal is desirable and so they recommend that their shareholders do not sell. This leads to a take-over battle in which the bidder is trying to buy up the shares against the wishes and advice of the victim company's directors. This often involves a public relations campaign on both sides. They argue their cases (reasons to sell, reasons not to sell). The share price often creeps upwards – as the bidder becomes more desperate to gain control, they may have to increase the price they offer. Sometimes a third party also makes a bid; the victim may even ask another company to launch a take-over attempt instead (in this case, the new bidder is called a '**white knight**').

FACT FILE

There is an estimated 20% of overcapacity in the European car industry; this has led to a number of mergers and take-overs (such as the creation of DaimlerChrysler and Ford's takeover of Volvo) to reduce capacity. The reduction in the number of car companies has also led to restructuring in component suppliers – there were 173 domestic mergers and acquisitions amongst suppliers in 1998, involving $8.5 bn of assets.

KEY TERM

Firms which decide to integrate believe in the idea of **synergy** (i.e. 2+2=5). They think that by combining with another business, whether it be through take-over or merger, the new organisation will be more successful than the sum of the two parts operating separately.

The Take-over Panel

The Take-over Panel imposes various rules for company take-overs, including a strict timetable of events. For example, once one firm has 5% of a plc it must let that company know. Once it has 30% it must make a full bid. It then has 60 days to gain control.

Cash and paper offers

The bidder usually offers shareholders a price subject to the company gaining over 50% of the voting shares; if it does not get enough shareholders to agree, it withdraws the offer. The bid may be in the form of cash, in which case the bidder simply buys up shares, or in the form of paper, in which case the bidder offers shares in its company in return for shares in the victim company. Whether or not people give up their shares depends on the price offered (or the value of the alternative shares) and whether they think the deal is good for the business.

A paper offer is cheaper to carry out in that the bidder is not using up cash. However, it does mean that it will have new shareholders who may be hostile to the firm's policies. The success of a bid, therefore, depends on how much is being offered relative to the perceived value of the company and how well executed the deal is. If the bid is launched at a time when the victim company's directors are unprepared, they are less likely to be able to put together an effective defence. In the late 1990s, GUS launched a bid for Argos when the Chief Executive of Argos was ill. Faced with a hostile take-over, Argos had to hire a new Chief Executive to come in to help save the business from the GUS bid.

How do firms finance a take-over?

A firm may be able to finance a take-over with its internal capital. Firms sometimes build up a 'cash mountain' and this is often in preparation for a bid. It is the cheapest way of financing a deal because it avoids borrowing. Alternatively, a bidder can raise finance by selling shares to its existing shareholders. If it cannot raise the money internally, it can borrow. In the 1980s and 1990s in particular, there were a number of highly publicised take-overs which were financed through high levels of borrowing. This type of bid means that, after the take-over, the business may be burdened with high levels of interest to pay back. In some cases, this leads to 'asset stripping' whereby many of the assets of the victim company are sold to raise enough money to pay off the debt. A number of commentators are worried by the fact that some companies borrow money, launch a take-over of another business and then immediately cut back on capital investment spending such as training, research and new product development to repay the loans. This can severely damage a firm's long-term competitiveness (although it boosts short-term profits).

PROGRESS CHECK

Analyse the ways in which a firm might finance a take-over bid.

NUMERICAL INVESTIGATION

In 1999 Wal-Mart, the huge American retailer, made a last minute bid for Asda (which had previously agreed to be taken over by Kingfisher). The all cash offer was for £6.7 bn and topped the £5.8 bn all paper bid from Kingfisher.
On average, Asda's stores are about 40,000 square feet whereas Wal-Mart's are four to five times bigger.

Company	Country of origin	Value (euro bn)
Wal-Mart	US	117.2
Metro	Germany	38
Intermarche	France	30.8
Carrefour	France	30.8
Rewe	Germany	29.2

Company	Sales £ bn
Wal-Mart	82.9
Tesco	17.2
Sainsbury's	16.4
Marks and Spencer	8.2
Asda	8.2
Safeway	7.5
Kingfisher	7.5

Table 7.3 a and b Europe's top food retailers by worldwide sales, 1998
Source: Goldman, Sachs and Co, Reuters

	Wal-Mart	Asda
Market capitalisation	£120 bn	£6.65 bn
Profit	£4.6 bn	£405 m
Sales	£83 bn	£8 bn
Employees	910,000	78,000
Stores	3,620	229

Table 7.4 A comparison of Wal-Mart and Asda, *Financial Times*, 15 June 1999

In 1998, Wal-Mart derived around 9% of its $138 bn sales from its overseas operations. On the announcement of the bid, Sainsbury's shares fell 18.5p to 372p; Tesco shares fell 12¾ to 178p.

a) Compare the size of Wal-Mart's worldwide sales to its nearest European competitor.
b) How much higher was the Wal-Mart offer compared to the Kingfisher offer in percentage terms?
c) Why might Wal-Mart be willing to pay this much more?
d) Distinguish between a cash and a paper offer.
e) Calculate the value of Wal-Mart's sales from its overseas operations in 1998.
f) Calculate the average sales per employee, sales per store, profit per employee for Wal-Mart and Asda. Comment on your findings.
g) Calculate the percentage fall in the share price of Tesco.

FACT FILE

The Take-over Panel is the UK's acquisitions watchdog and it has a Code of Practice for firms undertaking take-overs. Between March 1997 and March 1998 it adjudicated 288 bids, 177 of which led to a take-over. However, the European Commission is developing a framework to regulate all take-overs in member states.

Do take-overs and mergers really work?

Most analysts do not think that take-overs and mergers are a particularly effective means of improving performance in the long run. In many cases, the profitability and market share of the new business is less than that of the individual firms before the integration. There are often one-off gains, such as the revenue gained by closing outlets or factories, but in the long term performance is not particularly impressive. However, when the idea of a take-over or merger comes up, the managers involved often believe that they can buck the trend – integration may not normally be successful, they argue, but in this case it will be!

Problems with integration

The problems of integration are often connected with the human resource and cultural aspects of business. If you look at any two firms, even if they are in the same industry, they almost certainly have different ways of operating – people are paid different rates, have different entitlements and are managed in different ways. If these two firms are pushed together, there is often a cultural clash. Employees resent changes in the way they are being managed and often become demotivated by redundancies and a feeling that they do not know what is going on. Another problem with integration is that, simply to make the merger or take-over worthwhile, the new business must do better than the firms did individually to cover the costs of the deal. In the case of a take-over, for example, the bidder may have to pay 15–20% over the value of the target firm's assets on the balance sheet to be able to buy enough shares to gain control. They must recover this money through higher revenue or cost savings elsewhere simply to stand still in financial terms.

In the case of hostile take-overs, there is the additional problem that the bidder may not know exactly what they are buying. Whilst they may have had access to the company's published accounts and will have analysed the financial situation, the bidder may be surprised by what they find once the bid actually happens. The stock may not be in the condition that was expected, the premises may be worth less than the accounts suggested and some of the debtors may be very unlikely to pay. Hostile bidders must proceed with caution.

In the case of vertical and conglomerate mergers or take-overs, a bidder also faces the problem that they are operating in unfamiliar markets. This provides an element of risk and may explain why the returns from integration are often disappointing. To be successful, therefore, mergers and take-overs have to be managed effectively. The target company must be chosen carefully and the bidder must take into account whether the styles and approaches of the two firms are compatible. It is also important to keep people informed and to reassure them where appropriate; employees need to know why the deal has happened and what the future holds.

PROGRESS CHECK

Discuss the possible problems one firm might face following its take-over of another.

Considerations before a merger or take-over

Both mergers and take-overs usually involve a substantial change in the structure of both organisations and should not be entered into lightly. Before going ahead, the companies should be clear on their objectives. What are the benefits of combining?

PROGRESS CHECK

Lack of employee support
Other
Poor communications
Business issues
Poor integration strategies
Poor management
Cultural differences

Figure 7.1 Reasons why mergers are not successful
Source, Roffey Park Management Institute

Discuss ways in which firms that are merging could overcome the above problems.

How substantial are they? The firms involved should also be aware of the dangers. How will employees react? Will there be redundancies? What implications does the integration have for other stakeholder groups? There may also be ethical considerations to take into account. Will the deal reduce consumer choice? Will it lead to factory closures in already depressed areas? The firms must also consider how well the two firms will 'fit' together. Do they have similar aspirations, approaches and styles? Is there likely to be a culture clash which will hinder the success of the deal?

Whether a deal goes ahead is likely to be determined by the expected financial outcome. Is the deal profitable or not? Managers will use a range of investment appraisal techniques to assess the deal such as average rate of return, net present value and payback. They must be careful how they interpret such data and consider its reliability. If the numbers suggest the rate of return is poor, it is unlikely that the deal will go ahead.

Should governments allow take-overs?

To many commentators, take-overs are a legitimate form of business growth. They allow firms to grow quickly, to develop their businesses and increase their competitiveness. The threat of a take-over may also provide an incentive for all managers to perform more effectively. If they do not, they may be vulnerable to a take-over bid. However, take-overs can also be undesirable. Faced with the threat of a take-over, managers may become short-termist and seek to boost immediate profits rather than plan for the long run. This may result in insufficient capital investment and a failure to develop enough new products. Take-overs can also lead to

KEY POINTS

Mergers and take-overs are more likely to be successful if:

- the administration costs are not too high
- the information about each firm's assets and skills is good
- the process is managed effectively.

FACT FILE

In 1998, Citigroup and Travelers merged to form the world's biggest bank. The deal was the world's largest take-over to that point, with a value of $72,558 m. Soon afterwards, the president of newly created Citigroup left the business. Commentators believed there had been major disagreements about how to manage the new company and that the new president was forced out. The exit triggered a fall in Citigroup's shares, which had already fallen 40% in the months after the merger. There had already been many rumours about the cultural clash between the two organisations. Only weeks before, the co-chairman of Citigroup had appealed to his colleagues to put aside their 'tribal ways' and work as a 'single tribe'.

monopoly power and work against the public interest. With too much market power, firms can charge high prices and provide a poor quality service. Governments may, therefore, want to restrict the total amount of take-over activity because it prevents long-term planning. It will almost certainly intervene in particular take-overs if it raises competition issues. Take-overs are not in themselves assumed to be undesirable in the UK, but they are monitored by the Competition Commission (formerly the MMC) to protect the public interest.

FACT FILE

BPAmoco was formed by the £32.6 bn ($55.0 bn) take-over of Amoco by British Petroleum in 1998. Following the deal, the company was expected to spend around $2 bn on severance payments and restructuring, These costs are expected to be covered by annual savings of $2 bn which the company hopes to achieve. These will be achieved partly through job losses. Amoco executives insisted their relatively high salaries and compensation were maintained. Advisory and legal fees on the deal added up to over £100 m.

NUMERICAL INVESTIGATION

	1987	1988	1989	1990	1991	1992	1993	1994	1995	1996	1997
Qualifying mergers	321	306	281	261	183	125	197	231	275	277	186
Mergers referred to the MMC	6	11	15	26	6	10	3	8	9	9	10

Table 7.5 Mergers qualifying for and actually referred to the Monopolies and Mergers Commission 1987–1997

a) Why do you think so few mergers are referred to the MMC compared to the number which qualify?
b) On what basis do you think mergers should be referred to the MMC?

PROGRESS CHECK

Consider the factors that a government might take into account when deciding whether to allow a merger.

KEY POINTS

Managers are more likely to decide on a take-over if:

- they want fast growth
- the bid is unlikely to be referred to the Monopolies and Mergers Commission
- they find a company which they think is significantly undervalued
- they can raise the finance easily
- the organisational cultures are similar.

Alliances and ventures

If firms want to work together but do not want to integrate they could consider an alliance or venture. An alliance occurs when two or more firms agree to co-operate on certain business activities. A venture occurs when two or more firms create a new company to undertake activities of common interest. For example, in the 1980s Labatts and Femsa formed a venture to help both companies expand in the American market. Labatts was a Canadian brewer which had some experience selling in the northern part of the American market; Femsa was a Mexican brewer with experience of the southern part of the American market. By forming a venture they were able to share expertise and distribution channels. The advantage of an alliance or venture is that it leaves the member firms free to pursue their own activities in other areas. They can co-operate in areas which are mutually beneficial whilst keeping their overall independence. This type of arrangement avoids many of the cultural problems of mergers and take-overs.

Alliances and ventures have been used by several western companies to gain access to Asian markets, which only allow local firms to trade. By joining up with local companies, western firms can get their products to the market.

PROGRESS CHECK

Consider the possible reasons why one firm might form an alliance with another business.

Management buy outs (MBOs)

Why sell a business to the managers?

Management buy outs occur when the existing managers of a company buy the company (as opposed to a *management buy in* when managers from outside of the business form a team and gain control). In some cases, management buy outs occur when a parent company wants to sell off non-core businesses and gives first option to the existing managers. This can lead to a relatively quick deal and can reward the managers for their work. In the 1990s, there was a great deal of corporate restructuring as firms attempted to increase efficiency and focus on their core activities; this has led to a large number of buy outs.

MBOs have also been a common occurrence during the process of privatisation. The government is often eager for a relatively quick sale – offering the business to people who already work within it can speed up the process. Selling to the managers may also help ensure the privatised business is run efficiently. The argument is that those managing the business will want it to be especially successful if they are the owners as well as the employees. Shareholders may sell the company if they receive an offer that is too good to refuse. If managers believe they can generate higher returns from the business than the owners can envisage, they may offer a price which the shareholders will want to accept.

FACT FILE

In 1998, Glaxo and SmithKline Beecham proposed a merger. This would allow them to share their research and development. At the time, Glaxo was spending approximately £1.2 bn on R&D; SmithKline Beecham was spending £0.8 bn. The deal was attractive to Glaxo, whose main products Zantac and Zovirac were coming to the end of their patent. It would also allow cost savings of around £1 bn with job losses of around 15,000. In the end, the deal failed as the management could not agree terms. Part of the problem was rumoured to be that Glaxo's Chief Executive was earning £1 m but SmithKline's boss wanted to continue with his £8 m salary!

Advantages of management buy outs

By buying the company for themselves, the managers are removing the problem of the 'divorce between ownership and control'. In most companies, the owners do not actually run the business; they leave this in the hands of the managers. This can cause problems if the managers begin to pursue their own aims at the expense of the owners. In the case of a management buy out, however, there is no such problem. Given that the owners are the managers, there can be no conflict of interest.

A MBO also serves to make managers more focused on the way in which the business is run. Although they were previously accountable to the owners for the performance of the business, as manager-owners, they are likely to become much more aware of costs, wastage, inefficiency and poor working practices. As managers they may have fought hard to retain their right to first class business travel, for example. As owners they may well volunteer to make more basic travel arrangements and save money.

Disadvantages

There are problems with MBOs. Buying a business may involve a high level of debt. To finance the deal, managers may have approached venture capital companies or banks, as well as investing a significant amount of their own money. If managers have to borrow a high percentage of the funds to take over a company, this is called a leveraged buy out. This means the managers must generate relatively high returns from the business to meet the interest payments; this is stressful (particularly because managers' own money is at stake) and it may also encourage short-term planning. Training, brand building, R&D may be cut to provide the short-term funds needed for the interest. On the other hand, it can be argued that this need for high returns forces the managers to achieve a higher level of performance.

After the buy out, the managers have to take *complete* responsibility for their decisions because they are now the owners; before they reported to the Board of Directors. They may find this additional responsibility difficult. The new business may lack the support of a parent company; if the buy out is a result of a larger company divesting one of its businesses, the new owners may find it more difficult to survive in their markets.

FACT FILE

In 1999, Unilever restructured its businesses in China to try and end cost and control problems in the region. The company decided to take full control of its businesses by replacing the many joint ventures with local partners which had proved difficult to manage. Under the new plan, Unilever will create a more streamlined centralised structure.

PROGRESS CHECK

The problem with many companies is that there is a 'divorce between ownership and control'. With a management buy out this problem no longer exists.

1 What is meant by a 'divorce between ownership and control'?
2 Why might this be a cause for concern for shareholders?

FACT FILE

In 1998, the number of UK management buy outs and buy ins was 320 companies with a value of £2.7 bn, (£2.1 bn in 1996). High technology was the most popular sector, attracting £707 m in funding – 15 times as much as in the mid-1980s.

Are management buy outs ethical?

Management buy outs do pose some ethical issues. Managers will presumably want to buy the business as cheaply as they can. This means it may be in their interests to ensure that the firm underperforms in the months and years building up to their bid. Clearly, the owners may be suspicious of a bid from the managers: the managers know how to improve the business but may be deliberately holding back until they are in complete control.

Buy ins and buy outs compared

As mentioned previously, a management buy in occurs when managers from outside the business take over the company. This can happen when a venture capital company brings together a team of managers from different businesses and organises the finance needed for the deal. The finance is likely to be a combination of the managers' own money and loans.

The advantages of a management buy in, compared to a buy out, are that more specialist, experienced managers can be brought in. On the other hand, outsiders may not know the business as well as the existing managers and may be resented by staff. The success of a buy in will depend on the price paid, the ability of the managers and the underlying state of the business.

KEY POINTS

A management buy out is more likely to be successful if:

- the managers can cope with the transition to owners
- the firm is not too highly geared
- there are clear areas of improvement
- the price paid is reasonable.

PROGRESS CHECK

What problems might face managers who take over a company via a management buy in?

Summary charts

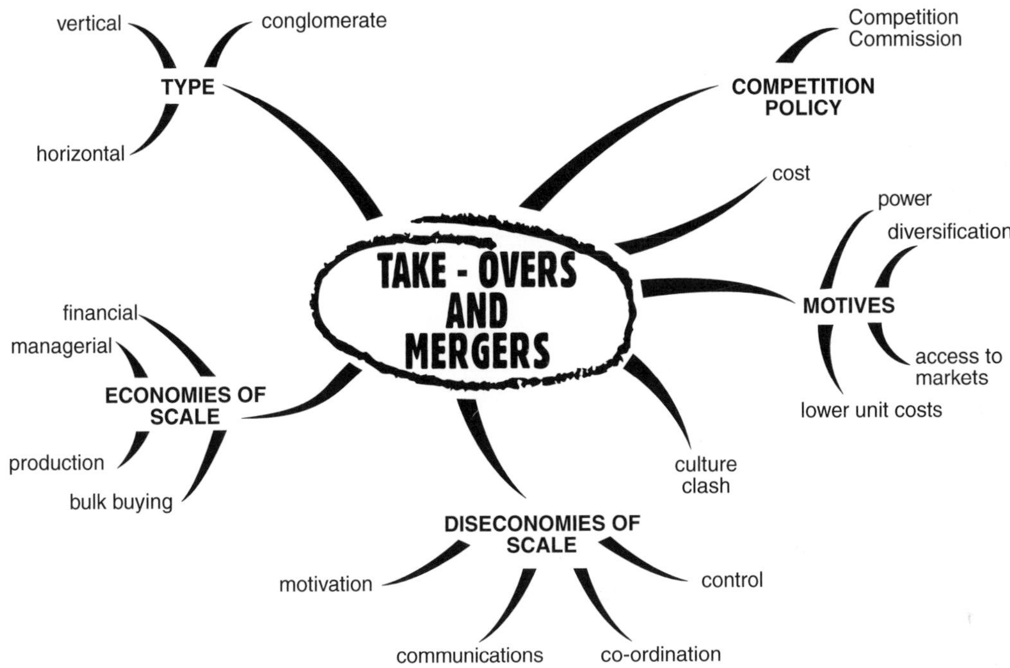

Figure 7.2

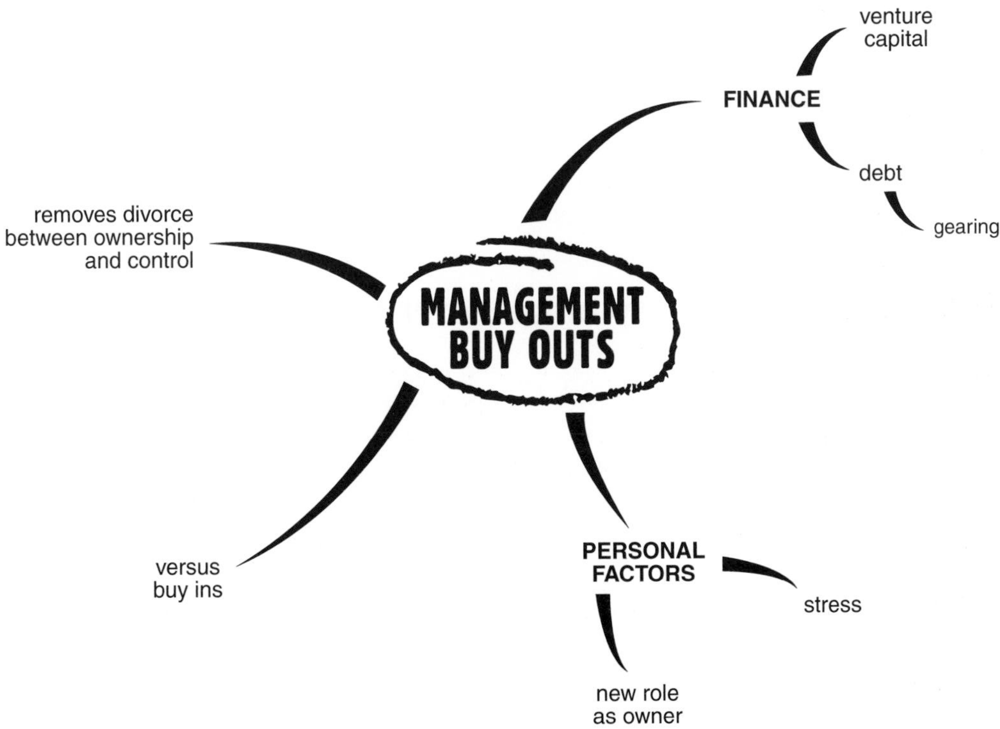

Figure 7.3

Approaching exam questions: Change in ownership

Discuss the view that the government should prevent all takeovers.

(11 marks)

A good answer to this question will focus on the case for and against takeovers and highlight that intervention may be necessary in some but not all cases. The precise level of intervention will depend on factors such as the costs of intervening, the impact on competition and the extent to which the government takes a laissez faire approach. Candidates should certainly pick up on the use of the word 'all', which is extreme and should be challenged.

Answers may include the following ideas:

- *Take-overs may lead to monopoly power* – this could bring about higher prices, less innovation and poorer quality goods and services. For this reason, the government may want to intervene and prevent certain takeovers. However, this depends on the nature of the takeover. What is the market share of the firms involved? Are they in the same industry? What is the likelihood of them acting against the public interest?
- *Take-overs can provide benefits* – they can lead to lower unit costs, which may be vital for international competitiveness. They can lead to synergy and a more effective service to the customer.

Even if there was a threat of monopoly power, such companies can be regulated. Therefore, the government needs to consider each case individually. It also needs to think about the costs of intervention (and the opportunity cost) and the likely negative effects – too much intervention may deter firms, leading to slower growth rates.

Should all managers try to take over their company?

(40 marks)

Once again this question uses the word 'all', which should be challenged. It deliberately adopts an extreme position and the stronger candidates will spot this and question it. A good answer will highlight possible reasons for a buy out, but also identify potential problems. Whether managers should undertake a buy out will depend on how positive and negative factors balance.

Answers might include the following ideas:

- *The advantages of owning a company rather than just managing it* – the rewards from your efforts go to you and not someone else.
- *Considerable cost and risk* – the managers would have to consider the price they would be expected to pay for the business (and all the other costs involved in a take-over, such as legal fees) compared to the expected return. They must also think about their view of risk. Manager-owners are likely to have to stake a con-

siderable amount of their own wealth as part of the deal. If they are approaching retirement or have considerable financial commitments, they may be reluctant to take this risk.

- *Personal stress* – all the problems of the firm are now the managers' problems and their relationship with the staff is likely to change.

So, whilst there may be gains, it is unlikely that all managers will want the problems that can come with a buy out, or that all shareholders will want to sell. Managers may prefer to obtain some shares in the business as part of their remuneration package, so they share in the prosperity of the organisation.

'The results of many organisations which have merged are actually worse than they were before the merger.' Discuss the possible reasons for this poor performance post-merger.

(40 marks)

Candidates wanting to do well with this question should analyse the possible reasons for poor performance, but also highlight that not every merger fails. It would be interesting to know more detail about the disappointing mergers. Do they involve firms of a particular size? Is performance worse for conglomerate, vertical or horizontal mergers? Also, over what time period is performance measured and how is performance measured? Strong answers will take a critical approach and not just accept the idea that mergers do lead to poor performance.

Answers may include the following ideas: Mergers create a larger firm and this brings with it all the dangers of diseconomies of scale – difficulty communicating, co-ordinating and controlling more people and more diverse activities. Also the merging firms may have very distinct ways of operating and values. This can lead to discontent, unhappiness and poor decision-making. Furthermore, any change can lead to uncertainty and resentment as some people lose their jobs, others do not get the job they had hoped and working practices change. The challenge of a merger is the effective management of change.

However, there are also potential benefits to merger (such as economies of scale) and it is not true that all mergers are unsuccessful. The success of a merger will, therefore, depend on factors such as the costs of restructuring, the degree of the culture clash and the ability of both sets of management to exploit the opportunities.

'Take-overs are only likely to succeed if they are between firms in the same industry. All other types are bound to fail.' Discuss.

(40 marks)

The given statement is extreme and needs to be attacked. It claims that 'all other types are bound to fail' which is clearly not true – although they may be more difficult to manage, some are obviously successful. A good answer to this question would explore the underlying logic (namely that horizontal integration is easier to control – the firms are in the same industry and so there is greater likelihood of similar technology, issues and culture). The answer could also discuss some of the problems of the other types of merger (e.g. conglomerate or vertical merger – moving into new areas may pose problems of co-ordination and management). Success depends on:

- which firms are involved
- the way the deal is carried out
- the cultures of the firm.

Student answers

'The danger of take-over forces managers to take a short-term view which damages a firm's long-term competitiveness.' Discuss.

(11 marks)

Student answer

If there is a high level of take-over activity, firms must be careful not to become victims. Managers will be aware of this and will want to protect the business (and themselves) by maintaining the share price as high as possible. One way of doing this is to have high dividend pay outs but this may mean that the firm's ability to invest long term may be restricted – it may have to cut back on building brand loyalty, investment in research and development and training. All of these might affect the firm's ability to innovate and develop new products, which in turn may restrict its competitiveness.

However, it does depend on the extent to which managers feel they are vulnerable to attack (e.g. take-over activity may vary between sectors) and the extent to which investors look for a short-term approach. Investors, however, may favour long-term policies as the best way to defend the company and to build long-term competitiveness. In the UK, however, shareholders are said to be short-termist, forcing managers to adopt short-term policies. This is because they are mainly institutional shareholders who are interested in immediate rewards, rather than the long-term success of the business.

Marker's comments

An excellent answer which covers the ground well!

Mark: Content 2/2, Application & Analysis 6/6, Evaluation 3/3. Total = 11

'The main motive for take-overs is personal pride and the desire to manage a bigger business.' Critically assess this view.

(11 marks)

Student answer

People like to be in charge of growing businesses because this makes them more important (ego needs – Maslow). They will have more people to be in charge of and this makes them more powerful. This makes one company want to take over another. There is no question that this is the motive for many take-overs – merged companies do not tend to do well financially and so what else could be the motive?

Marker's comments

This is not a particularly strong answer because it does not address the question of whether personal pride is the main motive. Whilst it may well be one motive – is it the main one? This of course will depend on the people involved and the precise details of the deal – in some cases people may be driven by pride, in others it may be pure financial logic. The candidate makes an interesting observation that take-overs do not do well financially, so the driving force must be pride. However, it is worth noting that some take-overs do succeed and that managers may still believe their deal will be profitable (whether or not they are).

Mark: Content 1/2, Application & Analysis 2/6, Evaluation 0/3. Total = 3

'The problems of integration outweigh the benefits.' Discuss.

(11 marks)

Student answer

Integration means merger or take-over. There are three types: horizontal, vertical or conglomerate. A horizontal merger involves two firms at the same stage of the same production process. This can lead to economies of scale. A vertical merger involves firms at different stages of the same production process. This means a firm can have control over its suppliers or its distributors. A conglomerate merger involves firms in different markets. This can spread risk. Integration is therefore a good thing which helps firms do better.

Marker's comments

This is a very factual answer which does not actually address the question. There is no discussion of the problems or whether the problems outweigh the benefits. Overall, a very limited approach which fails to explore ideas.

Mark: Content 2/2, Application & Analysis 0/6, Evaluation 0/3. Total = 2

'Alliances provide all the benefits of mergers and none of the problems.' Consider this view.

(11 marks)

Student answer

Alliances occur when firms work together and this can have advantages – they can share ideas or resources. Firms can use each other's distribution channels, for example, or share the cost of marketing in a joint promotional campaign. Unlike mergers they still remain separate companies and so retain their independence; this can mean it is easier and quicker to set up and some of the cultural clashes of merger can be avoided. Firms can co-operate in areas where there are genuine benefits, e.g. gain economies of scale in transport without having to work together in other areas where there is not such a natural fit. Alliances, therefore, offer benefits without having the costs and restructuring involved in a full scale merger; firms retain their flexibility.

Marker's comments

This is a fairly strong answer which identifies the relative strengths of alliances and highlights their possible advantages over mergers. However, it does not really challenge the notion that it offers all the benefits or none of the costs; this is a fairly dramatic claim which could be usefully explored. Also, it might be worthwhile considering some of the problems of alliances (such as agreeing terms and what to do if objectives differ).

Mark: Content 2/2, Application & Analysis 4/6, Evaluation 0/3. Total = 6

End of section questions

1 Discuss the factors which may influence the success of a management buy out.
(9 marks)

2 Consider the factors which should determine the price paid for a business in a take-over.
(9 marks)

3 Analyse the possible motives for one firm merging with another.
(8 marks)

4 Many mergers are unsuccessful due to a culture clash between the two organisations. Discuss ways in which the problems of culture might be reduced in a merger.
(9 marks)

5 Discuss the view that take-overs are doomed to failure.
(11 marks)

6 Should a firm which is taking over another business try to use internal or external funds? Justify your answer.
(11 marks)

7 The managers of Joolun plc are eager for the business to grow faster. Would you advise them to pursue external or internal growth? Justify your answer.
(11 marks)

8 Is bigger really better? Discuss the view that all firms should try to increase their size.
(11 marks)

9 Analyse the possible reasons why a firm might choose to form an alliance rather than merging with a competitor.
(9 marks)

10 Discuss the factors which might influence the price paid for a business in a take-over.
(9 marks)

Essays

1 The UK government prevents relatively few take-overs. Discuss the view that it needs to intervene more to prevent take-overs.
(40 marks)

2 'Ventures and alliances are much more desirable than take-overs.' Critically assess this view.
(40 marks)

3 'The high level of take-over activity leads to a short-termist approach which is undesirable.' Discuss this view.
(40 marks)

4 Management buy-outs give control of the company to those who know best what to do with it. The government should, therefore, actively encourage management buy outs.
(40 marks)

5 'Take-overs rarely succeed so the government should ban them.' Discuss.
(40 marks)

Contingency planning and crisis management

FACT FILE

In 1998, the merger deal between Grand Metropolitan and Guinness to create Diageo was apparently put together in record time. In reality, it was the result of years of planning and preparation by Guinness. In 1994, Guinness formed a specialist team to prepare for a deal to take Guinness into the 21st century. The group built models for every conceivable take-over, merger or alliance, including the possible reaction of governments to different deals. When the Grand Metropolitan merger appeared as an option, they were ready.

As we have seen, an essential element of effective management is planning. Managers must plan ahead to identify, not just likely changes, but possible changes in the external and internal environment. They also have to prepare accordingly. In this section we examine a specific type of planning called contingency planning.

What are contingency planning and crisis management?

A contingency is a possible future occurrence. Therefore, contingency planning is the process through which firms attempt to look into the future and make preparations for opportunities and threats that may occur. It is applicable at both a strategic level, as well as at all the different functional levels of the firm. Unlike other plans, contingency planning is based on probabilities rather than on solid data. Because of this, some firms do not see the point.

A crisis occurs when an event which poses a real threat to the existence of the firm occurs. Crisis management is, therefore, an extension of contingency planning – it deals with the issues facing a firm before a crisis occurs, during the actual event and during the aftermath.

KEY POINTS

Contingency planning is more likely when:

- an event is believed to be likely to occur
- the firm believes the event will have a serious impact on its activities.

Contingency planning

What should firms plan for?

This will vary considerably from industry to industry, and from function to function within the business. The aim is to identify possible situations that might prevent a firm from achieving its objectives set out in its existing plans. Having identified these possible situations and assessed the likelihood of their occurrence, alternative plans that would meet the new situation are developed. A firm might look at any aspects of the **P**olitical, **E**conomic, **S**ocial and **T**echnological (PEST) environment which could change in the future and develop plans to deal with this. Essentially, anything that might have a sudden impact on the firm can be included in a contingency plan. Clearly, the more complex the firm and its environment, the more issues it is likely to have to consider.

Obviously a firm cannot prepare for every possible occurrence and so it will look at the *likelihood* (probability) of an issue arising and the *size of impact* that it would have. This enables managers to prioritise their contingency plans. The more probable the firm thinks it is that an event will happen and the more serious the impact, the more likely it is to plan for it.

In the case of *crisis* planning, a firm attempts to look at improbable and unfamiliar events which pose a very high risk. Crisis planning is therefore part of contingency planning, but focuses on particularly threatening potential occurrences.

FACT FILE

In the 1990s, the headquarters of HSBC was bombed. Most of the windows were blown out and the area was sealed off by police. Unfortunately the telephone numbers of many of the staff were only held on computer in the building. As a result of this problem, HSBC changed its procedures; its new contingency plan called for all staff 'phone numbers to be kept off-site as well as in the firm's headquarters. When, a year later HSBC was hit by another bomb, contacting employees was much easier and quicker.

Source: *Human Resource Implications of City Bombs*, Barry Hine

Who should use contingency planning?

If a firm can develop a framework to deal with possible changes in its environment, it should be better prepared to cope. Given the very volatile nature of today's business world, it is rarely possible to have an exact plan, but a plan that has to be adapted is usually better than no plan at all. Companies with well developed contingency plans tend to recover much faster from sudden shocks than those that do not. Any firm can make use of contingency plans, although the faster the rate of change in the environment and the more uncertainty there is in the markets, the more contingencies a firm is likely to have to deal with.

PROGRESS CHECK

Consider the possible impact on a manufacturing firm of a major supplier going into liquidation. What might the firm do to protect itself against this event?

KEY POINTS

Formal contingency planning may be more useful:

- for firms in market places that are unused to sudden shocks
- for firms where line managers are less experienced
- in times of volatility in the external environment.

Firms in dynamic markets

Obviously contingency planning tends to be of more use to firms in dynamic markets than those in static ones, but no firm can ever be wholly isolated from changes in the external environment. In some ways, firms in static markets are *more* at risk from changes, simply because they are unused to dealing with them.

PROGRESS CHECK

Consider whether Sainsbury's or a local corner shop would be more likely to plan for the threat of a new Tesco opening nearby.

Managers in volatile markets are more likely to adopt an 'ad hoc' approach to contingency management and are more likely to be able to draw on previous experience of change; managers in stable markets will not have this experience and might, therefore, be *more* in need of formal contingency planning.

FACT FILE

Shell has disaster plans covering all sorts of crises which might threaten its oil rigs – fires, explosions, terrorism and so on – so that it can respond immediately and effectively. However, when faced with a different type of crisis (the case of bad publicity surrounding the disposal of the Brent Spar North Sea platform) the firm was unprepared and slow to respond because of its bureaucratic culture, meaning that its reputation was badly dented.

KEY POINTS

Effective contingency plans:

- are communicated fully and effectively
- are up to date and easy to update
- cover most relevant contingencies
- are easy to use when a contingency arises.

KEY POINTS

Contingency planning is less likely to work well if:

- top management are not committed
- plans are not regularly reviewed
- a structured approach is not used
- adequate resources (both financial and managerial) are not available
- too much information is generated.

Problems with contingency planning

- *Using an unstructured approach* – a firm with an unstructured approach to contingency planning is more likely to make a mistake: lack of rigour makes it more likely that an oversight will occur. For example, it is more likely that firms which are not using a structured approach will fail to identify all the relevant potential problems. Such firms are also less likely to commit an appropriate amount of resources – contingency planning may be a mere gesture towards current management trends, rather than a genuine attempt to look into the future. Planning in this way can do more harm than good, as the firm may be lulled into a false sense of security.
- *Errors of human judgement* – the problem with human judgement is that it is not objective. Previous experience, whilst often useful, may be counterproductive in new situations. Sometimes humans simply get it wrong: the plan may not be appropriate for the conditions.
- *Consumption of management time* – contingency planning requires considerable input of management time, since all the contingencies have to be analysed by a team of experienced staff. This means that other areas of the business may be made less effective whilst the process is taking place; in many cases, contingency planning suffers because it is rushed to save time and money. Managers often deprioritise it, meaning that the process suffers.
- *Information overload* – as computers become more and more prevalent and powerful, the danger of information overload becomes increasingly likely. Computers cannot take decisions, they can only provide information for those decisions – the more information that is gathered, the better the decision, in principle.
- *Failure to review assumptions and plans* – a contingency plan based on out-of-date information and assumptions that are no longer valid is potentially more dangerous than no plan at all. This is because, if the firm relies on such a plan, the recommended course of action is unlikely to be appropriate. For example, a redundancy plan that failed to take into account changes in the rights of part-time workers could land the firm in serious legal difficulties.

PROGRESS CHECK

A manufacturing firm develops a list of alternative component suppliers, but fails to keep it up-to-date. Consider the possible impact on the firm of a collapse of one of its current suppliers.

The costs and benefits of contingency planning

Whether the costs of contingency planning outweigh the benefits is difficult to judge. The costs are short term and are often hidden (e.g. the impact on managers' time). The benefits will only ever be felt in the long term and, even then, only if a particular contingency occurs. The judgement is especially difficult to make, because the firm can never know what would have happened had there *not* been a contingency plan in place.

Deciding to plan for contingencies

For shareholder-driven organisations, the cost of contingency planning can be difficult to justify, since it eats into short-term profits and dividends – not something institutional shareholders, such as pensions funds and insurance companies, are likely to welcome. For a stakeholder-driven organisation, or one under private control, the decision may be easier – contingency planning fits well with the sort of long-term outlook that those organisations are likely to adopt. Even if the cost cannot be justified in strictly financial terms, a stakeholder-driven organisation may consider social costs important.

Another element in the decision to invest in contingency planning is the attitude of the organisation towards risk. A risk-neutral organisation is less likely to engage in contingency or crisis planning, arguing that the risk of the crisis is small enough to mean that the expected value of investing will be negative. A risk-averse organisation might be more likely to argue that a sudden shock could finish the business, and that a lower average profit is a worthwhile price to pay. A further element in the equation is the extent to which preparing for contingencies may make them less likely to occur. By looking at the risks facing a business, the crisis management and contingency planning process may help managers to spot problems. The adverse contingency is, therefore, prevented from occurring. Thus, the expenditure on planning in the short term may have substantial (unquantifiable) long-term benefits.

The final element is how changeable the market is; firms in markets prone to sudden change are likely to get more use out of their contingency plans than firms in stable markets. On the other hand, they are likely to have more contingencies to cover, so the cost of planning will be more in the first place. However, it is likely that economies of scale are going to be present; a large scale contingency plan is likely to cost less per contingency than a small scale one, due to the fixed costs of getting the programme up and running.

FACT FILE

When planning the launch of the Challenger space shuttle and looking at the various contingencies affecting success, the scientists examined past data detailing the outcomes of previous launches under various environmental conditions. However, it has been suggested that, when using the mass of data, they failed to apply probability theory correctly. Had they done so, they might have concluded that they were planning to launch the shuttle under critical conditions – the chance of disaster was outside acceptable limits of risk. Had the theory been used correctly, the explosion which killed all the crew might not have occurred.

PROGRESS CHECK

Is contingency planning worth it?

Differences between crisis and contingency planning

In his book *Communicating out of a Crisis*, Michael Bland describes a crisis as 'an issue in a hurry'. Contingency planning may prepare for issues where the firm has weeks to respond. In the case of a crisis, there may only be hours and the issue could prove fatal for the organisation. A crisis is, therefore, defined as a sudden event which poses a severe threat to a firm.

Crisis management tends to emphasise the need for a *flexible* response to any situation, whereas contingency planning contains more detail on predictable issues facing the firm. Contingency plans for issues arising, such as an increase in exchange rates, can be specific because the risk is predictable and quantifiable. The need to respond immediately is less. In the case of a crisis, such as a terrorist attack, the firm's survival may depend on an immediate response.

Crisis planning generally involves selecting a crisis team who will deal with *any* crisis and operate on general principles. An attempt to follow a systematic set of rules on how to react in a crisis situation is unlikely to succeed – in a crisis, there simply isn't time to read them!

FACT FILE

AT&T provides information for air-traffic control at New York's airports. During a summer heatwave a few years ago, the power supply dropped due to heavy use of air conditioning systems in the city. AT&T had a back-up generator, but this failed. The further back-up to this was a battery with a 6 hour life, which kicked in. This battery had an alarm and a countdown, but this wasn't heard until 6.5 hours later, by which time aircraft were circling blind overhead.
The reason the alarm wasn't heard? The systems operators were attending a contingency planning meeting to teach them about a new backup system.
This illustrates the point about consumption of management time and the failure to dedicate appropriate resources to the process. Had the systems operators been provided with cover while on the course, the disaster would have been less likely to occur.
Source: 'Thinking about the unthinkable' *Across The Board*, September 1996

Crisis management involves preparing for sudden, highly threatening events which need an immediate reaction.

PROGRESS CHECK

How might a firm's response to a possible increase in interest rates differ from its response to a claim that its products are dangerous?

How far is it possible to plan for a crisis?

It is clearly very difficult to prepare for *specific* crises. By its very definition, a crisis is sudden and dramatic. Firms that attempt to plan may end up producing giant manuals, hundreds of pages thick, that few managers have time to read and that are of little use. Because of their complexity, such manuals become rapidly out-of-date. They may actually make the organisation *less* prepared for crisis, by encouraging complacency.

However, it may be possible to prepare for crisis *in general*, provided the preparations are very flexible. For most firms this tends to involve creating a crisis team drawn from all areas of the business. At the same time, funds are set aside to provide the key resources that the crisis team needs to handle a crisis – at the least, a meeting room, communications equipment and lots of phone lines. After this, the key is to ensure that staff are well trained in crisis psychology, media management and run through regular simulations. Given this, they should be able to handle most crises through flexibility and the application of general principles.

Dealing with a crisis

How a company deals with a crisis will depend on whether it has a crisis plan. In particular, it depends on how well the firm can communicate with the various groups involved, including the media. Given the severe nature of the event, good communication is essential to keep up with events and to bring about a quick reaction. Firms with an effective crisis plan should be able provide information to the general public and to co-ordinate their response internally. Effective plans, for example, usually involve only one point of contact for the press and this person is named in the plan. This means that the organisation finds it easier to provide a coherent response to the public, which in turn makes it more able to protect its image.

Speed of reaction

By reacting quickly, a firm may be able to get its side of the story into the press, thereby helping to create a more favourable public image. The press usually assigns a large amount of column space to any major disaster and, if the company fails to give information, the column space will be filled with speculation. This is unlikely to be to the firm's advantage. Furthermore, if an organisation is seen to be acting, this usually reduces the adverse reaction of the general public; they feel that at least something is being done.

Resources required in a crisis

As mentioned, the two types of resource required are finance and communications. Which is more relevant will depend on the nature of the crisis. If the crisis is one affecting the firm's *reputation*, the key to success will be communications links, both internal and external. If, on the other hand, the crisis affects the firm's ability to operate (without immediately damaging its reputation) then financial resources are more likely to be important. In the early 1990s, adverse market conditions led to IBM making a loss of $4 bn. IBM devised a restructuring plan and had the resources to carry it out. It was able to absorb the impact of the crisis far better than a smaller organisation would have been able to do.

PROGRESS CHECK

Suppose a firm such as Tesco faced a major scare because of glass contamination in its own-brand tinned tomatoes. Discuss the factors that will determine whether it is able to handle the scare effectively.

FACT FILE

An example of a failure to look deeply enough into relevant assumptions was seen in Japan in the case of the Kobe earthquake in 1995. Japanese firms make heavy use of lean production techniques (just in time) and have contingency plans to deal with temporary problems. However, the scale of the earthquake affected many firms and their suppliers; existing contingency plans were simply not adequate for dealing with a problem of that size. Disruption was, therefore, widespread as lean production methods avoid holding buffer stocks. Following this event, more Japanese firms are utilising disaster planning and crisis management techniques, which are specialised forms of contingency planning, than had previously been the case.

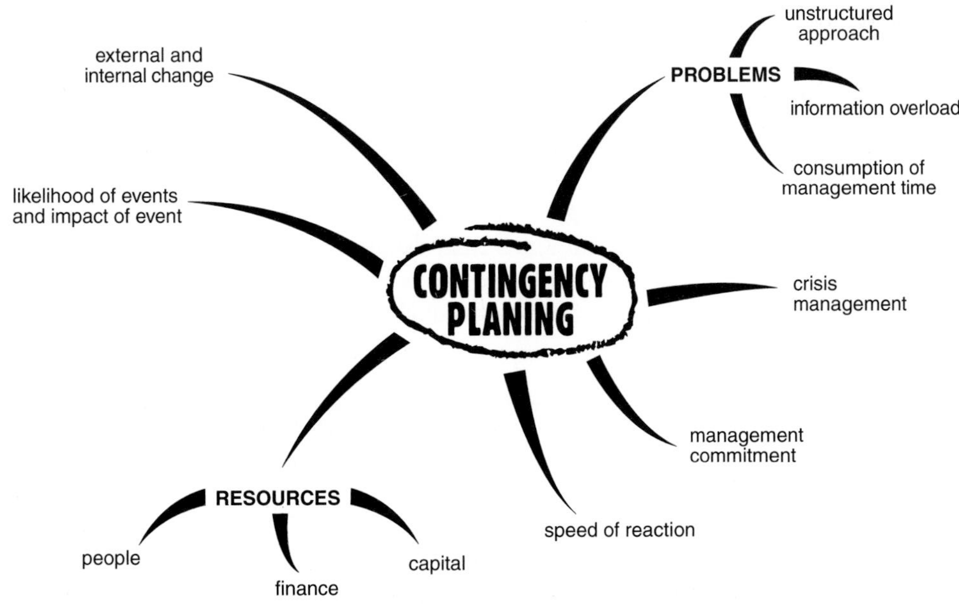

Figure 8.1

FACT FILE

It has been alleged that the tobacco industry has been aware of the health and addiction problems of tobacco for many years, but only incorporated warnings on the packets when forced to by legislation. The US courts are now citing this as part of their case against the tobacco firms. This could be seen as a failure of contingency planning – *if* the companies were aware, at the time, of the dangerous nature of their product, contingency planning might have prepared for eventual legal action. However, voluntary incorporation of warnings at an early stage would have hit short-term profits.

KEY POINTS

The benefits are more likely to outweigh the costs for:

- firms adopting a long-term (stakeholder-driven) outlook
- firms that are risk-averse
- firms that are prepared to plan thoroughly
- firms in volatile markets.

The impact of a crisis

Many factors influence the impact that a crisis may have on an organisation. These are discussed below.

- *The reaction of the firm's allies and enemies* – generally, the public is more likely to believe a firm's statements if they come from or are endorsed by a third party. Figures with power, such as journalists and other commentators, are more likely to put a favourable gloss on events if they know the organisation fairly well. Consequently, contacts in politics, local authorities, emergency services and key newspapers are likely to be important in a crisis.
- *The reaction of the firm's rivals* – if other firms can show a much better safety record, for example, and are prepared to go on the news to announce it, this can have a major impact on the ability of the firm in trouble to survive the crisis. If competitors decide to say nothing, the impact is likely to be less.
- *Blame* – if the organisation is seen to be wholly at fault, public reaction is likely to be adverse. If the firm is shown to be negligent, the public tends to see it as uncaring and, in some cases, hypocritical, especially if it has previously been critical of other firms for similar failings.
- *The early stages* – the way the firm deals with the early stages of a crisis can affect the impact of the crisis. If a firm appears to be genuinely sorry for any incident that has occurred, and is open and honest throughout the crisis, the perception of blame is often considerably diluted.
- *Luck* – in the case of a financial crisis, the impact will depend on the firm's exposure at the time. For instance, when the pound dropped out of the ERM in 1992, the direct financial impact on individual firms was dependant on the firm's foreign currency position at the time. If the firm owed large amounts in foreign currency, the impact of the crisis was much greater than if it did not. Therefore, some would say that the impact of some crises is simply a matter of luck, although others would argue that the crisis could have been foreseen. In the case of a crisis affecting reputation, the amount of damage done may also be a matter of luck. The press tend to run stories that are in vogue – if a firm has a food poisoning incident at a time when the press has been reporting on this issue, generally, the adverse exposure is likely to be far greater.
- *How well prepared the organisation is, and how it reacts* – if the organisation is set up to deal with a crisis, the impact will be less. Therefore, the more an organisation has done to plan for similar events, the less damage a crisis is likely to do. If a firm responds quickly and with integrity to a crisis, the impact is reduced.

PROGRESS CHECK

Examine the factors which might influence the impact of a crisis on a firm.

Are crises always bad?

For some organisations a crisis can be the thing that drives them over the edge into liquidation. For others a crisis is an opportunity, particularly if the organisation is not directly to blame. By handling a crisis effectively, a firm can boost its reputation. In Tom Peters' book *In Search of Excellence*, he points out that a customer complaint is a chance to be in direct contact with the customer and to really shine. He showed that in some cases, firms with an inferior product reliability record had *higher* satisfaction ratings, simply because of the way they dealt with complaints.

Crises can provide an opportunity for a company to show its colours. BP was actually praised by the US emergency service following the 'American Trader' oil slick of the 1980s, because of the swift way in which it responded and the responsibility it took for its own actions. Consequently, crises are not necessarily a bad thing. Generally, peoples' memories are quite short, which means that, if the firm can deal with an incident effectively, after a period of time all that will remain in the mind is the company's name and the knowledge that it acted in a responsible way.

PROGRESS CHECK

Discuss the factors that might influence whether a crisis has an unfavourable impact on a firm.

FACT FILE

Over the last few years, there has been a wide range of crisis situations for many well known firms:

- Marks and Spencers, Nike and Manchester United have all been accused of using child labour in developing countries to manufacture their products.
- Pepsi, SmithKline Beecham (Lucozade) and Perrier have all had product-related crises.
- Barings Bank, and several major Japanese banks, have faced financial ruin.
- BA has had its reputation damaged through its 'dirty tricks' campaign against Virgin.
- HSBC has had its headquarters blown up twice in 2 years.
- The US tobacco giant RJR Reynolds has lost a major legal challenge over the marketing of its products.
- the BSE crisis hit many British farmers.

Clearly, crises are often unpredictable and varied, making preparation and handling all the more difficult.

KEY POINTS

An effective crisis management team will be:

- senior enough to take decisions
- trained in dealing with the media
- cool under pressure
- drawn from all areas of the business
- well resourced.

Approaching exam questions: Contingency planning and crisis management

To what extent can crisis threaten the survival of a firm?

(40 marks)

A common problem with this type of question is to assume that it is only asking about one type of crisis. A classic weak answer might imply that a crisis will greatly reduce a firm's sales, and therefore it will be unable to survive. This is not the case and a strong candidate will attempt to look at a number of different crises in a structured manner. The structure might centre around these questions:

- Is the crisis internal or external?
- Does the crisis affect the firm's reputation immediately or in the longer term?
- Is the crisis financial (e.g. the firm is defrauded of large sums of money) or non-financial (e.g. large numbers of key staff leave simultaneously)?
- Does the crisis affect the whole organisation or only a part?

Another problem with many answers to this question is that students do not think through the last part of the question: 'threaten the survival of the firm'. What is meant by 'survival' – continuing with the same market share as at present or avoiding liquidation at all costs? Some firms will be in a better position to survive than others. A good candidate would take one of the crises identified above and apply it to firms in different situations:

- Does the firm have substantial financial resources at its disposal?
- Did the firm have a good public image before the crisis?
- Has the firm been involved in similar scares before?
- Does the firm deal directly with the general public?

The final problem with this sort of question is that students often assume that firms will not or cannot respond. Candidates treat firms as if they are passive victims of crisis, rather than able to influence events. Consequently, a good answer might look at:

- *The firm's readiness for a crisis* – the extent to which it has engaged in contingency management. This means the firm will be able to respond in a more structured and coherent way.
- *How quickly the firm responds* – a fast response generally makes the crisis less serious.

The more you talk about specific crises, firms and responses, the tighter focus your answer will have. It will naturally strengthen your analysis, and because a number of different viewpoints have been considered, coming to a conclusion will be easier. As ever, a conclusion is essential if a top level response is to be generated.

Consider whether contingency planning is of use to all firms.

(11 marks)

This question contains a classic phrase which might trip up the unwary: 'all firms'. There is very little in the business world that is equally applicable to *all* firms, and contingency planning is no exception. A strong answer might use the opening paragraph to deal with this issue.

Having done this, the answer might look at the phrase 'contingency planning', and consider whether it has a clear cut meaning. In general, questioning the question is quite an analytical approach. In this case, a distinction could be drawn between formal contingency planning on the one hand, and just thinking about the future on the other – most firms would benefit from informally looking into the future; not all would benefit from formal contingency planning processes.

Finally, a strong candidate will show an awareness that there are costs involved – they will show an evaluative approach. The very last element of a top quality answer is a conclusion, summarising the key points, and referring back to the question directly.

To what extent is it possible to plan for the unexpected?

(40 marks)

This question has an obvious split – there are some things that can be planned for and some that cannot. Those that can be planned for tend to be problems that the firm encounters regularly, for example:

- suppliers delivering late
- customers failing to pay
- changes in interest rates and exchange rates.

A good answer though, would point out that these factors are not really *unexpected* – although the firm does not know *when* they will happen, it must be fairly sure that at some point they will. A strong answer would then move on to talk about genuinely unexpected events, such as a bomb, fire, fatal product defect and so on. While it is not possible to plan for a *particular* event, it is possible to plan for *types* of event, or for crises in general.

A strong answer might go on to argue that effective crisis planning rests on flexibility and that, even if it was *possible* to plan in detail for the unexpected, it might not be desirable to do so. Each event will have its own particular characteristics and a pre-planned response might not be appropriate. Therefore, it is only possible to plan for the unexpected in general terms. If this is done well enough, most unexpected events can be dealt with.

The title asks about the extent to which a firm can plan for the unexpected. The best conclusion might be related to how unexpected the event is – if the event is unexpected, but part of the firm's normal business, planning should be possible. If the unexpected event is completely out of the blue, (for example, a meteor destroying the firm's factory), planning may be more difficult, except in the most general terms.

Discuss the main factors a firm should consider when deciding how to respond to a crisis.

(11 marks)

This is a relatively straightforward question, requiring the student to analyse two or three possible responses and then come to a conclusion about the *key* factor. The sort of factors that should be considered are:

- *How serious is the crisis?* – does the firm need to respond?
- *Does the firm have a plan?* – if so, is it applicable to this situation? Is it up to date?
- *What resources are available?* – if limited, there may be little that can be done.
- *What sort of firm is it?* – large or small? National or multinational? A multinational firm will be of greater interest to the media, meaning that it may have to react more quickly.

The answer should look at each of the factors and explain why they are important in the context of a crisis.

The main thing to avoid is over-generalising about 'responses', 'crises' and 'firms' – each of these can be very varied. This allows for an evaluative response!

Student answers

Consider whether the use of contingency planning might have reduced the adverse impact of the Asian crisis on UK exporters.

(11 marks)

Student answer

Contingency planning makes firms better prepared for possible issues arising in the future. Therefore, it might be argued that firms with contingency plans for such an eventuality would have been better prepared. The development of a contingency plan would have assessed the risks in the area and would have come up with strategies to deal with a crisis. Firms might have developed plans for exploiting other markets in the event of a crisis in Asia. Better still, having identified the risk, they might have developed an export strategy that was not over-reliant on sales in one area, which would have meant that the loss of sales to Asian firms would have had less of an impact.

However, even if the firm had used a contingency planning process, they might not have considered the Asian crisis as a likely eventuality. After all, it came as a surprise to many of the world's leading economic analysts. A firm has only a certain amount of resources available for contingency planning, and will, therefore, tend to devote them to the most likely scenarios. At the time when something could be done about it, the Asian crisis might not have been thought to be plausible – after all, just before the crisis, the economies were still growing strongly.

Even if the crisis had been identified as a possibility, the most sensible contingency plan, that of selling less there and looking for other markets, might well have not been adopted. After all, sales to the area were very profitable, and there are few firms that would be willing to sacrifice those profits to cater for a very unlikely event.

Overall, contingency planning has the potential to help with such crises – that is what it is designed for. However, the practicalities of day-to-day management may mean that a short-term drive for profit outweighs the long-term benefits of contingency planning. In the case of the Asian crisis, however, the more likely situation was simply that the crisis was not considered a likely enough contingency to plan for. In the end, it is unlikely that a contingency planning process would have helped.

Marker's comments

This is a top quality answer. The question is a difficult one because it cuts across a number of different syllabus areas. Rather than panic, the student takes the question in parts. The opening paragraph begins with a standard explanation of contingency planning, which can be dangerous if it is allowed to degenerate into a regurgitation of notes. By the end of the first paragraph, the student has started to relate his or her knowledge to the question.

The second paragraph shows an awareness that this is a 'consider' question and the student moves directly on to put the other side. The candidate clearly has a thorough knowledge of contingency planning and is well aware of its limitations. These are well applied to the Asian crisis, showing an awareness that firms' resources are finite, a point often missed by candidates.

By the end of the third paragraph, the examiner would already have the answer marked down for a top mark. This paragraph shows that the student is aware that contingency planning is mainly a long-term tool, and that many firms have only a short-term outlook. This is a highly sophisticated argument, showing a practical awareness of business.

In the final paragraph, the answer simply drives home the point about short-termism. The candidate has also chosen a deliberately unexpected conclusion – the majority of candidates would be reluctant to question the validity of contingency planning.

Mark: Content 2/2, Application & Analysis 6/6, Evaluation 3/3. Total = 11

Discuss the pros and cons of increased Information Technology (IT) use in the contingency planning process.

(11 marks)

Student answer

IT has made a major difference to contingency planning because firms can now handle much more data. With computers today being much more powerful than even 5 years ago and with hard disks of up to 15 gig of memory, contingency planners can handle many more scenarios than they could in the 1980s. If managers can look at more possible situations, contingency planning should be better.

Supermarkets can build up huge databases of customer spending patterns, and can then use them to predict the likely impact of things like price changes. Oil companies can build up computer models of their oil and gas fields, so that they can develop plans for what they might do if there was an explosion. Given that firms can look at all these different possibilities, it means that whatever happens the firm will have a plan for it. The firm will be able to respond quickly, so the damage done by any event should be less.

Therefore, because computers are now more powerful, more contingencies can be looked at and, therefore, planning is better.

Marker's comments

This is a moderate answer. There is only one main point that is explained in many different ways; essentially that firms can project a much greater range of scenarios than they could in the past. As a consequence, their plans will be more complete. This is true to an extent, but the candidate overlooks the fact that there are many situations that cannot be planned for at all, with or without a computer, and that, in fact, the use of IT might actually make contingency planning less effective, because the firm might overlook the importance of qualitative data and scenarios.

The basic problem is that the answer is one-sided – it looks only at the pros of IT use. Nevertheless, it is fairly analytical, especially in the second paragraph.

Mark: Content 2/2, Application & Analysis 4/6, Evaluation 0/3. Total = 6

Analyse the steps needed to develop effective contingency plans in an organisation.

(9 marks)

Student answer

Contingency plans make a firm better prepared for future eventualities, by considering what might happen and then by looking at what the firm could or should do. If the firm would be unable to respond to certain events, the contingency planning process might lead to changes in business practice.

However, to work, contingency planning needs to be a structured process, otherwise the firm will overlook important possible threats. The first stage is the identification of contingencies – until the firm has identified the threats that it faces, it will be unable to do much about them. Therefore, the firm must gather experienced managers to assess the threats facing the firm. These managers will be able to draw on past experience, possibly in other firms, to improve the contingency coverage. In many ways this step is the most important, since if a firm omits to assess certain contingencies, then the whole process is fundamentally flawed.

Having done this, the firm can assess the impact of the contingencies that it has identified. In some cases, it may be possible to quantify the contingency and use computer models. In other cases, the threat will be non-numerical, and human judgement will be needed. This stage is also vital – if the firm underestimates a threat then it may fail to plan for it, resulting in disaster should the contingency occur.

The next stage will be the creation of detailed plans. When assessing contingencies to plan for, the firm will look at the salience of the contingency. This will be based on an assessment of its probability and impact. The more probable the event is and the bigger its impact, the more important it is to have plans, because it is more likely to damage the firm in a serious way.

The final, and also vital stage, is the constant review of assumptions and plans. If the firm just creates a set of contingency plans and leaves them to gather dust, the exercise will have been a waste of money. This is because the world is always changing – new threats appear and existing plans may no longer be appropriate to deal with new threats. Therefore, unless the firm constantly updates its plans, it will have a plan that is out of date when an event occurs. The advice contained might be of little use, or worse still, be counterproductive – for example, if there has been a change in the law since the plan was prepared, the plan might advise the firm to respond to the crisis in a way that is actually against the law.

Overall, the key is to develop a structured approach that follows the normal rules of effective management – set objectives, gather data, develop plans, implement them, review them. If this is done, then the contingency planning process should be effective, provided the resources are there to support it.

Marker's comments

This answer is clearly extremely strong. It has a number of good features. Firstly, it defines the terms of the question clearly in the introductory paragraph – by stating what is meant by contingency planning, the candidate gives focus to the answer. Secondly, the answer does actually answer the question set – it looks at the ***steps needed to be taken*** *to ensure contingency planning is effective, rather than the usual mistake which is to look at the effectiveness of contingency planning. Finally, the answer is well structured – it looks at each of the steps in turn, giving plenty of detail as to why each step is necessary.*

Mark: Content 2/2, Application 4/4, Analysis 3/3. Total = 9

Consider what is the key factor in determining whether a firm can survive a crisis.

(11 marks)

Student answer

There are many factors that will determine whether a firm can survive a crisis. The main ones are money, luck and planning.

If a firm has plenty of money, then it can survive almost any crisis. It will have the money to meet any costs which come up. It is usually lack of money that forces firms under.

Luck is another factor. Some firms happen to have crises when lots of other things are being covered on the news. Therefore, the firm's crisis might not get that much attention, meaning that less people hear about it. If less people hear about it, the damage to the firm's reputation is reduced and it is more likely to survive.

Finally, planning can help. If the firm has a detailed product recall plan or whatever, then it will be able to respond faster to the crisis meaning that less damage is likely to be done, because the firm will have sorted it out before many people notice.

Overall the key factor is probably luck, because without it a firm might have any sort of thing happen.

Marker's comments

This candidate does attempt to answer the question and there is evidence of some analysis, especially in the second and third points made. The answer is let down by the poor quality of English, and the failure to decide on the key factor. The answer is clearly not evaluative – the last paragraph has no evidence supporting the conclusion, and no examiner would be fooled into thinking that this was genuine evaluation.

Overall, a relatively promising answer but one which would score only a weak analysis mark.

Mark: Content 2/2, Application & Analysis 2/6, Evaluation 0/3. Total = 4

End of section questions

1 Consider whether all major manufacturing firms should develop crisis management procedures. (11 marks)

2 Analyse the factors determining the likely impact of a scandal on a major service sector firm, such as an insurance company. (9 marks)

3 Examine the factors likely to make crisis management procedures in a firm more effective. (9 marks)

4 To what extent can a crisis threaten the survival of a firm? (11 marks)

5 Consider the extent to which previous experience can guide a manager when dealing with a new crisis. (11 marks)

6 Consider the issues that might need to be considered when setting up a contingency plan. (11 marks)

7 Discuss the likely impact of increasing amounts of Information Technology use in business on contingency planning. (11 marks)

8 Analyse the Human Resource implications of the contingency planning process. (9 marks)

9 Outline the arguments you might use to convince the Managing Director of a major manufacturing firm of the benefits of contingency planning. (9 marks)

10 What steps would need to be taken to ensure minimal disruption if a key member of the IT department left the Company? Issues might include succession plans (i.e. will it be necessary to recruit externally or internally), standardisation of programming language, documentation of work and so on. (11 marks)

Essays

1 'The success or failure of any contingency plan depends less on the plan itself than on those required to administer it.' Discuss. (40 marks)

2 'The costs of contingency planning outweigh the benefits.' Discuss. (40 marks)

3 Consider whether crisis management is a waste of valuable resources. (40 marks)

4 A cosmetics firm discovers that one of its products has been linked with cancer in rats. Discuss the possible impact of this discovery on the firm and consider how it should respond. (40 marks)

5 'Contingency plans are so rarely used that they represent a waste of a firm's resources.' Discuss. (40 marks)

Recent issues

Information and knowledge management

Western economies continue to move towards the service sector and away from manufacturing. As technology continues to develop at an incredibly fast rate, the key to competitive advantage is increasingly being seen as the effective management of knowledge. This was directly acknowledged in the UK government's White Paper on competitiveness in 1998 which stressed the importance of the 'knowledge economy'.

KEY TERM

A **knowledge-driven economy** is one in which the generation and exploitation of knowledge has come to play the predominant part in the creation of wealth . . . it is about the effective use and exploitation of all types of knowledge in all manner of economic activity.
Source: DTI

Information Technology (IT)

At the heart of knowledge management is information technology (IT). Spreadsheets, databases, e-mails, voice mail and the Internet all make information easier, quicker and cheaper to transfer from one place to another. As a result of developments in IT, information is no longer difficult to find or to access; the skill is not so much in *getting* information but in *knowing what to do with it.* Making sure the right information gets to the right person, at the right time, at an appropriate cost is the key. These are all areas of 'knowledge management'. Whereas information technology provides the mechanisms for capturing, storing and retrieving the raw data that forms the basis of knowledge, knowledge management makes sure that the right data is collected and is used effectively. The management of knowledge involves bringing together the right people, systems and technologies to collect and distribute information to build and maintain a competitive advantage.

Knowledge comes from information. Knowledge is power.

Knowledge in different industries

The value of managing knowledge may seem obvious in industries such as software development, film-making and biotechnology which rely heavily on peoples' ideas. But it is also important in manufacturing where greater knowledge provides a better understanding of its customers and enables a firm to meet their needs more precisely. With more knowledge, employees can do their jobs more successfully and better processes can be developed to improve performance. The need to actively manage knowledge is growing all the time as firms seek ways of increasing their competitive advantage. In Bill Gates' words every organisation needs to be building a 'digital nervous system' to provide a well integrated flow of information to the right part of the organisation every time. 'The most meaningful way to differentiate your company from your competition, the best way to put distance between you and the crowd is to do an outstanding job with information. How you gather, manage and use information will determine whether you win or lose.'

Dell provides a good example of how a firm can successfully use information. Dell's competitive strategy focuses on producing personal computers to order and selling them direct to customers. This strategy is based on a very sophisticated system of managing information. Dell has invested heavily and built up a detailed inventory of available components. Customers choose the various specifications they want, suppliers then provide the components which are needed and the manufacturing system schedules and begins assembly. In 1997, Dell sold 11 million personal computers. These were produced from 40,000 configurations (competitors usually offer around 100) meaning that configurations were used on average 275 times. The direct link with customers, the flexibility of production and the re-use of information of different configurations allows Dell to provide a highly flexible service at a relatively low price.

FACT FILE

According to a key survey by Price Waterhouse-Coopers in conjunction with the World Economic Forum, 95% of chief executive officers saw knowledge management as an essential ingredient for the success of their company.

FACT FILE

KMPG is a financial consultancy. Its mission is 'to transform knowledge into value for the benefit of clients, people and communities.'

Knowledge is information put to productive use.

Knowledge and culture

The importance of managing the gathering and flow of knowledge around the organisation and between stakeholders is now being explicitly recognised by firms, some of whom have appointed Knowledge Officers. Their task is not always an easy one! A major barrier is that the culture of many organisations makes individuals reluctant to share the information they have. Many people believe their power and status is closely linked to what they know. As a result they are reluctant to give information away. Managers may have to change the culture of their organisation to one where sharing information is the norm and where collaboration is embraced. Employees need to appreciate that how information is used is more important than who provides it.

Knowledge and accounts

The *value* of knowledge is difficult to quantify and certainly does not appear on companies' balance sheets. This means that traditional accounts are often limited because they can significantly underestimate the 'true' value of a business. 'Our primary asset, which are our software-development skills, do not show up on the balance sheet at all' says Microsoft's Bill Gates. The failure to measure the worth of knowledge can be seen by the massive differences between the book values of firms (i.e. the value in their published accounts) and their market values. This gap is particularly significant in firms which have high levels of research and development. Analysts must look beyond the book value to the underlying abilities, skills and knowledge within the firm.

FACT FILE

In 1998, Microsoft's net asset value was $16.6 bn; property, plant and equipment accounted for just $1.5 bn of a $22 bn balance sheet total. The bulk of its market value is the brain of Bill Gates.
Source, *Financial Times* 8 December 1998

NUMERICAL INVESTIGATION

	SALES	BOOK VALUE	MARKET VALUE	ESTIMATE OF KNOWLEDGE CAPITAL*
Merck	23.6	12.6	139.9	48.0
Bristol Myers Squibb	16.7	7.2	107.0	30.5
Johnson & Johnson	22.6	12.4	92.9	29.7
DuPont	39.9	11.3	87.0	26.4
Dow Chemical	20.1	7.7	21.8	10.2
Monsanto	7.5	4.1	33.2	6.0

Table 9.1 Knowledge capital in selected companies ($bn).
Source, *The Economist*, June 1999

(Based on 1995–7 actual results and 1998–2000 IBES projected results; market value as at 3 May 1998.)

a With reference to the table above which company is the second largest according to its published accounts?
b With reference to the table above which company is the second largest according to its market value?
c With reference to the table above which company is the second largest according to sales?
d Explain why these answers differ.

Why is knowledge management becoming more important?

In its 1998 White Paper, the government highlighted a number of reasons why knowledge management is becoming increasingly important. These included:

- *Developments in Information and Communications Technology* – increasing amounts of information can now move around at greater speeds more cheaply. Entirely new products (e.g. digital cameras) and services (e.g. Internet travel agents) have been created. Firms must harness the knowledge they have internally and develop knowledge links with their stakeholders to be ready and able to exploit their market opportunities.
- *Increased speed of scientific and technological advance* – an increase in scientific research, and research and development has increased the amount of knowledge which exists. These findings are more available because of developments in information technology. However, if this information remains an unexploited asset it is wasted. Firms need to access and use this information before their rivals do.
- *Global competition* – this has been facilitated by cheaper communication costs which has opened up markets to consumers by reducing search costs. Transport costs have also fallen and some businesses can deliver their services down the

phone line. The ease with which information can be transferred has made it easier to imitate products and processes. Firms must be ready to seize opportunities and defend themselves from attack.

- *Changing demand patterns* – demand is changing due to increasing incomes and changing tastes, e.g. an increasing desire for more leisure. With rising prosperity, a smaller proportion of income is spent on essential goods. Consumers place more emphasis on the quality of the goods and services they buy and their quality of life. People also put more emphasis on environmental factors. This implies increasing pressure on firms to reduce their dependence on physical components of production, limit pollution and give more emphasis to innovation, creativity and technical excellence.

PROGRESS CHECK

In what ways can the effective management of knowledge help a firm's competitiveness?

Globalisation

FACT FILE

Rolex is the same certified chronometer anywhere in the world. Its positioning as the time piece for the elegant achiever is the same in every country, as is its advertising message. It is always found at an upmarket distribution outlet and sold at a premium price.

In the last 20 years there has been a tremendous growth in world trade, aided by the opening up of markets in Central Europe and the Far East, and increased competition from the emerging economies. Companies must now think globally, not locally. With amazing improvements in technology, communication, transport and the removal of many barriers to trade, the whole world is a potential market for supplies, for staff and for sales. Organisations can now look far and wide to source their inputs or to export their goods and services. This does not mean that there is free trade everywhere or that differences between markets have vanished overnight, but we have moved a long way towards a global economy. Brands such as Coca Cola, Nike, Sony and Marlboro are known all over the world.

Increasingly people are drinking the same drinks, wearing the same types of clothes and listening to the same music all around the world. Markets are converging, providing enormous opportunities for firms to produce more standardised global products and benefit from economies of scale. Promoting the same brand in each country and producing a universal version of a product, rather than altering it for several different markets, can lead to major cost savings and drive down the price for the customer.

Operating globally can reduce input costs. By seeking the cheapest supplies worldwide (which is increasingly easy given the developments in communication, such as the Internet) or by locating in the lowest cost location, a firm can increase its profit margin or lower its prices to be more competitive. According to the business writer Theodore Levitt:

> 'A powerful force drives the world toward a converging commonality and that force is technology. It has proletarianised communication, transport and travel. It has made isolated places and impoverished peoples eager for

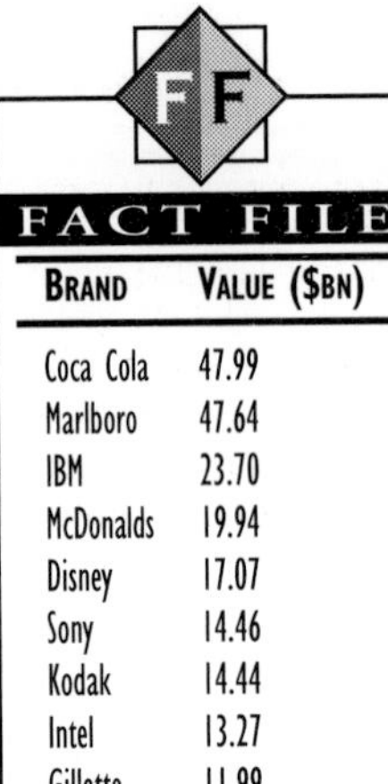

FACT FILE

Brand	Value ($bn)
Coca Cola	47.99
Marlboro	47.64
IBM	23.70
McDonalds	19.94
Disney	17.07
Sony	14.46
Kodak	14.44
Intel	13.27
Gillette	11.99

Table 9.2 Most valuable global brands, 1998.
Source: *The Economist*, 12 June 1999

FACT FILE

In the 1990s, Heinz introduced 'Project Millenia' to enable the organisation to compete more effectively throughout Europe. The company was restructured around a limited number of product areas which were to be managed in the same way across Europe. A regional structure was replaced by a product-based approach. Heinz Tomato Ketchup carries the same name and similar packaging all over the world and the company wants to extend this approach to its other product categories.

modernity's allurements. Almost everyone everywhere wants all the things they have heard about, seen or experienced via the new technologies.'

'The result is a new commercial reality – the emergence of global markets for standardised consumer products on a previously unimagined scale of magnitude. Corporations geared to this new reality benefit from enormous economies of scale in production, distribution, marketing and management. By translating these benefits into reduced world prices, they can decimate competitors that still live in the disabling grip of old assumptions about how the world works.'

However, the process of globalisation has been faster in some markets than others. It is most noticeable in consumer products such as videos, TVs, jeans, perfumes and alcohol. Well known brands in the UK in these markets are also strong in most other countries. In other markets, strong regional differences exist; in food, for example, regional tastes differ considerably. Companies such as Saatchi and Saatchi have struggled to build a global brand in the advertising industry (this may be because clients prefer 'local' agencies or that market tastes are too different). Language can also be a problem in terms of packaging and promotion.

The danger of developing a 'global offering' is that the *precise* needs of the local consumer will no longer be met. Economies of scale may be achieved at the cost of sales. More profits may actually be made by adjusting the product for local needs. The solution to this dilemma seems to lie in 'glocalisation' or 'thinking globally, acting locally'. Firms must seek to benefit wherever possible from standardisation, but at the same time be flexible to regional requirements. This flexibility is becoming easier with improvements in manufacturing technology, enabling firms to adopt 'mass customisation' processes. This approach uses a platform strategy in which the basic elements of the product are built in a standard manner, but add-on features can enable it to be adapted for different customer demands.

The distinction between a global and a local approach can be seen in the operations of Ford and of Honda. In the past Ford operated locally. Each country had its own regional manager and cars were heavily adapted for the local markets. Honda, by comparison, operated out of Japan, exporting from there and paying little attention to different market requirements. Interestingly both companies have now moved nearer in approach to each other. Honda now produces overseas and makes some adaptions to its models, whilst Ford has reorganised its activities to base them around global product lines.

In some cases, firms have actively decided not to compete globally. Whilst Cadbury Schweppes set out to build a global non-cola soft drinks company in the 1990s, AGBarr, owner of IrnBru, was content to focus mainly on the Scottish market. Not every company has the desire, the resources or the products to go global. Indeed, there are only a handful of companies which could be said to be genuinely 'global' in their thinking, their recruitment, their sourcing and their sales.

Globalisation is an important business trend and one which is likely to continue to grow. It does not affect markets equally, but nevertheless most firms need to think more broadly. If they do not, they will find themselves attacked by those that do. In the UK, a firm's competitors are no longer other UK firms; they could be anywhere in the world. Similarly, their markets could be global. However, at the same time as thinking globally, a firm must try to maintain a flexible process which gives them some ability to meet local needs.

Corporate governance

FACT FILE

In 1999, the Chief Executive of Cable and Wireless announced his vision for the company. He wanted to transform the firm from a collection of separate business units into a focused business-to-business telecom provider with standard products and services all over the world. He highlighted the importance of 'identifying and exploiting global benefits and synergies', and expressed an intention to create an integrated group, combining voice and data, fixed and mobile services and cable television in all its regions.

In the 1990s, there has been increasing concern over the way in which firms are managed and the extent to which the owners are kept informed. Many commentators have been concerned that directors and managers have pursued their own aims and that, on occasion, this has been at the expense of the owners. The very high rewards of some directors and managers has been used as evidence of a lack of control on their activities. The way in which the owners monitor the firm's activities and are kept informed is known as corporate governance. The government has taken an increasing interest in corporate governance to try and ensure that shareholders' rights are protected. Corporate governance is concerned with these questions:

- How do shareholders know that the directors and managers are really acting in their best interests?
- How do shareholders make it more likely that managers act in their interests?

Typically, most individual shareholders have very little idea of what managers are actually doing (certainly in the case of plcs). This is because the majority of shareholders own relatively small numbers of shares; in many cases they are content to monitor the share price and trust in the directors. Their individual power is usually limited and they have little access to information. All shareholders receive a copy of the annual accounts and an invitation to the annual general meeting, but this may not give them much of an insight into what is really happening. The reports are fairly technical and can make use of various accounting techniques to create a favourable impression. Furthermore, there is not usually much time for real discussion at the annual general meeting. In many cases, an individual shareholder, therefore, has very little understanding of the workings of the business and has to assume that the directors are protecting their interests (as indeed they are *legally* required to do). Institutional investors, such as pension funds, are likely to be more influential (as they usually own more shares) and are generally kept better informed. Even they may not know exactly what is happening within the firm. They may be told what they want to hear (or what the directors want them to hear) rather than having the 'true' picture.

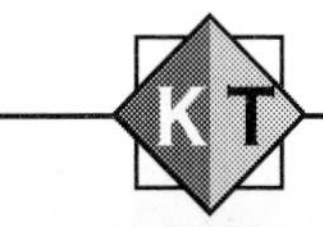

KEY TERM

Corporate governance is the system of rules and procedures which attempts to ensure that businesses are run in the interests of the shareholders.

The real problem lies in the divorce between ownership and control. The shareholders own the company, but the managers control it on a day-to-day basis. What the owners want and what the managers want may be very different. For example, the owners may seek relatively high pay-outs in the form of dividends, whereas the managers may want to retain profit to invest, so the company grows and they gain in status. This disagreement may not be a problem provided it is discussed openly and both sides have access to the same information. The danger is that shareholders have to believe what they are told because they lack any other information. Managers may put forward investment proposals in a way which makes them seem necessary, when in reality there is much more room for more discussion. Directors and managers may even disguise their real actions.

FACT FILE

According to *Management Today* magazine, the chief executives of the UK's top 350 companies received pay rises in 1998 averaging 17.8%, bringing their total average pay to almost £395,000.
This is 25% more than French chief executives, the next highest paid on £318,000. The UK is second only to the US, where CEOs last year pocketed an average £655,000.
Jan Leschly, chief executive of SmithKline Beecham, has a package of options and other incentives that has given him a fortune of more than £90 m.

FACT FILE

Many believe that institutional shareholders do not do a particularly effective job when it comes to ensuring companies behave in the interest of their owners. Interestingly, only about 40% of shareholders vote in the UK, compared with more than 80% in the US.

In the 1990s, there were many examples of unethical or illegal behaviour by managers or directors who were certainly not acting in the best interests of their shareholders. For example, Robert Maxwell of the Mirror Group and the Polly Peck company were involved in dubious financial dealings about which shareholders were not kept informed. There have also been several instances of directors awarding themselves very high salaries and benefits, even if their companies appeared to be performing badly. This has led to a great deal of criticism of the 'fat cats' in the boardroom and calls for controls on their earnings.

The growing concern over corporate governance in the 1990s led the government to set up various committees to report on this area, namely the Cadbury Committee, the Greenbury Committee and the Hamel Committee. These committees made a number of recommendations, including the need for more non-executive directors who might be able to provide a more objective view of the business. Non-executives do not have a position within the firm so should be able to bring different experiences to the company and provide an outsider's view. Other proposals included the separation of the role of Chairman and Chief Executive (if the job is held by the same person, the Chief Executive is reporting to him or herself) and greater transparency of the rewards of the directors. Companies were also advised to appoint an audit and remuneration committee to review the rewards for directors.

The latest proposals in this area have come from the Turnbull Committee which published its Report in 1999 and pulled together the findings of the other groups to create a corporate 'supercode'. It also went further than previous recommendations and dealt with the area of corporate risk. How do directors deal with risks such as product obsolescence or unethical suppliers? How do they ensure these situations do not happen or, if they do, that they do not threaten the firm's existence? Turnbull recommended that companies should have an ongoing risk assessment programme which is regularly reviewed. Directors must also be prepared to own up if the internal control systems have failed. Non-executive directors will be expected to ensure that what is stated externally matches what happens internally. These recommendations are incredibly far reaching and substantially increase the responsibilities of directors, who must now ensure that they are taking *all* reasonable steps to prepare for non-financial, as well as financial, risks, including those posed by environmentally unfriendly policies, changes in markets and technology, and others beyond a narrow definition of financial controls. It is fascinating to see how greater controls are now being introduced to try and ensure that directors act in the interests of their owners. It is also interesting to see how our view of their responsibilities is growing, so that directors are being held much more to account for the performance of the business. Even so, the rights of shareholders may need yet more protection from the possible abuse of power by directors.

PROGRESS CHECK

To what extent should the government legislate to control directors' actions?

CHAPTER 10

Numerical data

1 *Supermarkets and small firms*

MARKET SHARE OF FOOD PURCHASES (%)	1988	1993	1998
Tesco	9.3	11.7	17.3
Sainsbury's and Savacentre	9.6	12.4	13.3
Asda	4.9	6.7	8.8
Safeway	6.8	7.8	8.0

AVERAGE WEEKLY HOUSEHOLD EXPENDITURE	1988	1993	1997/8
Commodities and services (£)	204.41	276.68	328.78
Food (£)	38.28	49.96	55.92

a Calculate the percentage change in market share for the four main supermarket chains listed above between 1988 and 1998.

(3 marks)

b(i) Calculate the change in the value of average weekly household spending on food between 1988 and 1998.

(3 marks)

(ii) Calculate the percentage of weekly expenditure that was on food for each of the periods shown above. Comment on your findings.

(4 marks)

c If the trends in market share shown above continue, consider the possible implications for a small retail outlet's business strategy.

(8 marks)

d Discuss whether the trends in market share shown above are likely to benefit UK consumers.

(7 marks)

Total: 25 marks

2 *Alliance & Leicester and the Bank of Ireland*

In May 1999, the Alliance & Leicester bank (having converted from building society status in 1997) and the Bank of Ireland proposed to merge. The following are pre-merger figures for both banks.

	Alliance & Leicester	Bank of Ireland
Market capitalisation	£5.43bn	£6.65bn
Pre-tax profits	£455.2m	£696.7m
Earnings per share	54.6p	98.4p
Net assets	£1.85bn	£1.88bn
Cost/Income ratio	57.2%	55%
Mortgages	£20.6bn	£13.9bn

Source: *Financial Times*, 25 May 1999

The resulting merger would create the largest bank in Ireland and the 8th largest in the UK. Analysts expect annual cost savings of £120 to £140m, and overall gains of over £200m when the increased range of products can be sold through the entire banking network. The Bank of Ireland owns the Bristol and West brand in the UK, and sources suggest that about 10% of the combined UK branches might be closed.

a What is meant by 'market capitalisation'?

(2 marks)

b Using the data, consider which of the two banks is the larger.

(3 marks)

c Using the data above, comment on the financial performance of the two companies.

(5 marks)

d Analyse the possible reasons for the proposed merger.

(7 marks)

e Discuss the possible difficulties that might be faced by the combined business in its first few years of trading.

(8 marks)

Total: 25 marks

3 EMI and the internet

Music sales via the Internet ($m)				
Area	**1997**	**1998**	**1999***	**2004***
US	35.7	145.2	312.2	2 276.2
Europe	6.7	15.9	36.9	833.9
Asia	1.4	4.2	12.2	582.5
Rest of the world	1.9	4.6	13.7	293.8
Total	**45.7**	**169.9**	**375.0**	**3 986.4**

* forecasts (Source: *Financial Times*, 26 May 1999)

In 1999, EMI, the global music group, showed an interest in marketing its music catalogues over the Internet. With profits down by £80 m to £227 m on a turnover of £2.37 bn (down from £2.41 bn in 1998), the music group is looking for a new direction. Internet users are downloading increasingly large amounts of, often unauthorised, music clips from web pages (which often infringe copyright laws), and businesses such as EMI are beginning to feel that the only way to control this growing trend is to get involved themselves.

a What is meant by copyright?

(2 marks)

b Calculate the following:

(i) the percentage change in sales via the internet sales between 1998 and 2004 in the US.

(2 marks)

(ii) If the £/$ exchange rate is £1=$1.60, calculate EMI's turnover as a percentage of the total world sales of music over the Internet in 1998.

(4 marks)

(iii) Calculate EMI's profit margin in 1999.

(2 marks)

c Analyse the factors which might have led EMI to change their business strategy.

(7 marks)

d Consider the difficulties that EMI are likely to face in changing its strategy from an over-the-counter to an over-the-net business.

(10 marks)

Total: 25 marks

Business report 1: Phillippe Marcaux

(40 marks)

Phillippe Marcaux plc is a major European high street clothing retailer, renowned for high-quality men's suits and shirts. It is considering a take-over bid for Y2K, a new and rapidly growing UK chain in the expanding youth fashion market. In your role as management consultant and using an appropriate format, write a report outlining the case for and against the bid and recommending whether the bid is advisable. Refer to the appendices supplied.

(2 marks for report format)

Appendix A – Portfolio analysis of Phillippe Marcaux in the UK

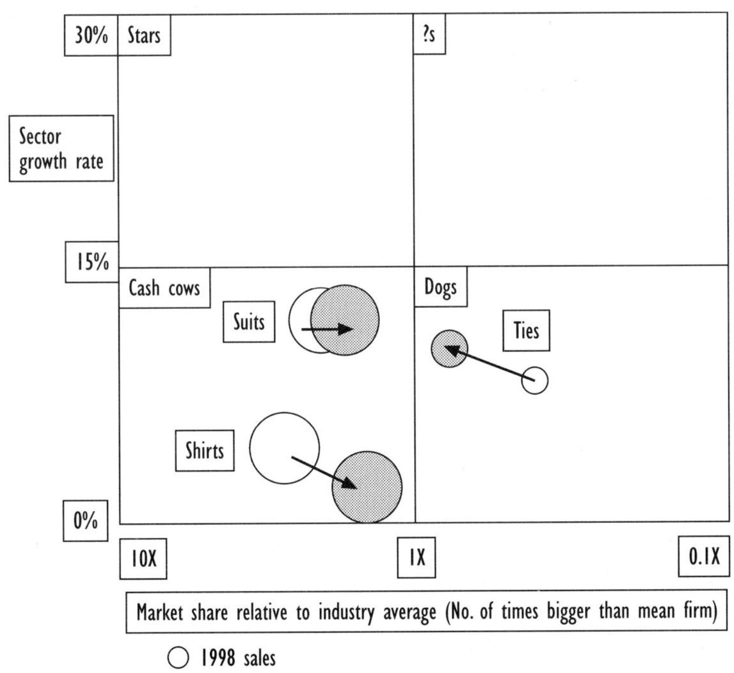

Figure 10.1 Portfolio analysis

Appendix B – Phillippe Marcaux plc

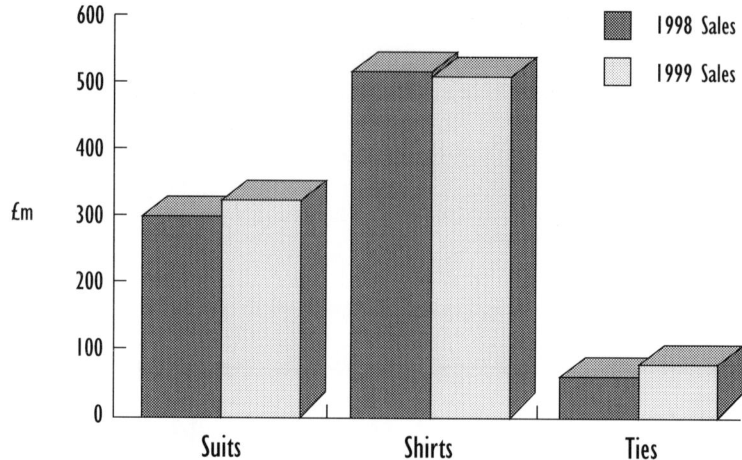

Figure 10.2 Analysis of sales

Phillippe Marcaux results	1998	1999
Total UK profits	£98 m	£96 m
Total group profits	£425 m	£396 m

Appendix C – Y2K plc

	1998	1999
Sector growth rate	25%	28%
Y2K's sector market share	2.1%	5.8%
Mean market share in sector	7.1%	7.5%
Sales	£32 m	£118 m
Profit	(£7 m)	(£15 m)
Fixed assets	£130 m	£400 m
Market capitalisation	£205 m	£745 m
Gearing	65%	60%

Appendix D – Demographic breakdown of sales

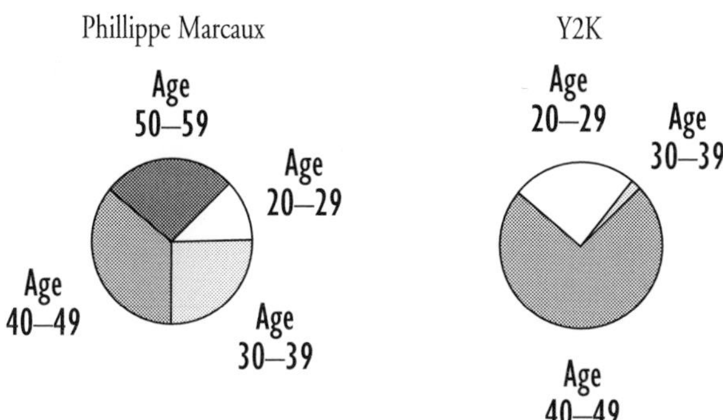

Figure 10.3

Appendix E – Probability tree looking at possible outcomes

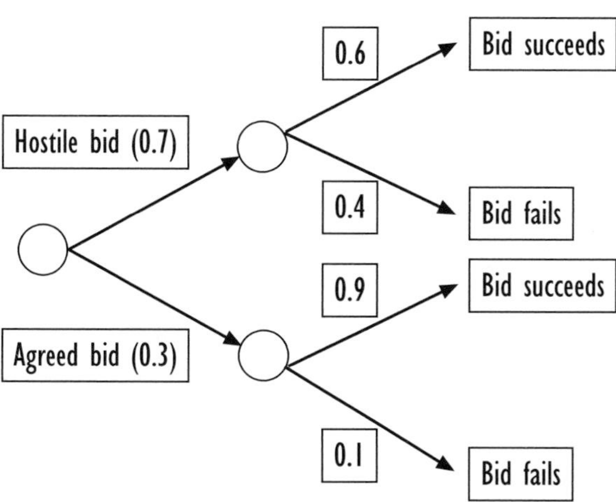

Figure 10.4 Probability tree

Appendix 6 – Finance costs (forecast)

	Hostile bid	Agreed bid
Advertising costs	£85 m	£35 m
Cost of acquiring equity	£1.25 bn	£1.05 bn
Debt finance needed	£ 1.1 bn	£840 m
Annual repayments (of interest and capital)	£175 m	£125 m
Combined gearing (post take-over)	55%	45%

Appendix 7 – Employees and management

	Phillippe Marcaux plc	Y2K
Labour turnover	25%	15%
Average age of managers	52	23
Average age of assistants	26	18
Average managerial salary	£27,000	£21,000*
Pay of shop assistants	£3.75	£4.75
Training spend per employee	£700 p.a.	£2500 p.a.

*plus performance-related bonus: 1999 average = £3500

Business report 2: CountyBank

(40 marks)

CountyBank is a major UK high street bank that is considering a policy of closing 3,026 of its 4127 branches, countrywide, over the next 5 years, at a cost of 28,000 jobs. The closed branches will be replaced with a central call centre and Internet banking service. In the remaining 1,101 branches, customers will be charged between £2 and £5 for all over the counter transactions. You have been called in as a management consultant. Write a report using an appropriate format outlining to the Board the case for and against this strategy. Come to a fully justified recommendation on whether the firm should go ahead with the plan.

(2 marks for report format)

Appendix A – Mission statement for CountyBank

CountyBank exists to:

- Deliver above industry average dividends to shareholders in the long term.
- To provide a caring and family-friendly work environment.
- To deliver quality, low cost, banking services to rural and urban communities, especially lower income and disadvantaged groups.

Appendix B – Profitability of CountyBank

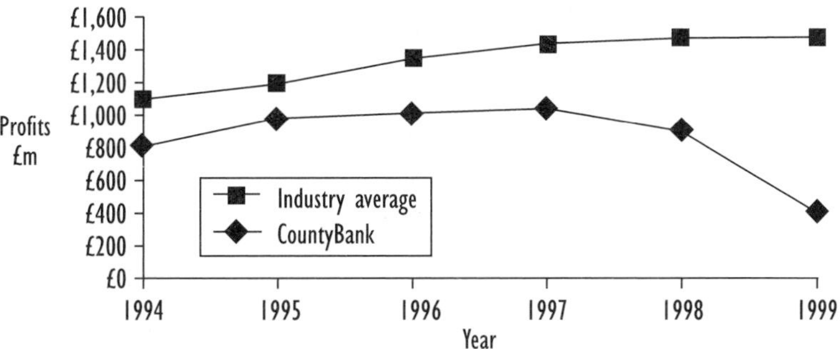

Figure 10.5 Profitability of County Bank

Appendix C – CountyBank customer survey

These are the results of a questionnaire which asked: Do you agree or disagree with the following statements?

	Agree strongly	Agree slightly	Neither agree nor disagree	Disagree slightly	Disagree strongly
Telephone and internet banking would be useful to me	23%	42%	17%	14%	4%
I rarely use my local branch	14%	17%	18%	31%	20%
Most of my banking business could be conducted over the 'phone	19%	25%	17%	29%	10%
It is important to me to be able to meet my bank manager face-to-face	6%	29%	20%	32%	13%
I would be seriously inconvenienced if my local CountyBank branch closed	12%	34%	23%	22%	9%
My bank charges are too high	19%	34%	22%	20%	5%

Survey of 2,097 CountyBank customers (6 November 1999 to 11 November 1999)

Appendix D – Costs and benefits of the change, if fully implemented

Costs of closure

- Redundancy payments: £294 m
- Call centre set-up costs: £379 m

Benefits from closure

- Asset sales: £1 756 m
- Staff costs: £469 m/year
- Other branch costs: £397 m/year

This would allow an average reduction in bank charges of 34% per year, weighted towards customers using the telephone and Internet banking facility.

Appendix E – Breakdown of CountyBank's customers and branches together with industry comparison

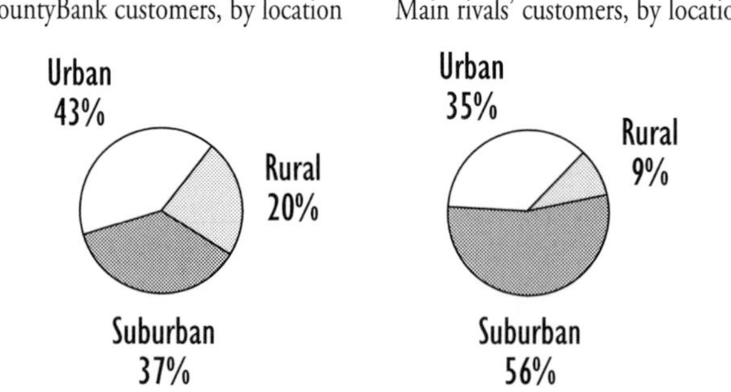

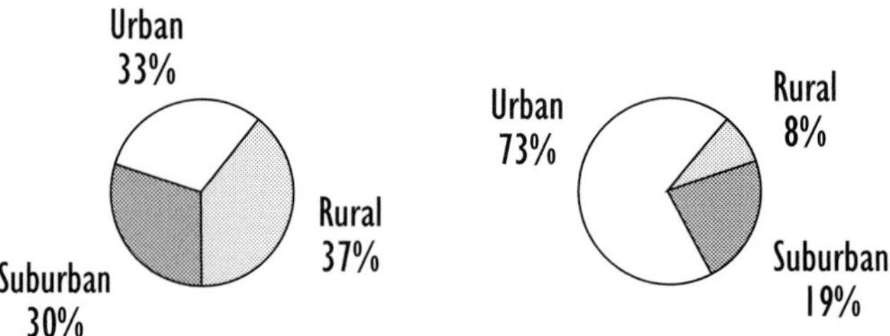

Figure 10.6

Appendix F – Forecast home internet access, 1999–2009

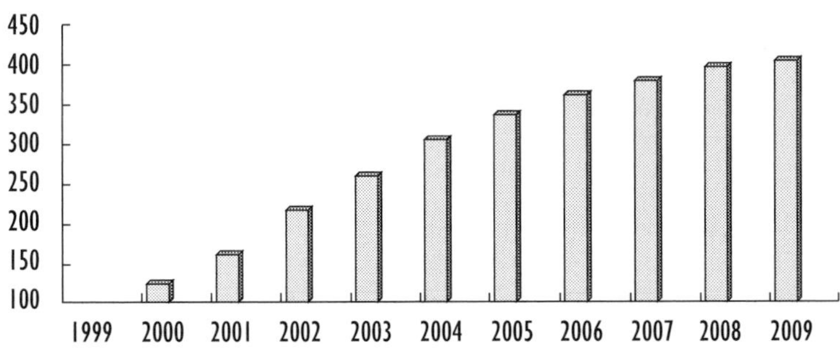

Figure 10.7 1999 = 100

Examining tips

The topics covered in this book are integrating themes which are crucial to business success. They are often assessed in the form of business case studies, because they are the key determinants of a firm's performance and pull together all the different strands of business studies as a subject. A firm's strategy, for example, depends on its resources, its strengths and the market opportunities. Strategic planning will, therefore, involve an understanding of the various functions of a firm (such as marketing, finance, human resources and operations), the external environment (such as the economic and social climate) and the firm's objectives. To identify the best strategy for a firm involves a detailed analysis of its situation and an appreciation of all the areas of business. You should also be able to discuss topics, such as objectives and strategy in data questions, since all of a firm's actions should relate to what it is trying to achieve, and to its long-term plan.

The business in question

When answering questions on these topics it is important to think carefully about the particular business involved. The objectives of one firm may be very different from another one, for example; it depends on the values of the owners, their personal ambitions and the stage of development at the firm. Similarly, the strategy a firm pursues is very much linked to its own circumstances. There are no set solutions, no set ways of winning – successful companies tend to have certain features in common, such as good communication, high levels of motivation and good planning, but they are still unique. It is important to remember that firms operate in different markets, in different ways, with different styles. Compare, for example, the decisions of an ambitious, young, inexperienced manager to those of an older, highly experienced manager looking forward to retirement; the aims, culture and strategy of a relatively small, family-owned business to a growing multinational. Your answer should take account of such differences, and try to ensure that your responses are rooted very heavily in the actual context of the firm described. If you are working through a data question or case study, for example, make sure you have a clear idea of the objectives of the owners and managers, the situation of the firm at present (e.g. strengths and weaknesses) and the nature of the environment. The strategy of a firm in a growing market will be very different from that of a business operating in a declining market. The strategy of a firm with high levels of liquidity, low gearing, a strong brand and good research and development will be different from a firm with cashflow problems and no new products coming on line.

Breadth of discussion

When answering a question you should try and be quite broad, highlighting the interrelationships between functional areas. A change in marketing, for example, must be supported and complemented by operational and human resource changes. Pricing decisions naturally have financial implications. One approach when answering these questions is to consider how the different functional managers would react in the given situation. Imagine you are talking to the marketing manager, then the operations manager, the finance manager and the human resource manager – how do they each respond? Then imagine the Chief Executive's response – having heard all their views how would he or she co-ordinate their ideas to develop a coherent strategy?

Specific advice on topic areas

Objectives

It is very important to try and identify a firm's objectives if you want to know how they will react in a particular situation. After all, the objectives should determine everything the firm does. Whenever you are asked to assess a firm's actions you need to put them in the context of its aims. Should it be pleased with a 10% growth in sales of Brand A? This depends on what it was hoping to achieve – if it wanted an 80% increase or wanted the sales of Brand B to increase, the managers would be disappointed. So, whenever you are asked about the suitability of a particular course of action, it is important to stand back and think what the firm was hoping to achieve.

If you are considering a particular situation write down the firm's objectives before answering the questions and make sure you identify what it is the people involved want to achieve. If this is not clear, this fact may be revealing in itself – why is there no clear sense of direction? If there seem to be several conflicting objectives, comment on it – for example, if the marketing departments are promoting tailor-made products whilst the operations department are going all out for volume production of standardised items, this should be a cause for concern. In some cases, you may identify a clash of objectives between the people involved in the business. Donna may want to sell up and retire; William may want to expand within the existing business area; Jav may want to diversify. The fact that the owners or managers disagree amongst themselves may mean the firm lacks the clear direction needed to succeed. Remember that objectives set out where the firm is headed – look out for these as they will guide you in the rest of your answers.

Strategy

A firm's strategy determines the way in which it competes and is a major factor in its success. However, many student answers fail to identify the strategy of firms, or appreciate the significance of this as a topic. There is often an acceptance of a firm's actions (they did it because they did it), rather than an attempt to identify the plan behind the decisions. When France won the World Cup in 1998, did the players just go out and kick the ball, or did they have a plan about how to play each match? Undoubtedly they had a strategy which determined how they played at each stage of the competition. Ask a football fan how France played in the tournament and no doubt he or she will be able to talk you through their strategy and tell you why it was so successful. Similarly, the strong answers in business studies look for the overall plan and then see how (or whether) everything else fits into this.

Managers have all sorts of business options – at any moment there are numerous plans they could choose. What makes them decide to compete in one market rather than another? To distribute their products in one way rather than another? To focus on reducing costs rather than providing additional benefits? To sell only in the UK rather than internationally? These decisions all depend on the firm's strategy – its masterplan.

Once the strategy has been identified, all other decisions should fit into place. For a UK firm pursuing a strategy of overseas expansion, the possibility of a take-over of a French firm is of interest; for a business wanting to operate purely within the UK it is not. For a firm focusing on growth in the fast food market, the chance to open 10 new burger outlets is relevant; for a firm concentrating on diversifying into new markets it may be less interesting.

Whenever you are faced with a business situation, try to identify what the firm is trying to achieve and how it is trying to do it. Is it operating in particular niches? Or going for the mass market? What range of markets does it want to be involved in? Typical questions in these areas will involve the importance of strategy in determining success and a consideration of the influences on the firm's plan. Why has it chosen to compete in this way? Is the strategy appropriate?

In your answers you need to focus on the role of strategy as a unifying force within the firm, determining the actions of all the different functions. Look at the way in which strategy is derived from a match between the firm's strengths and the opportunities in the external environment. It is vital that the strategy is built on the firm's resources and skills and fits with the possibilities developing in the market. You also need to consider the objectives and the extent to which the strategy will help the firm achieve these.

Decision-making

This is a fascinating topic for anyone interested in business success. How do the great business leaders decide what to do? To what extent do they rely on data? Or do they simply go by their gut instinct? This area of the syllabus has increased in importance in recent years. Examiners want you to appreciate the value of the scientific approach to decision-making but also be willing to question whether it is appropriate in all circumstances. You need to consider issues such as the time available to the decision-maker, the nature of the decision and the skill and experience of the decision-maker. All of these will influence the mix of data, experience and intuition involved in a particular decision. You are likely to need an awareness and understanding of scientific techniques used in decision-making such as decision trees, ratio analysis, investment appraisal but you should also highlight the role of qualitative factors and how intuition can also have an impact. Not all decisions are as logical and rational as we might think.

Managing growth

A very common theme in business studies questions concerns the issues facing a business as it grows. Growth provides many challenges such as controlling the finances, keeping people focused and motivated, and ensuring a common set of objectives. Firms must develop mechanisms and systems to cope with such issues; these include budgeting, appraisals, team briefings and effective use of information technology. You may well encounter a firm which is having problems keeping control of the business as it grows – it may be struggling with communication, motivational and strategic issues. You will have to advise on how these problems can be solved. It is also quite common to ask about the benefits of growth; this includes issues such as economies of scale and market power. Ultimately, the best size of firm will depend on factors such as the objectives of the managers, the cost conditions of the market and the systems developed by the firm to keep control. In many cases, entrepreneurs do not want their firms to get too big and prefer to keep a smaller size, so they feel personally involved in all the various aspects of the business. In other cases, the market may not support a large firm.

Change in ownership

Another common theme in business studies questions involves a change in the ownership of the firm or restructuring by an organisation. Managers may take over the business, one firm may gain control of another; two businesses may merge. Typically, you will be asked to assess the issues involved. Why has one firm taken over another? What are the strategic gains of such a deal? How does it fit with its objectives? At the same time you may have to consider the problems involved in reshaping, such as employee resistance, raising the finance, and problems changing culture. This is a highly integrative topic allowing you to discuss issues from all areas of the business.

Contingency planning

When studying contingency planning, you should consider the value of such planning to a firm. To what extent should a firm invest resources in this area? How do managers assess what events to plan for? A firm will need to weigh up the potential costs and benefits and your role is to highlight the case for and against. Once again, it is important to think about the industry or firm under examination – what particular events might it be necessary to plan for in retailing or oil refining, for example? To what extent is this firm particularly vulnerable to such shocks?

Summary

A key skill in answering questions based on the topics in this book is the ability to look at the big issues involved in business decision-making and avoid focusing too much on one or two specific details. What is the overall aim of the business you are studying? What do its owners want? What is its dominant culture? How does it compete? These are key questions when analysing a business situation.

In particular, you should consider:

- Who are the owners, and what do they and the managers want the business to do in the future?
- What are the firm's resources – its finances, marketing strengths, operational skills, human resource skills, its position in the market?
- How do they intend to fulfil their objectives? Does the strategy make sense? Is it coherent given the market conditions and the firm's own strengths and weaknesses?
- What obstacles are there to its success?

Finally, be specific

It is very important if you are answering a question to make sure your response is based around the particular firm described: 'this firm in this situation at this time should do . . .'. Make sure you avoid very general comments. If you are asked what strategy a firm should adopt and you write 'strategy depends on a firm's strengths such as its brand name, its distribution, the skill of its people, its capacity and its financial situation', you are not answering the question. What are the strengths of *this* firm? What is *this firm* trying to achieve? What opportunities exist in *these* markets? It is very important that your answer is based on the firm actually described in the case study, rather than writing an answer which is so vague that it could apply to any business.

Whatever the situation, the firm's objectives, strategy, business format and decision-making style are crucial determinants of its behaviour and success. Your answers should try to identify these concepts, highlight the people, finance, marketing, operational and managerial issues involved and place these firmly in the context of the particular firm and its environment wherever possible.

Index